Trading Catalysts

Trading Catalysts

How Events Move Markets and Create Trading Opportunities

Robert I. Webb

FT Press
FINANCIAL TIMES

Vice President, Editor-in-Chief: Tim Moore
Executive Editor: Jim Boyd
Series Editor: Robert I. Webb
Editorial Assistant: Pam Boland
Development Editor: Russ Hall
Associate Editor-in-Chief and Director of Marketing: Amy Neidlinger
Cover Designer: Solid State Graphics
Managing Editor: Gina Kanouse
Project Editor: Jennifer Cramer
Copy Editor: Kelli Brooks
Indexer: Lisa Stumpf
Compositor: Nonie Ratcliff
Manufacturing Buyer: Dan Uhrig

FT Press © 2007 by Pearson Education, Inc.
FINANCIAL TIMES Publishing as FT Press
Upper Saddle River, New Jersey 07458

Financial Times Press offers excellent discounts on this book when ordered in quantity for bulk purchases or special sales. For more information, please contact U.S. Corporate and Government Sales, 1-800-382-3419, corpsales@pearsontechgroup.com. For sales outside the U.S., please contact International Sales at international@pearsoned.com.

Company and product names mentioned herein are the trademarks or registered trademarks of their respective owners.

Printed in the United States of America

First Printing October 2006

ISBN 0-13-038556-5

Pearson Education LTD.
Pearson Education Australia PTY, Limited.
Pearson Education Singapore, Pte. Ltd.
Pearson Education North Asia, Ltd.
Pearson Education Canada, Ltd.
Pearson Educatión de Mexico, S.A. de C.V.
Pearson Education—Japan
Pearson Education Malaysia, Pte. Ltd.

Library of Congress Cataloging-in-Publication Data

Webb, Robert Ivory, 1952-

   Trading catalysts : how events move markets and create trading opportunities / Robert I. Webb.

      p. cm.

   Includes bibliographical references.

   ISBN 0-13-038556-5 (hardback : alk. paper) 1. Stock price forecasting. 2. Business cycles. 3. Speculation. I. Title.

   HG4637.W43 2006

   332.64'5—dc22

                        2006019367

*To my wife, Mary Beth, and my children,
Alexander, Elizabeth, and Diana.*

CONTENTS

ABOUT THE AUTHOR

Robert I. Webb is the Marvin J. Patsel, Jr., Research Professor and Director of the Center for Financial Innovation at the McIntire School of Commerce of the University of Virginia. He is also a visiting professor at the Darden Graduate School of Business Administration at the University of Virginia where he teaches Financial Trading. Bob serves as editor for the *Journal of Futures Markets*—a leading academic journal that specializes in publishing articles on derivative securities and markets. His experience includes: trading fixed income securities for the Investment Department of the World Bank; trading financial futures and options on the floor of the Chicago Mercantile Exchange; designing new financial futures and option contracts for the Chicago Mercantile Exchange; analyzing the effects of deregulating the financial services industry, among others, at the Executive Office of the President, Office of Management and Budget; and examining issues related to international futures markets at the U.S. Commodity Futures Trading Commission. Bob has also consulted on risk management issues for the Asian Development Bank. He formerly taught at the Graduate School of Business at the University of Southern California. Bob received his M.B.A. and Ph.D. in finance from the University of Chicago and his B.B.A. from the University of Wisconsin Eau Claire. He has written articles for a number of academic journals and the financial press. Bob is the author of *Macroeconomic Information and Financial Trading* (Blackwell, 1994).

PREFACE

This book owes its origin to my long fascination with the behavior of speculative prices, in general, and extreme market moves, in particular. My interest is driven by both intellectual curiosity about how news is incorporated into market prices and fascination with the potential for large gains or losses associated with trading around extreme market moves. This book is the culmination of many years of observing changes in financial market prices up close, as a trader, and at a distance, as a professor.

I was a doctoral student at the University of Chicago Graduate School of Business when the finance faculty included Fischer Black, Eugene Fama, Merton Miller, and Myron Scholes, among others; and the statistics faculty included Arnold Zellner—the brilliant Bayesian econometrician. Chicago was the birthplace of the *efficient markets hypothesis*—the notion that security prices fully and correctly reflect available information. However, the process by which new information was impounded into market prices was largely a *black box*. Although I was a student at Chicago during arguably the peak of the influence of the efficient markets hypothesis on academic research, the fundamental takeaway from my studies at Chicago was not the presumptive validity of market efficiency, or any other theory for that matter, but rather the importance of empiricism—that is, what do the data tell us? Indeed, the theory of market efficiency originated from seemingly puzzling observations by Maurice Kendall, Holbrook Working, and Harry Roberts that changes in speculative prices appeared to follow a random walk.

I was a newly minted Ph.D., and an assistant professor at the University of Southern California, when I watched silver and gold prices sometimes rise or fall sharply on a number of days during the autumn of 1979. Clearly, the movements were too large and volatile to be explained by the arrival of new information alone, as the efficient markets hypothesis would suggest. Equally clearly, the actions of certain traders played a key role in many of the price moves. This episode eroded my belief in the validity of the efficient markets hypothesis, but increased my curiosity over how news is impounded into speculative prices.[1] It also led me to secure a two-year leave of absence from the University of Southern California and accept an appointment at the Commodity Futures Trading Commission in Washington, D.C. in 1980.

At the time, the Commodity Futures Trading Commission was a relatively new Federal Agency, having been created in 1974. Not surprisingly, the then-recent attempted "silver corner" was a common topic of conversation among Commission staffers as were other issues related to market surveillance. My work at the Commission gave me an opportunity to see raw news as it was reported. The Commission had a teletype machine that received news bulletins. The machine was located in a hallway closet next to the water fountain. I would stop by several times a day to read the latest news off the wires. I quickly recognized the important role that news editors play as I sorted through mounds of fluff for the occasional nugget of news. However, even bona fide news did not always seem to have the predicted impact on market prices.

My career took a slight detour when I was offered an opportunity to serve in the Executive Office of the President, Office of Management and Budget (OMB) in 1981. My boss at OMB was Larry Kudlow. The emphasis on domestic economic policy during President Reagan's first term meant that OMB was the place to be in the Reagan Administration at the time—until OMB Director David Stockman was "taken to the woodshed" by the White House for some ill-advised comments.

When my two-year leave of absence was up at USC in 1982, I chose to enter the private sector and accepted a position as Senior Financial Economist at the Chicago Mercantile Exchange (CME), where I helped design new financial futures and option contracts. It was an exciting time to be at the CME as stock index futures contracts had only been introduced in April 1982, just months before I arrived. Working at the CME also afforded me the opportunity to observe the open outcry system on a daily basis from the vantage point of the exchange floor. The only thing that I was precluded from doing was entering the trading pits themselves—that was reserved for CME members (i.e., seat holders) and CME pit reporters. Active days were especially exciting to watch and I availed myself of every opportunity to do so. Although I was closer to the market, I was not closer to understanding how news is impounded into market prices. I left my position as an employee of the CME in 1983 and became a member of the Index and Options Market division of the CME. I was inside the "black box" at last. Finally, I hoped to get an answer to my question of how news is impounded into market prices.

An open outcry futures trading pit provides an unusually good vantage point from which to view the determination of market prices because a large fraction of total trades in an open outcry environment are between locals. Life as a "local" was fast-paced and exciting on active days, boring on tranquil days, but always intellectually challenging. I quickly found that many of the preconceptions I had about how speculative prices should behave were wrong. My advanced training in finance was initially a disadvantage in the pit because it made me intellectually rigid rather than flexible and open to new ideas. Some intellectual baggage was discarded. At the same time, my training at Chicago also helped me discover many potentially profitable trades. I saw firsthand the wide range of factors that could impact market prices in the short run.

In 1986, I returned to academia when I accepted a position at the University of Virginia. Almost immediately upon my arrival, I was approached by the World Bank. At the conclusion of my first academic year at Virginia, I took a 15-month leave of absence to work in the Investment Department at the World Bank in May of 1987. At the time, the Investment Department was an active trader in fixed income markets—trading almost as much as a primary government securities dealer. The Investment Department managed a *liquidity portfolio* of about $19 billion to $22 billion, depending upon whether International Development Association and International Finance Corporation funds were included. (The purpose of the liquidity portfolio is to allow the Bank to continue to perform its principal function of lending to developing countries in the event of a financial crisis.) These monies were invested in high-grade sovereign securities. Befitting its status and its immense trading volume, the World Bank had direct telephone lines to the major investment and commercial banks. I rotated around the trading desk. My experience trading on the floor of the CME proved to be immensely valuable when I traded fixed income securities for the World Bank.

However, the experience of trading in the Investment Department of the World Bank also presented me with a new set of anomalies to think about. One group of these anomalies—the often puzzling reactions of fixed income prices to scheduled economic reports—inspired my book *Macroeconomic Information and Financial Trading* (Blackwell, 1994). I was fortunate to be on the trading floor during the stock market crash of Monday, October 19, 1987 where I observed the limited (and initially negative) reaction of the U.S. Treasury bond market to the crash. A few hours after the U.S. stock market closed, however, Treasury bonds scored their largest one-day rally ever in a *delayed* reaction to the stock market crash.

After my leave of absence was up, I returned to the University of Virginia. In addition to writing articles for academic journals, I wrote a number of opinion pieces for various publications including *The Wall Street Journal*, the *Nihon Keizai Shimbun*, the *Nikkei Weekly*, and *Investors Business Daily*. In 1994, at the request of students, I started teaching a course on Financial Trading at both the McIntire School of Commerce and the Darden Graduate School of Business Administration at the University of Virginia. One of my former students, Andrew Peskin, was a particular help to me in that regard. A number of prominent traders, fund managers, and fund of fund managers have lectured to students in the course over the years including Arki Busson, John Henry, Paul Tudor Jones II, Peter Matthews, Drew Millstein, R. Jerry Parker, and Jeff Yass, among others. The comments of many of these speakers on the issues of the day have also influenced my views on the behavior of speculative prices. In 1998, I was appointed editor of the *Journal of Futures Markets*—a leading academic journal on derivative securities and markets. The *Journal of Futures Markets* has had two special issues on trading during my editorship.

This book has benefited from many conversations that I have had over the years with Hesham El-Naggar, Rick Gerson, Richard Jaycobs, Gary Schirr, Paul Staneski, and Jules Staniewicz on a whole host of financial topics. I would also like to thank Victor Canto and Richard Leonard for their steadfast encouragement to write this book. A special note of thanks is due to Jim Boyd, Executive Editor at FT Press, and to Melody Koh for her research assistance in producing the various figures included in this book.

Finally, I would like to thank my wife, Mary Beth, my three children, Alexander, Elizabeth, and Diana, as well as members of my immediate family, for the patience, love, and encouragement that they showed me while I was writing this book.

Robert I. Webb

Endnote

[1] That said, the concept of informational market efficiency is a useful benchmark by which to measure the value of private information and assess whether there are any hidden risks associated with potential trades. Grossly inefficient market prices are unlikely to persist for an extended period of time.

1

INTRODUCTION

"In War more than anywhere else in the world things happen differently to what we had expected, and look differently when near, to what they did at a distance."

—Carl von Clausewitz[1]

Federal Reserve Rate Cut Announcement

At approximately 1:14 in the afternoon of January 3, 2001, the Federal Reserve announced a 50 basis point cut in the targeted Fed funds rate.[2] The announcement was intended to surprise market participants, and it did—coming almost four weeks before the next regularly scheduled meeting of the Federal Reserve Open Market Committee on January 30, 2001. The impact on the stock market was immediate. Stock prices rose sharply in reaction to the news. Many large Nasdaq-listed stocks soared. JDS Uniphase closed up 36.6%. Sun Computers

1

closed up 29.9%. Amazon closed up 26.5%. Adobe Systems closed up 23.9%. Oracle closed up 21.3%. Even Microsoft managed to eke out a double-digit gain and closed up 10.5% for the day. Not surprisingly, the Nasdaq Composite Index reflected the broad gains enjoyed by many of its component stocks.

The performance of the *cubes* or *QQQs*—the tracking stock for the Nasdaq 100 stock index—also mirrored the rally in the underlying stocks of the index.[3]

Perhaps, the strength of the rally is best illustrated by the reaction of Nasdaq 100 stock index futures contract prices to the announcement.[4] At one point, the price of Nasdaq stock index futures contracts—which usually leads the underlying Nasdaq 100 stock index—was up more than 20% in response to the announcement.

Nasdaq 100 stock index futures contracts are traded on the Chicago Mercantile Exchange. For many commodities, the most actively traded futures contract is the *nearby* or *front month* contract (i.e., the contract closest to expiration).[5] This was certainly true for the Nasdaq 100 stock index futures contract on January 3, 2001, when the March 2001 futures contract was the most actively traded Nasdaq 100 stock index futures contract.[6]

Prior to the Fed announcement, Nasdaq 100 stock index futures were trading in 1 to 2 full point increments—that is, the change in notional value of the contract when futures prices changed ranged from $100 to $200. The Nasdaq 100 stock index futures contract traded at 2173 immediately before the announcement. Immediately after the announcement, the Nasdaq stock index futures price jumped by 5 full points to 2178. This was only the beginning of the move. For the next 48 seconds, the contract largely moved up (but sometimes down) in 5-point increments rising to 2240. The reaction then accelerated. For the next 75 seconds, the contract largely moved in 10-point increments rising to 2340. The reaction continued. Over the next 34 seconds, the contract had a 30-point move followed by 20- and 10-point moves.

All of this occurred within three minutes of the announcement. Then, incredibly, the reaction intensified even further, and the market started moving in 50-point increments up or down. The market continued to bounce between 2400 and 2650 largely in 50-point increments over the next minute and one half. That is, the market went from bouncing $100 to $200 between price changes before the Fed announcement to bouncing $5,000 between price changes a few minutes after the Fed announcement. The bid ask spread was not recorded. However, if one regards the bounce as a proxy for the bid offer spread, then it widened by as much as 25 to 50 times its pre-announcement amount after the Fed announcement. At this point, the Nasdaq stock index futures market was up a stunning 22% *intra-day* (i.e., during the trading day).

To put the size of this price move in perspective, on Black Monday, October 28, 1929—the first day of the two-day 1929 stock market crash—the Dow Jones Industrial Average (DJIA) was down 13.5%. On Black Tuesday, October 29, 1929, the DJIA was down another 11.5%.[7] The percentage decline in the DJIA on Monday, October 19, 1987—another stock market crash—was more than 23%. Stock market crashes are considered extreme events, yet the Nasdaq index was up in a few minutes almost the same percentage amount as these indexes fell in one or two days. Another way of looking at it is that the average *annual* return earned on a diversified portfolio of stocks of large U.S. companies over the 1926 to 1999 period was 13.3% and 17.6% for a portfolio of small company stocks according to Jack C. Francis and Roger Ibbotson.[8] Yet, the intraday move in the Nasdaq 100 spot and futures exceeded both of these *annual* stock returns. Clearly, this was a large reaction in stock prices by any measure.

The initial reaction, however, apparently entailed a substantial *overreaction* as the futures price subsequently fell from the high of 2650. The size of the price changes narrowed to mostly $25 moves over the next two minutes as the market fell to 2425. This was followed by a period of largely 5-point moves and some 10-point moves over the next 21 minutes as the market rose back up to 2480. The Nasdaq 100 stock index futures contract closed up for the day approximately 16.7%, whereas the underlying Nasdaq 100 index closed up 18.77%.[9] The more widely reported and related Nasdaq Composite Index closed up 324 points, or about 14%. In contrast, the S&P 50 stock index closed up 64 points, or 5%, whereas the Dow Jones Industrial Average closed up 299 points, or 2.8%, for the day.[10] Figures 1.1, 1.2, and 1.3 depict the daily trading range (high to low) of values for the Nasdaq Composite Index, Nasdaq 100 stock index futures contract, and the Dow Jones Industrial Average for a number of days before and after the surprise cut in the targeted Fed Funds rate.[11]

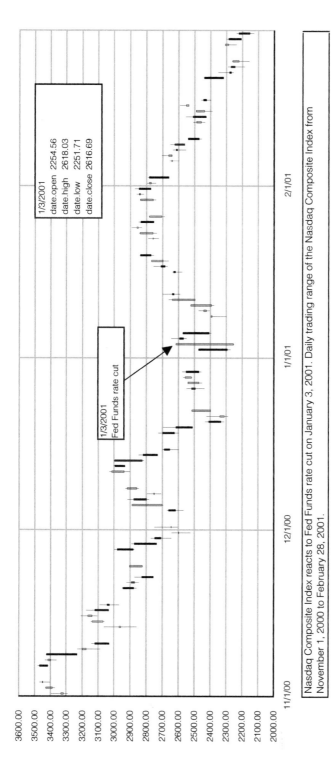

1/3/2001
date.open   2254.56
date.high   2618.03
date.low   2251.71
date.close 2616.69

1/3/2001
Fed Funds rate cut

Nasdaq Composite Index reacts to Fed Funds rate cut on January 3, 2001. Daily trading range of the Nasdaq Composite Index from November 1, 2000 to February 28, 2001.

FIGURE 1.1   The Fed sparks a rally on Nasdaq.

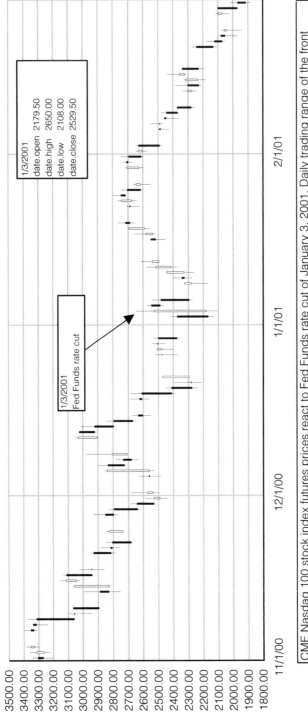

FIGURE 1.2   Nasdaq futures soar higher than the Nasdaq Composite.

CME Nasdaq 100 stock index futures prices react to Fed Funds rate cut of January 3, 2001. Daily trading range of the front month CME Nasdaq 100 stock index futures contract from November 1, 2000 to February 28, 2001.

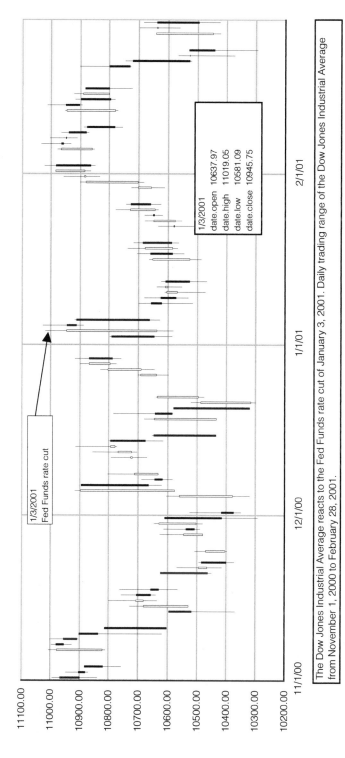

1/3/2001
Fed Funds rate cut

1/3/2001
date.open 10637.97
date.high 11019.05
date.low   10581.09
date.close 10945.75

The Dow Jones Industrial Average reacts to the Fed Funds rate cut of January 3, 2001. Daily trading range of the Dow Jones Industrial Average from November 1, 2000 to February 28, 2001.

FIGURE 1.3 Blue chips rally but not as much as the Nasdaq in percentage terms.

Analyzing the Market Reaction

The financial market reaction to the Federal Reserve announcement is both fascinating and puzzling. It illustrates the powerful impact that a trading catalyst can exert on financial market prices. To be sure, the size of the market's reaction was likely exacerbated by the expectation that this rate cut would be the first in a series of rate cuts by the Federal Reserve and by the fact that the announcement came as a surprise to most market participants. The reaction may also have been exacerbated by the fact that the Nasdaq Composite plunged 7.23% the day before. However, the size of the reaction in the Nasdaq spot and futures markets was enormous. And, other potential trading catalysts were not readily apparent.

The market's reaction to the announcement also raises some disturbing questions. Was the reaction of Nasdaq stocks and futures a case of euphoria or a logical response to the arrival of new information? Why did the Dow Jones Industrial Average and the Nasdaq spot and futures markets react so differently in magnitude to the same piece of news? Why did the Nasdaq futures market apparently overreact to the Fed announcement? Was the reaction of market prices to the catalyst alone or did the market feed on itself? What role did the electronically traded Nasdaq e-mini futures contract play in impounding the news of the rate cut?

The behavior of financial market prices in response to trading catalysts is of keen interest to traders, investors, and policymakers alike. Traders are less interested in whether the response of market prices to a particular trading catalyst accords with what financial economic theory would predict than with how the response impacts their trading opportunities and affects their trading strategies.

Traders have a different, but related, set of questions to answer when an unexpected trading catalyst occurs.

1. Which market or markets are most likely to be affected? The answer to this question depends on the prevailing *trading*

thesis (i.e., the perceived relationships between the catalyst and financial market prices). The belief that an unexpected increase in employment would cause the overall bond market to tumble is an example of a trading thesis.

2. What is the likely direction of the price move? (The answer to this question depends, in turn, on what market consensus expectations, if any, were before the catalyst occurred.) For instance, many participants believe that a larger than expected increase in employment would cause bond prices to fall, whereas a smaller than expected increase in employment would cause bond prices to rise.

3. What is the likely magnitude of the price move?

4. What is the likely speed of response of market prices to the catalyst? Although many academics would regard a market reaction lasting several minutes as exceedingly quick, most traders would not. A minute can be a lifetime in the world of trading. A few seconds is often more than enough time to enter, exit, or even reverse a position. The relevant question is do you have enough time to execute a trade?[12]

5. What is the likely duration or half-life of the trading catalyst's effect on market prices?

6. Will the price move intensify or deteriorate as time passes?

7. Will prices overshoot?

Given the answers to the preceding questions, the trader must then determine the size of the position to put on. The more uncertain the answers to these questions, other things equal, the smaller the position size the trader will put on.

Many traders think in terms of what might be called *event time*— that is, the market's reaction to similar events in the past is used as a guide to how the market will likely respond to similar events in the future.[13] Thus, a trader's prediction of how the market will react to a second U.S.-led war against Saddam Hussein's Iraq is influenced by how the market reacted to the first such war. Although such an approach is understandable, the market need not be *consistent* in its response to similar trading catalysts over time. The principal problem with the use of event time to forecast market reactions to trading catalysts is that it inevitably entails the use of a small number of observations from which valid statistical inferences cannot be drawn. This drawback is unlikely to stop many traders from using event time. Another problem with using event time as a predictor of how the market will respond to a trading catalyst is that the timing of the impact might be off as more traders attempt to exploit the same perceived relationship. Sometimes in the rush to simplify the analysis to use event time as a guide for trading decisions, traders miss potential offsetting factors that make the analogy inexact.

Notice that the impact of the Fed rate cut announcement was not limited to affecting the level of market prices alone. Rather, the Fed announcement affected both the bid/offer spread (as noted previously) and the volatility of financial market prices. This illustrates two other ways that some trading catalysts (particularly those whose timing can be anticipated) influence trading decisions. In this way, scheduled or anticipated trading catalysts facilitate bets on changes in volatility. Finally, the volume of trading often rises sharply after a trading catalyst occurs.

The Nature of Trading Catalysts

Volatile financial markets create both risk and opportunity—that is, the risk of substantial losses and the opportunity for substantial gains. However, not all volatility is created equally. Sudden jumps or breaks in prices can impart a roller-coaster-ride quality to trading or investing in financial markets. This book examines the catalysts that spark large changes in prices suddenly or over time. These include the following, among other factors: ill-advised comments by policymakers, news of natural disasters, elections, certain economic reports, company-specific announcements, and factors internal to the market itself.

The *direction, magnitude, speed, duration, intensity,* and *breadth* of influence of trading catalysts on market prices are important to understand. It is also important to understand how trading catalysts differ in their influence on market prices and how the same trading catalyst may differ in its influence on market prices over time. Part of the difference in the influence of trading catalysts on market prices at any point in time, as well as over time, is a function of *market conditions* and *sentiment*, both of which are discussed in detail in Chapter 2, "Market Conditions and Sentiment."

The identification of which market or markets are most likely to be impacted by a trading catalyst seems easy but may sometimes be difficult as the preceding Fed rate cut example shows. Again, from a trading perspective, a trader wants to take positions that will achieve maximum benefit from the occurrence of the trading catalyst at minimum risk. Imagine a trader who anticipated the surprise Fed rate cut announcement shortly before it occurred or had advance knowledge of it. Which market or markets would the trader have placed his bet or bets on? It is not apparent that most traders would have selected the Nasdaq as the market most likely to have the largest reaction to the Fed rate cut announcement. Yet, in retrospect, it is clear that a long position in the Nasdaq 100 stock index or Nasdaq 100 stock index futures was the place to be immediately following the Fed rate cut announcement on January 3, 2001.

A trader needs to know the direction of the likely response to a trading catalyst to determine whether he should go long or short. Determining the likely direction of market prices in response to a trading catalyst seems easy. However, the implicit simple assumption that markets always behave a certain way in response to arguably the same trading catalyst is also not true. Sometimes, there is a shift in how a given trading catalyst is interpreted. Sometimes, the information content of the trading catalyst is simply ignored. For example, the Merchandise Trade Balance is a monthly report issued by the U.S. Department of Commerce. Yet, as discussed in Chapter 7, "Periodic Economic Reports," the conventional interpretation of the information content in the report changed 180 degrees between 1986 and 1987. Other times, the market seemingly ignores a trading catalyst. During most of the 1990s, the merchandise trade balance report—which was so important during the late 1980s—was largely ignored by bond market participants.

Financial and economic theory provides only limited guidance in how market prices should react to various trading catalysts. More important than financial or economic theory are traders' perceptions of both economic theory and how other market participants will react to the catalyst.

The *speed* of response in market prices ranges from immediate to extensive delays. The speed of a market's response to a given trading catalyst is usually fairly fast. However, as will be shown later in this book, sometimes there is a perceptible delay in the market's response. In any event, the relevant question for a trader is whether there is sufficient time after the trading catalyst occurs for the trader to position herself and profit from it. Other things equal, the speed of the market's response tends to increase the greater the liquidity and transparency of the market.

Consider once again the Fed's January 3, 2001 rate cut discussed previously. Most traders, of course, did not anticipate the surprise Fed action and may not have been positioned to take maximum advantage of it. Yet, a trader who was *flat* (i.e., had no position on) in Nasdaq futures before the Fed rate cut announcement still had time to put on a long position and profit from the attendant rise in prices sometime after the announcement came out. To be sure, prices moved quickly, but there was sufficient time to place a trade if one was willing to tolerate the risk associated with it.

A closely related issue is the *duration* of the response—that is, how long the trading catalyst continues to impact financial market prices. The length of the impact of a trading catalyst ranges from transitory to permanent. The impact of many trading catalysts is fairly short-lived. Indeed, sometimes the impact of a trading catalyst is entirely erased in the course of a single trading session, even in the absence of the arrival of any other trading catalysts. Consider, for instance, the following example reported in the January 11, 2005 issue of *The Wall Street Journal*.

> Energy prices have turned volatile again, driven up by the impact of production outages and unfavorable weather that have prompted traders to snap up oil and gas contracts...
>
> Crude oil surged to a five-week high of $47.30 a barrel during trading yesterday before retreating to end moderately lower, as a broad rally in oil-related futures markets stalled. Analysts said the various production problems, combined with forecasts of cold U.S. temperatures, spurred the nearly $2 rally, but the supply snags were overshadowed by a sense that the market had gotten ahead of itself. February crude oil fell 10 cents on the day to settle at $45.33 a barrel on the New York Mercantile Exchange...[14]

The preceding example illustrates how two different trading catalysts—production outages and the weather—combined to impact crude oil prices on the upside. Although a single "fuzzy" factor—the "sense that the market had gotten ahead of itself"—caused a price break. In this case, the effects of two trading catalysts on market prices were short-lived because the market reversed course due to other concerns. Notice that the entire gain and some 10 cents more were supposedly wiped out by fears "that the market had gotten ahead of itself."

Another dimension by which to measure the influence of a trading catalyst is the *intensity* of trading in the reaction to market prices that they induce. The intensity of trading varies from infrequent trading at one extreme to a *trading frenzy* at the other extreme. The intensity of trading refers to the frequency as well as size of individual trades.

A trading frenzy might arise from either panic buying or panic selling—euphoria or despair. At first glance, one might suppose that trading catalysts that precipitate either panic buying or panic selling must be very significant because of the large price changes they induce. However, there is no necessary relationship between the significance of the trading catalyst and the panic buying or panic selling that ensues. Simply stated, panic selling or panic buying need not be precipitated by a momentous event. The trigger for episodes of panic buying or selling may be seemingly innocuous enough. It is also important to point out that trading frenzies need not start out as such—that is, trading may accelerate sometime after the trading event occurs, as it did in the Fed rate cut example discussed previously.

Consider another example. News of the assassination of President John F. Kennedy on Friday, November 22, 1963 sparked a sell-off in stocks and a sharp decline in stock prices that threatened to turn into a selling panic. The initial sell-off prompted the New York Stock Exchange (NYSE) to stop trading and close early. When the market reopened on Tuesday, November 26, stocks not only quickly recovered but rallied sharply higher. Indeed, in his book, *101 Years on Wall Street: An Investor's Almanac*, John Dennis Brown characterizes the trading activity on Tuesday, November 26, 1963 as a "buying panic" that resulted in a 4.5% gain in the value of the Dow Jones Industrial Average.

This episode is interesting from another perspective: namely, how a news-oriented trading catalyst, the assassination of President Kennedy, which was only partially responded to because the market was closed early, can be quickly followed by a larger, and arguably, *reflexive* trading catalyst. Although it is impossible to know how far the Dow Jones Industrial Average would have fallen if the NYSE had not halted trading early, the sharp rally on Tuesday, November 26, 1963 illustrates the powerful impact that purely reflexive trading catalysts can exert on market prices.

At the other extreme is a slow market with infrequent trading following the occurrence of a trading catalyst. These catalysts are relatively rare but may occur when prices jump to reflect the impact of the trading catalyst without inducing additional trading activity. A variant of this is sometimes observed in satellite or related markets where there is a considerably more muted reaction than occurs in the primary market, even after adjusting for any differences in risk.

Another dimension of the impact of trading catalysts is the *breadth* of the market's reaction—that is, whether the response to a trading catalyst is *localized* (i.e., limited to one market or one sector) or *generalized* (i.e., affects multiple markets). In other words, a trading catalyst in one market can act as a trading catalyst for prices in another market. A frequent example in this regard is the impact that changes in oil prices have on equity prices and the impact that price changes in the equity market have on other markets. The reaction of other markets may be quick or slow.

Consider the following example reported in the Thursday, October 28, 2004 issue of the *Financial Times*.

> World oil prices dropped sharply yesterday after the US reported a bigger than expected rise in crude stocks…sending equity prices scurrying higher.
>
> The dollar climbed broadly…as the fall in oil prices alleviated the threat to the US economy posed by further rises in energy prices.
>
> Nymex crude oil futures fell swiftly as news of a bigger-than-expected rise in stocks of crude oil and gasoline outweighed a fall in heating oil stocks…

Nymex December crude fell almost 5 per cent to $52.46 per barrel...

...The Dow Jones Industrial Average gained 1.2 per cent to 10,002.30...The Nasdaq Composite put on 2.1 per cent.

Yet while oil was the clear catalyst for yesterday's gains, next week's presidential election, the result of which is too close to call, is casting an uncomfortable pall over financial markets...[15]

There are several lessons to be gleaned here. First, it is important to understand that every trading day new catalysts can impact the marketplace. Consequently, some trading catalysts may have short lives. Second, other trading catalysts—like the impending presidential election in the U.S.—could exert an influence on day-to-day trading and otherwise color the market environment for some time. The underlying concern—in this instance, the uncertain outcome of the impending U.S. presidential election—could dampen the overall sensitivity of equity prices to oil price changes. Third, notice that the market seemingly chose to ignore certain information, namely the drop in heating oil stocks.

Trading catalysts can be defined in a number of different ways. The approach taken in this book is to divide trading catalysts into two principal categories: those external to the market and those internal to the market. *External* trading catalysts can be further subdivided as follows: the comments of policymakers and politicians; domestic and geopolitical risk; weather and natural disasters; scheduled economic reports; unscheduled economic news; earnings announcements, court or regulatory decisions, and other company-specific news; rumors; and noise—non-fundamental factors that affect prices among others. *Internal* catalysts can be subdivided into the following: reflexive catalysts; cases where trading feeds on itself and exacerbates the price move (i.e., *positive feedback trading*) because of stop loss orders being hit, margin calls being made, or perceived technical barriers violated; and cases where price changes in one market spill over and affect price actions in other markets.[16] The latter category includes cases where the price action in foreign markets affects the subsequent price action in domestic markets as well as cases where the price action in one commodity, say crude oil, affects the price action in the stock market. Other ways of categorizing trading catalysts also exist.

One might classify reflex rallies as being precipitated by internally generated trading catalysts. However, the spark that causes the rally is more frequently a change in market perception rather than a specific event marking the end of the panic and a reversal of opinion. This is illustrated in the historic behavior of U.S. stock prices as measured by changes in the Dow Jones Industrial Average. Significant price reversals oftentimes seemingly come out of nowhere. John Dennis Brown, who examines the behavior of the Dow Jones Industrial Average from 1890 (the first full year that statistics were available) through 1990 in his book, *101 Years on Wall Street*, includes a list of important one-day buying panics.[17] These days are associated with substantial positive percentage changes in the Dow Jones Industrial Average ranging from a low of 4% to a high of 15.3%. Brown categorizes the rallies as "news-oriented," "war-influenced rallies," and "reflex from panic conditions." Of the 29 examples listed, 12 are classified as reflex rallies from panic conditions.[18]

Two examples of reflex rallies are the 12.3% rally on October 30, 1929 following the market crash of October 28 and 29, 1929 and the 10.1% rally in the Dow on October 21, 1987 following the market crash of October 19, 1987. As noted earlier, one problem with using event time to predict future market sensitivity to trading catalysts is the small sample sizes that one has to deal with. The idea that prices should recover some of their losses from a major sell-off or market crash seems reasonable but, once again, the sample size is too small to draw valid statistical inferences from. Nevertheless, when the next market crash occurs, many traders may be looking for a major short-term rally following the crash based on what has happened in response to previous market crashes.

Probably most individuals would argue that news-oriented rallies or sell-offs would exert more impact on market prices than reflex rallies or breaks would. However, that need not be the case. Another interesting aspect of John Dennis Brown's list of important one-day buying panics is that many of the news-oriented rallies had a smaller impact on market prices than the reflex rallies did. This highlights the danger of relying on the arrival of new information to explain large moves in market price.

The preceding division of trading catalysts into external and internal factors is sometimes problematic. Consider, for example, a situation in which crude oil prices surge due to production disruptions also results in equity prices falling because of the fear that higher oil prices may have on the overall economy. Under the preceding definition, the trading catalyst for the oil price move would be classified as an external factor but the trading catalyst for the equity price move would be internal—namely the rise in crude oil prices. The relevant issue is whether the price changes in one market are driving the price changes in another market or whether fear has simply spread to other markets.

Another way of categorizing trading catalysts is to decompose them into informational and noninformational factors. A proponent of the efficient capital markets hypothesis would argue that only the first category should impact market prices. However, both types of trading catalysts exist. And, noninformational factors sometimes have a larger impact on market prices than fundamental news.

Do Perceived Trading Catalysts Really Influence Market Prices?

Most observers would regard a surprise Fed announcement of a targeted Fed funds rate cut as an unambiguous trading catalyst. This is not always the case for all trading catalysts. Sometimes, the trading catalyst that sparks a large move in prices may be a matter of contention. Other times, trading catalysts that have regularly sparked large price moves in the past occur without any appreciable response in market prices. An example in this regard is the inconsistent impact that large changes in crude oil prices have on the equity market.

Trading catalysts that spark large and sudden changes in market prices are more readily identified than trading catalysts that spark small changes. However, sometimes trading catalysts spark small changes in market prices immediately but accumulate to a large change over time. This category of trading catalyst may also have an effect on market prices by reinforcing market sentiment and thereby help create the conditions for a more abrupt change in prices later.

There is a natural human tendency to impose order on apparent chaos. This tendency applies to attempts to explain financial market behavior as well. This is especially true for large price changes. Intuition suggests that there must be a *reason* for a large price change. Most of the time there is. For instance, few observers would dispute that news of the Federal Reserve rate cut sparked a rally in equity prices on January 3, 2001. However, sometimes large price changes occur for no apparent reason. This occurs more frequently than one might think. During 2000 and 2001, there were a number of instances where the Dow Jones Industrial Average or the Nasdaq Composite changed by 3% or more from the previous trading day. Yet, there is no readily identifiable source for many of these price moves. These large price moves may be the result of internal trading catalysts discussed in Chapter 8, "Size Matters," and Chapter 9, "Bubbles, Crashes, Corners, and Market Crises."

The lack of a readily identifiable source for many large price changes may explain the sometimes seemingly inconsistent behavior of market prices in response to certain trading catalysts over time. It may also explain how seemingly innocuous events can precipitate large price changes.

The preceding discussion assumes that there is only a single trading catalyst affecting the market at a given moment in time. It is possible that there may be several competing trading catalysts of which the news media only highlights one or two. Multiple trading catalysts could reinforce or offset one another. This may also explain apparent inconsistencies in the impact of the same trading catalyst on market prices over time. Isolating the individual market impact of multiple conflicting trading catalysts would likely be difficult. In any event, perhaps more important than the potential existence of multiple trading catalysts is whether most traders perceive (correctly or incorrectly) that trading activity is being driven by a single trading catalyst.

The question naturally arises as to whether the attribution by journalists of a large price move to a given trading catalyst is accurate. After all, journalists are expected to provide their readers, viewers, or listeners with informative explanations of what prompted a market move. Are the explanations in media accounts accurate descriptions of the causes of price moves, or are the reported catalysts simply rationalizations or excuses traders use for doing what they intended to do all along? There are two aspects to this question. First, is the reported trading catalyst the correct reason for the price action? Second, if so, what fraction of the price move is explained by the presumed trading catalyst?

To be sure, news media stories typically try to account for the price action of the entire trading day rather than focus on the immediate reaction to the trading catalyst. In addition, news media accounts of the impetus of a given price change may also be biased by the choice of whom the media interviews or obtains its information from. In any event, it is often impossible to determine the fraction of a market's reaction that can be attributed to a given trading catalyst. That said, contemporary news media accounts of the apparent causes for large changes in prices, although not perfect, provide a good summary of the perceived causes of large price changes during the day.

If the reported causes of large price moves are simply rationalizations by traders for doing what they already intended to do, the market-moving power comes not from the arrival of the trading catalyst but from the acquisition, hedging, or unwinding of trading positions and the trading they induce. Although it is possible to "explain" virtually any price change, it is worth noting that the puzzling behavior of financial prices is not confined to cases with ambiguous trading catalysts. As the opening example in this chapter demonstrates, the behavior of financial market prices in response to unambiguous trading catalysts is also sometimes puzzling. Moreover, there are numerous examples of puzzling market reactions to various trading catalysts that will be discussed in this book.

Trading Catalysts and Market Efficiency

The perceived influence of trading catalysts on market activity is intimately intertwined with the notion of market efficiency. In an informationally efficient financial market, prices change only with respect to the arrival of new information.[19] There are varying degrees of market efficiency that reflect differences in the amount of information available to market participants. This decomposition is due to Eugene F. Fama, who divides market efficiency into *weak form, semi-strong form*, and *strong form*.[20] Weak form market efficiency refers to a market whose current prices reflect any information contained in the series of past price changes. The principal implication is that certain forms of technical analysis, such as trend following, should not be profitable. Semi-strong form market efficiency refers to a market where prices fully and correctly reflect all publicly available information. In such a market, an individual cannot profit from investing on publicly available information. Strong form market efficiency refers to a market where prices fully and correctly reflect all available information public or private. In such a market, it is not possible to consistently earn a superior return. Market efficiency does not suggest that it is impossible to earn superior returns. Rather, it suggests that it is not possible to *consistently* earn superior risk-adjusted returns.[21]

There are several implications for trading catalysts if the market is informationally efficient. First, true trading catalysts would be limited to the arrival of new information in the marketplace. Prices would not respond to *noise*—non-fundamental factors that influence market prices. Second, the impact of trading catalysts on market prices would be immediate and complete. Prices would jump or fall instantaneously upon the arrival of new information. Third, the market would interpret any information content of trading catalysts correctly. Prices would not react to a trading catalyst and then a few minutes later return to where they were before the announcement unless new information entered the marketplace during the interim.

There is a considerable amount of evidence in the financial economic literature that suggests that changes in financial market prices do not follow a *normal* or *lognormal* distribution. Rather, changes in financial market prices seem to be drawn from a distribution that is *leptokurtic*—a distribution that has more probability mass in the center and in the tails than the normal distribution does. This means that large price changes should occur more frequently than they would under a normal distribution. A stock market crash of the magnitude of either the 1929 or 1987 crashes should almost never occur if changes in stock prices are normally distributed. Even mid-single-digit daily returns are exceedingly rare in a normal distribution.[22] The observation of two stock market crashes in U.S. equities during the twentieth century and numerous days with high single-digit percentage price changes serve as a useful reminder of the practical importance of the distribution of changes in stock prices. It is also a potent reminder of the power of trading catalysts.

There is also a considerable amount of evidence in the financial economic literature that suggests that the volatility of changes in financial market prices tends to both cluster and persist. This leads to the question of whether trading catalysts also cluster. The answer to this question depends on one's view of what causes prices to fluctuate. Individuals who subscribe to the efficient markets hypothesis would argue that trading catalysts cluster because the arrival of new information, and hence volatility, clusters. Market participants who do not subscribe to the efficient markets hypothesis would tend to disagree. They might argue that the more frequently trading catalysts occur, the more potential there is for trading catalysts to reinforce one another and increase perceived volatility.

Trading Is a Game

Active financial markets are invariably dominated by traders and trading activity. Although traders and investors share the same objective—to make money—they frequently differ in their approach to decision making. These differences matter and can influence the short-term behavior of market prices. It is important to understand that trading is essentially a game. The objective—to make money—remains constant, but the "rules" change over time. John Maynard Keynes put it this way:

> [P]rofessional investment may be likened to those newspaper competitions in which the competitors have to pick out the six prettiest faces from a hundred photographs, the prize being awarded to the competitor whose choice most nearly corresponds to the average preferences of the competitors as a whole; so that each competitor has to pick, not those faces which he himself finds prettiest, but those which he thinks likeliest to catch the fancy of the other competitors, all of whom are looking at the problem from the same point of view. It is not a case of choosing those which, to the best of one's judgment, are really the prettiest, nor even those which average opinion genuinely thinks the prettiest. We have

reached the third degree where we devote our intelligences to anticipating what average opinion expects the average opinion to be. And there are some, I believe, who practice the fourth, fifth and higher degrees.[23]

When viewed as a game, some of the apparent inconsistencies and anomalous behavior in the reaction of market prices to trading catalysts appear more understandable. There may not be a rational explanation for all market reactions. The point is, to paraphrase legendary trader Richard Dennis, markets need not make sense.[24]

Trading Off of Catalysts

The timing of certain potential trading catalysts is known in advance. Examples include the release of periodic economic reports, elections, and certain presentations by politicians and policymakers. This allows traders the opportunity to position themselves in advance of the potential trading catalyst. It also provides more time for consensus expectations to form. And, it is the forecast error (the difference between consensus expectations and the actual results) that the market will respond to. One consequence of more precise consensus expectations is a smaller forecast error. In turn, this suggests a smaller market response for scheduled potential trading catalysts, other things equal, than for unscheduled potential trading catalysts.

Scheduled potential trading catalysts have another impact on trading activity, and that is to alter the timing of entry or exit of positions *unrelated* to a bet on the potential trading catalyst. For instance, the release of the monthly employment report by the U.S. Department of Labor often affects the bond, stock, and currency markets. A trader who wants to enter or exit some market might delay or accelerate doing so in order to avoid being stopped out from a position because of an adverse move caused by the release of a report that he does not have an opinion on.

In contrast, the timing of other potential trading catalysts may be unknown, but the outcome is fairly well-known. An example in this regard would be the invasion of Iraq during 2003. It was readily apparent to many observers that the Bush administration had already decided to invade Iraq months before it did. However, the timing of the action was uncertain to market participants. Another example would be the decision to end the 1:1 peg of the Argentine peso to the U.S. dollar. By late 2001 it was clear that the link would be broken; however, it was not clear as to when the peg would be ended.

The timing and content of many trading catalysts is unpredictable so that a trader cannot position herself in advance to take advantage of the perceived opportunity. Is it too late to profitably trade after a trading catalyst occurs? Not necessarily. Trading opportunities also exist after a trading catalyst occurs. Again, the nature and extent of the trading opportunities depend on the magnitude and duration of the market's reaction to a trading catalyst. In some cases, the market reaction may allow plenty of time to put a position on (albeit at less favorable prices than before the trading catalyst occurred). As noted earlier, a trader does not need a lot of time to put a position on or take a position off.

Not only is the *timing* or *content* of certain trading catalysts unpredictable but sometimes so is the market reaction. The Federal Reserve's cut in the targeted Fed funds rate illustrates the conventional view of the impact that a surprise central bank rate cut would have on equity prices. As will become apparent in this book, the market's reaction to trading catalysts is not always so predictable. As will be shown in the next chapter, market conditions and sentiment bias can influence the magnitude and duration of the market's response to a given trading catalyst. This adds a dimension of risk when trading off of scheduled economic reports and other potential trading catalysts whose timing is known in advance.

The opening example of a cut in the targeted Fed funds rate by the Federal Reserve illustrates a case where the price reaction is both relatively quick and large. Yet, as was noted, there is still time to put a position on. Sometimes, the reaction to a trading catalyst may not be as quick. Indeed, in some cases, the timing of the trading catalyst may not provoke an immediate reaction in market prices—that is, the reaction may be significantly delayed. Several examples of delayed reactions to events are discussed in the book. Delayed reactions create confusion over what the proper reaction to a trading catalyst should be but also create opportunities to put a position on.

In the January 3, 2001 Fed rate cut example, the impact on Nasdaq stock index futures prices grew as time passed during the first few minutes rather than declined in amplitude as time passed. This phenomenon is sometimes observed for trading catalysts that induce a delayed market reaction where the effect grows as time passes rather than diminishes. Another example in this regard is the reaction in the Indian stock market to news of the Congress' party's apparent victory in 2004. Yet another example is the reaction of Japanese markets to news of the Kobe earthquake in 1995. Both of these examples are discussed in more detail in Chapter 4, "Geopolitical Events," and Chapter 5, "Weather and Natural Disasters" respectively.

This book primarily focuses on trading catalysts that induce or seemingly induce large changes in prices. However, it also considers trading catalysts that may seemingly start a new trend in prices or reinforce an existing one. Basically, it is recognized that the impact of a trading catalyst may not be limited to a single trading day. Sometimes, there is a small reaction that accumulates into a large reaction over time. For instance, buying or selling frenzies or panics may extend and accelerate over time before climaxing. Most trend-following traders wait for the price action in the market to dictate when to enter or exit a position. The example that opens this chapter also illustrates a situation in which a positive short-term trend followed the Federal Reserve action.

Trading catalysts occur with great frequency. However, only a few induce large changes in prices immediately or cumulatively over time. Most daily changes in financial market prices are relatively small in percentage terms. Thus, large percentage price moves are of interest because they are both less common and because they tell us something about the process that generates changes in prices.

It would be wrong to think of traders as waiting for a trading catalyst to occur before responding to it by taking positions. To be sure, large price moves are often accompanied by large trading volumes. However, as explained in the next chapter, knowledge of market conditions and sentiment bias can create the conditions where the market can be subject to all manner of potential trading catalysts. Simply stated, a trader can react to a trading catalyst after it occurs or anticipate the market's reaction prior to the occurrence of the catalyst or catalysts and position herself accordingly.

Trading catalysts can affect the short-term liquidity of the market, as was shown by the dramatic impact the Fed rate cut had on the effective Nasdaq 100 stock index futures bid/ask spread on January 3, 2001. An increase in volatility may also be considered a trading catalyst by stimulating trading volume. It is also a factor that is internal to the market. Increased volatility leads to increased demand for vehicles to hedge the volatility. The additional trading may also create more short-term trading opportunities.

As will be discussed in more detail in later chapters, the market's reaction to a trading catalyst need not be consistent over time. Sometimes, the market focuses on one potential trading catalyst to the exclusion of other trading catalysts that might be announced at the same time. It seems that the market acts as if it has a one-track mind. Sometimes, it is not clear what the market really reacts to.

The price changes that trading catalysts induce are often transitory. This means that a trader seeking to position himself in advance of a potential trading catalyst will have to determine the appropriate time horizon for any prospective trade. Strong money management rules might keep a trader in a profitable position longer than the trader anticipated when he entered the trade. However, the trader is still subject to the risk of a sudden price reversal before the trader exits his position. For example, a trader who entered a buy order for the Nasdaq futures contract a few minutes late and was filled at 2650 on January 3, 2001 would find that he bought at the high of the day. All of this makes trading off of trading catalysts both difficult and risky.

References

Allais, Maurice. "Forgetfulness and Interest." *Journal of Money, Credit and Banking.* Vol. 4, Issue 1, February 1972, pp. 40-73.

Bahree, Bhusan, and Chip Cummins. "Energy-Price Volatility Returns Due to Output Outages, Weather," *The Wall Street Journal.* January 11, 2005, p. C5.

Brown, John Dennis. *101 Years on Wall Street: An Investor's Almanac.* New York: Prentice Hall, 1991.

Clausewitz, Carl von. *On War.* Edited and translated into English by Michael Howard and Peter Paret. Princeton: Princeton University Press, Revised edition, 1984.

Fama, Eugene F. "Efficient Capital Markets: A Review of Theory and Empirical Work." *Journal of Finance*, XXV, No. 2, May 1970, pp. 383-417.

Federal Reserve Board of Governors Web Site (http://www.federalreserve.gov/boarddocs/press/general/2001/20010103/default.htm), Federal Open Market Committee Press Release, January 3, 2001.

Francis, Jack C., and Roger Ibbotson. *Investments: A Global Perspective.* Upper Saddle River, New Jersey: Prentice Hall, 2002.

Jackwerth, Jens C., and M. Rubinstein. "Recovering Probability Distributions from Option Prices." *Journal of Finance*, December 1996, pp. 1611-1631.

Keynes, John Maynard. *The General Theory of Employment, Interest and Money*. New York: Harcourt, Brace and World, 1935.

Morgan, Michael. "Crude Price Dip Boosts Stocks." *Financial Times*, October 28, 2004, p. 28.

Roberts, Harry. "Stock Market 'Patterns' and Financial Analysis: Methodological Suggestions." *Journal of Finance*, Vol. 12, No. 1, March 1959, pp. 1-10.

Schwager, Jack D. *Market Wizards: Interviews with Top Traders*. New York: New York Institute of Finance, 1989.

Waters, Richard. "ebay Shares Fall by 11% as Earnings Falter." *Financial Times*, January 20, 2005, p. 15.

Endnotes

[1] Carl von Clausewitz, *On War*.

[2] The announcement was released at approximately 1:14 P.M. Eastern Standard Time. An examination of the wording of the announcement is interesting for what it says and what it does not say. The text of the announcement follows:

> The Federal Open Market Committee decided today to lower its target for the federal funds rate by 50 basis points to 6 percent. In a related action, the Board of Governors approved a 25-basis-point decrease in the discount rate to 5-3/4 percent, the level requested by seven Reserve Banks. The Board also indicated that it stands ready to approve a further reduction of 25 basis points in the discount rate to 5-1/2 percent on the requests of Federal Reserve Banks.

> These actions were taken in light of further weakening of sales and production, and in the context of lower consumer confidence, tight conditions in some segments of financial markets, and high energy prices sapping household and business purchasing power. Moreover, inflation pressures remain contained. Nonetheless, to date there is little evidence to suggest that longer-term advances in technology and associated gains in productivity are abating. The Committee continues to believe that, against the background of its long-run goals of price stability and sustainable economic growth and of the information currently available, the risks are weighted mainly toward conditions that may generate economic weakness in the foreseeable future. In taking the discount rate action, the Federal Reserve Board approved requests submitted by the Boards of Directors of the Federal Reserve Banks of New York, Cleveland, Atlanta, St. Louis, Kansas City, Dallas and San Francisco.

[3] The Nasdaq 100 index consists of the 100 largest nonfinancial companies in terms of market capitalization listed on Nasdaq, whereas the Nasdaq Composite reflects almost every firm traded on Nasdaq. Tracking stocks allow market participants to trade an index just like they would an individual stock.

[4] Stock index futures contracts allow market participants to bet on the future value of the index.

[5] This is not the case for some agricultural commodities. Another exception to this rule occurs during rollover periods when the trading volume of the futures contract that is the second closest to expiration exceeds the trading volume of the contract that is closest to expiration. Essentially, the second closest to expiration contract displaces the closest to expiration futures contract as the effective front month contract. The front month contract is *not* the futures contract that is closest to expiration for some commodities like Eurodollar futures.

[6] The *notional* or dollar value of the Nasdaq 100 futures contract is $100 times the Nasdaq 100 index value. Thus, an index value of 2000 would imply that the futures contract had a notional value of $200,000. In other words, one Nasdaq 100 stock index futures contract would be equivalent to buying a $200,000 diversified portfolio of Nasdaq stocks whose performance mirrors the Nasdaq 100 index. The minimum price move, or *tick*, on the contract is .50 point. Each tick has a value of $50 ($100 times .50).

[7] As John Dennis Brown points out in his book, *101 Years on Wall Street*, the high on the DJIA for 1929 was reached on September 3, 1929 when it hit 381.17. It should also be noted that the stock market had declined significantly from the high before the crash occurred in late October of 1929.

[8] Jack C. Francis and Roger Ibbotson. *Investments: A Global Perspective*. Upper Saddle River, New Jersey: Prentice Hall, 2002, p. 25. Francis and Ibbotson report that the *compound* annual return for large company and small company stocks over the same period was 11.3% and 12.6%, respectively.

[9] The Nasdaq 100 stock index futures contract settled at 2529.50 or 362 points higher than the previous day. The spot Nasdaq 100 index closed at 2528.38 or 399.60 points higher for the day. The Chicago Mercantile Exchange also lists an electronically traded version of the Nasdaq 100 stock index futures contract that is one-fifth the size of the pit-traded Nasdaq 100 stock index futures contract. It might be argued that the behavior of the e-mini futures prices were more representative of the market's reaction to the Fed rate cut trading catalyst. However, such an argument ignores the fact that the daily price change was essentially the same for both contracts. Moreover, the pit-traded Nasdaq 100 contract exceeded the trading volume of the Nasdaq e-mini futures contract on a size-adjusted basis. Note that the pit-traded volume was 35,677 contracts on January 3, 2001, virtually all of which were March 2001 futures contracts. The Nasdaq e-mini futures contract had record trading volume of 115,139 contracts on January 3, 2001, virtually all in the March 2001 contract.

[10] *Marketplace*. January 3, 2001.

[11] These and most other figures in this book are presented in Japanese Candlesticks format, where open, high, low, and close data are used to construct simple bar charts.

[12] The trader would also be interested in the position size that he could put on and the expected slippage associated with the prospective trade. Slippage measures the difference between the price at which the trader can actually execute the trade at and the price quote he observes when he submits the trade.

[13] Expectations of the future are often a function of individual past experiences or perceptions of the past experiences of others. To the extent that memory plays a role in formulating expectations of the future, the question arises as to how individuals weight past observations in formulating expectations about the future. Put differently, what is the rate of forgetfulness of individuals? This is not merely a function of calendar time. Nobel Laureate economist Maurice Allais discusses the rate of forgetfulness and argues that individuals form expectations adaptively.

[14] Bhusan Bahree and Chip Cummins. "Energy-Price Volatility Returns Due to Output Outages, Weather." *The Wall Street Journal*, January 11, 2005, p. C5.

[15] Michael Morgan. "Crude Prices Dip Boosts Stocks." *Financial Times*, Thursday, October 24, 2004, p. 28.

[16] Positive feedback trading refers to cases where a rise in prices spurs additional buying, which drives up prices even further, and a fall in prices spurs additional selling, which drives prices down lower.

[17] John Dennis Brown. *101 Years on Wall Street: An Investor's Almanac*. New York: Prentice Hall, 1991.

[18] Of course, this assumes that Brown's classification is correct. It is possible that other observers would identify other trading catalysts associated with the large percentage price changes on those days.

[19] An exception is changes in the value of default free discount securities (e.g., Treasury bills), which increase in value as time passes if the interest rate remains the same or lower.

[20] Eugene F. Fama. "Efficient Capital Markets: A Review of Theory and Empirical Work." *Journal of Finance*, XXV, No. 2, May 1970, pp. 383-417.

[21] Proponents of market efficiency argue that the observation of individuals who consistently beat the market is simply a product of chance. Proponents of market inefficiency argue that such observations are evidence that the market is inefficient.

[22] In a fascinating article, Jens C. Jackwerth and Mark Rubinstein use option prices to ascertain the relevant (risk-neutral) probability distribution that U.S. stock market participants face. They argue that large one-day returns of the magnitude earned or lost on the stock market crash of October 1987, for example, would be virtually impossible if security returns were lognormally distributed. They state (on pages 1611 and 1612):

> On October 19, 1987, the two month S&P 500 futures price fell 29 percent. Under the lognormal hypothesis, this is a -27 standard deviation

event with probability 10^{160}, which is virtually impossible. Nor is October 1987 a unique refutation of the lognormal hypothesis. Two years later, on October 13, 1989, the S&P 500 index fell about 6 percent, a -5 standard deviation event. Under the maintained hypothesis [of lognormality], this has a probability of 0.00000027 and should occur only once in every 14,756 years.

The fact that extreme price moves occur with greater frequency means that the relevant return distribution for traders and investors has fatter tails than a normal distribution does. J.C. Jackwerth and M. Rubinstein, *Journal of Finance*, 1996, "Recovering Probability Distributions from Option Prices," pp. 1611-1631.

[23] John Maynard Keynes. *The General Theory of Employment, Interest and Prices.* 1935, p. 156.

[24] Jack Schwager [1989] reports Richard Dennis' response to his question, "What is the biggest public fallacy about market behavior?" as "That markets are supposed to make sense" (p. 106).

2

MARKET CONDITIONS AND SENTIMENT

"Water shapes its course according to the nature of the ground over which it flows; the soldier works out his victory in relation to the foe whom he is facing. Therefore, just as water retains no constant shape, so in warfare there are no constant conditions."

—Sun Tzu[1]

Treasury Announcement Discontinuing Issuance of 30-Year Bonds

At approximately 9:50 A.M. on Wednesday, October 31, 2001, the U.S. Treasury announced that the 30-year Treasury (or *long*) bond would no longer be issued. The immediate reaction of Treasury bond prices did not reflect the significance of the announcement, in large part, because the announcement came from the inadvertent and premature posting of the text of then Treasury Undersecretary Peter Fisher's remarks on the department's Web site about 10 minutes before the news embargo was to be lifted. As a result, the long bond rose modestly at first, from about 102 27/64 at 9:50:09 to 103 1/32 at 9:55:33. However, prices quickly gathered steam as word of the announcement spread. Prices had risen to 104 1/32 by 10:00, the time of the scheduled announcement. This full-point move was only the beginning as the news set off a firestorm of panic buying. Prices rallied over the next 21 minutes or so, before falling back only to rally again to over 108 shortly after 1:00 P.M. The long bond was up over 5 1/4 points by the end of the day, and the yield had fallen by 34 basis points.[2] This is a huge move in the Treasury bond market. Indeed, the Treasury announcement sparked the largest one-day rally in Treasury bond prices since the October 19, 1987 stock market crash.

The rally did not end on Wednesday. On Thursday, November 1, 2001, the "long bond" rallied to a high of 111 13/32, or almost 3 3/4 points above the previous day's close, before pulling back and closing at 108 31/32. Market talk attributed the continuing rally on Thursday to the Treasury announcement the previous day and the actions of institutional investors in response to it. The massive rally in Treasury bond prices following the Treasury Department's announcement is depicted in Figure 2.1.

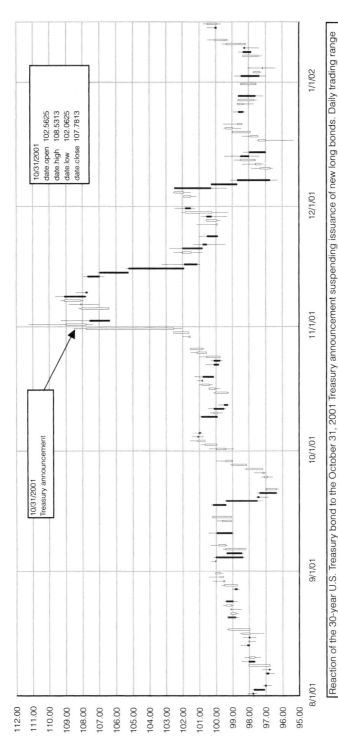

10/31/2001
Treasury announcement

10/31/2001
date.open 102.5625
date.high 108.5313
date.low 102.0625
date.close 107.7813

8/1/01   9/1/01   10/1/01   11/1/01   12/1/01   1/1/02

Reaction of the 30-year U.S. Treasury bond to the October 31, 2001 Treasury announcement suspending issuance of new long bonds. Daily trading range of the cash market 30-year Treasury bond from August 1, 2001 to January 15, 2002.

FIGURE 2.1   The Treasury suspends issuance of the long bond.

Note that contrary to what the efficient market hypothesis would predict, the bond market took a long time to digest the news of the Treasury decision. First, the market did not react fully to the inadvertent and premature posting of the announcement on the Treasury Department's Web site on Wednesday. Second, the market continued to react to the news throughout the rest of the trading day. Third, the Treasury bond market had an intraday move on Thursday, November 1, 2001 that was approximately half the size of the previous day's move when the news came out. The lack of other news suggests that the Treasury bond market was responding to either the previous day's news or the Treasury market's reaction to the previous day's news. Fourth, Thursday's market move was not all in one direction. After rallying another 3 3/4 points on Thursday, the market gave up almost 2 1/2 points—a significant correction. This suggests that the market overreacted to the Treasury announcement. Once again, there was plenty of time for traders to trade off of the news.

Where should a trader have placed her bets upon learning of the Treasury announcement? A trader learning of the news on the Treasury Web site prior to 10:00 A.M. might have been tempted to buy December 2001 Treasury bond futures contracts traded on the Chicago Board of Trade (CBOT) instead of buying Treasury bonds in the cash market. The Treasury bond futures market is deep and liquid and often leads the corresponding cash market. Traders can easily do size without significantly affecting transaction prices.

However, such a decision would have been a mistake as Figure 2.2 shows. The reason is that the strong reaction in the cash Treasury bond market was largely absent in the Treasury bond futures markets. An examination of time and sales data for the December 2001 Treasury bond futures contracts reveals that the futures price was at 108 21/32 at 9:50:12 A.M., shortly before the announcement was posted on the Web, and settled at 110 14/32 by the end of the day. Although the almost 1 3/4 point move would have resulted in a substantial profit, the profit pales in comparison to what a trader could have made given the almost 5 1/4 point move in the cash bond market. Anticipating the market's reaction to news is important, but it is also important to position oneself in the right market in order to maximize profits.

Why was there a substantially different reaction in Treasury bond cash and futures market prices? The principal explanation for this seeming anomaly is that the CBOT Treasury bond futures contract allows delivery of a whole array of Treasury bonds on the contract rather than just Treasury bonds that mature in 30 years.[3] Because the individual who is short Treasury bond futures has the option of choosing which Treasury bonds to deliver (and the rational short almost invariably chooses the cheapest bond), the Treasury bond futures contract tracks the *cheapest-to-deliver* Treasury bond. This is rarely, if ever, the *on-the-run* (i.e., most recently issued) 30-year Treasury bond. Consequently, buying the December 2001 Treasury bond futures contract on October 31, 2001 was tantamount to being long the cheapest-to-deliver Treasury bond on a day when news impacted longer maturity Treasury bonds much more than the cheapest-to-deliver Treasury bond. Not surprisingly, the 30-year Treasury bond futures contract did not rally as much as the cash 30-year Treasury bond did.

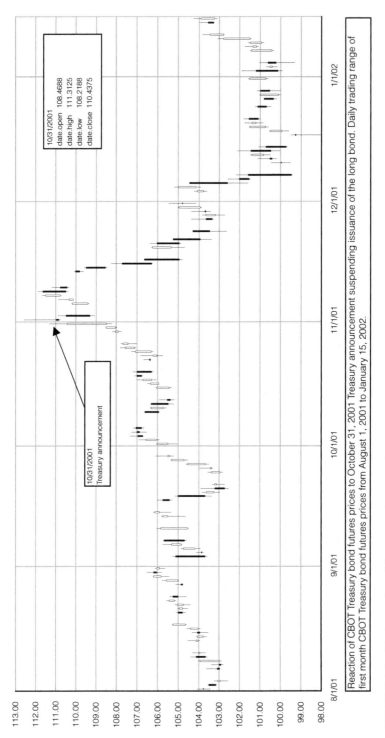

FIGURE 2.2 Treasury bond futures prices react.

Reaction of CBOT Treasury bond futures prices to October 31, 2001 Treasury announcement suspending issuance of the long bond. Daily trading range of first month CBOT Treasury bond futures prices from August 1, 2001 to January 15, 2002.

The market's reaction to the Treasury announcement on Wednesday, October 31 is further complicated by the subsequent discovery that a bond trading consultant (whom Treasury officials had thought was simply another reporter) had sat in on the Treasury's quarterly refunding press briefing and, in violation of the news embargo until 10:00 A.M., had conveyed the information to individuals at a major investment bank and a fixed income management firm shortly after the Treasury Department's press conference ended at 9:25 A.M.[4] This meant that news of the Treasury's impending action was known by at least two major bond market participants well in advance of the actual announcement. This knowledge enabled the recipients of the information to take positions in the Treasury bond cash and futures markets that would benefit when the information became publicly available. This is *insider trading* and is illegal in the United States.

Insider trading in the Treasury bond market is a rare event, in large part, because there is little information that is truly inside. Certain Treasury Department debt-management decisions and Federal Reserve monetary policy actions are exceptions. The details of the present case provide fascinating insights into insider trading ahead of a major trading catalyst and warrant close examination.

The Securities and Exchange Commission (SEC) announced enforcement actions on September 4, 2003 against some of the parties involved in the misappropriation of, and trading on, inside information involving the Treasury's decision to cease issuance of the long bond. Essentially, the Securities and Exchange Commission alleged that

> Peter Davis—a Washington D.C. based consultant—...attended the Treasury Department's quarterly refunding press conference on the morning of Oct. 31, 2001, where he learned of the Treasury's decision to cease issuance of the 30-year bond...Davis called numerous clients and tipped them to news about the cancellation of the long bond before the Treasury Department's news embargo was lifted and the news was made generally available to the public. John M.

Youngdahl,...formerly a Vice President and Senior Economist at Goldman Sachs & Co., [entered into an agreement with Davis in July 2001 whereby] Davis would provide Youngdahl with confidential information he learned at Treasury Department refunding press conferences...[A]fter receiving Davis's call on the morning of Oct. 31, 2001, Youngdahl tipped traders on Goldman Sachs' U.S. Treasury Desk to the news about the Treasury's decision to cease issuance of the long bond. While the news was still nonpublic, the traders purchased $84 million worth of 30-year bonds for Goldman Sachs' own accounts, generating illegal profits of over $1.5 million...[5]

In a related announcement, SEC staff indicated that Goldman Sachs made $2.3 million from purchasing 2336 CBOT Treasury bond futures contracts after learning of the Treasury's impending action.[6] Goldman's Treasury bond futures position had a notional value of $233.6 million, or slightly less than three times the size of the cash market position it took. Interestingly, Goldman did not maximize its potential profits from trading off of the advance information of the Treasury's announcement because it chose to trade mostly Treasury bond futures contracts.[7]

The Treasury Department's announcement to discontinue 30-year Treasury bonds induced an exceptionally powerful rally that lasted the better part of two days before subsiding. What made this trading catalyst so powerful and long-lasting? Was it the nature of the announcement or its timing, or did other factors play a significant role?

Market Conditions, Sentiment, and Trading Catalysts

As noted in the previous chapter, traders form *trading theses* about how financial and commodity markets should react to potential trading catalysts. However, the power of a statement, action, or event to serve as a trading catalyst is intimately intertwined with the *market conditions* and *sentiment bias* that prevail at any moment of time. Market conditions and sentiment bias can exacerbate a price move, mitigate it, change the direction of the reaction in prices from previous reactions to similar events, cause an otherwise potentially significant trading catalyst to be seemingly ignored by the market, or in some cases, even induce a significant change in prices to the occurrence of widely anticipated events. Market conditions and sentiment bias can also affect the duration of the impact of trading catalysts on market prices.

Markets are sometimes characterized by fads where a particular sector (e.g., biotech stocks) is considered hot. Less common are extreme market events such as *bubbles, crashes,* or *crises.* Fads and extreme market events have a dynamic all their own and not only influence the potential power of trading catalysts on market prices but also impact the set of potential trading catalysts. The interrelationship between trading catalysts and extreme market events is considered in Chapter 9, "Bubbles, Crashes, Corners, and Market Crises." This chapter focuses on the impact of market conditions and sentiment bias on the power of trading catalysts during more normal market conditions.

Market conditions refer to the underlying *economic situation, policy regime, political environment, risk preference level,* and *trading environment* that prevail at a given moment in time. Traders must assess a variety of factors to obtain a sense of market conditions. This task is made more difficult because some factors (e.g., the strength of the economy) may also depend upon other factors (e.g., monetary policy). It would be wrong to give the impression that traders are interested in making detailed assessments of the economy and politics. Rather, traders are trying to answer some recurring basic questions in order to improve their trading performance. For instance, is the economy *expanding* or *contracting?* Is central bank monetary policy *accommodative* or *restrictive?* Is the average level of *risk aversion* among market participants high or low? Is the market *tranquil* or *turbulent, choppy* or *normal, liquid* or *illiquid, overbought* or *oversold?* Are there concentrated trading positions in one direction by key market participants? Can one trade in size without unduly affecting market prices? These are only some of many potential market conditions. Some market conditions may also act as *internal* market catalysts.

Sentiment is a measure of the collective market bias of traders and other market participants—that is, market sentiment is a way of characterizing whether a given market overall has a *bullish* or *bearish* bias with respect to likely future price action and the extent of the bias. Of course, not every market participant shares the same point of view or market bias at any moment in time. After all, differences of opinions make markets. Sentiment bias can reinforce or retard a price move a trading catalyst precipitates. It can also exacerbate a price move opposite to the sentiment bias as traders move to cover losing positions.

There is a time dimension to sentiment bias as well—that is, sentiment bias may vary across the short-term, medium-term, and long-term. For instance, a trader could have a negative outlook on the stock market for the medium- or long-term but be bullish about its prospects for the short-term. The same is true for the market overall. These differences are important to understand as they impact how long a trade is held and may also impact the position size a trader puts on.

Market conditions and sentiment bias may interact with and depend on each other. It is easy to imagine various market conditions combined with various sentiment biases. Numerous combinations are possible.[8] In a sense, market conditions and sentiment bias are analogous to the amount of dead trees and other easily combustible material on a forest floor. Other things equal, the greater the amount of easily combustible material on a forest floor the greater the danger of a forest fire from a lightning strike and the worse the fire is likely to be. Similarly, gauging market conditions and sentiment bias is important in evaluating the potential power and duration of a trading catalyst on prices should a trading catalyst spark a move in prices.

Perceived market conditions also influence trading decisions in accordance with how one expects the market to behave. For example, there is a widespread belief that growing economies are characterized by rising interest rates. The reasoning is simply that there is a greater demand for credit when the economy is expanding. This means that interest rates should rise, holding the supply of credit constant. During the summer of 2004, many traders expected long-term interest rates to rise with the growing economy and long rates to rise more than short rates, causing the yield curve to steepen. Put differently, perceived market conditions were the essential premise behind this trade. In this instance, the trade did not work out and one investment bank reportedly lost several hundred million dollars on the trade.

It is important to recognize that traders are often looking for a *skewed* distribution when others see a *symmetric* distribution. When everyone is on one side of the market (figuratively speaking), the one-sided trade can easily reverse. Simply stated, traders are searching for trades with outsized rewards with little or moderate risk. It might be argued that skewed distributions are more likely to exist when market participants share common beliefs and market expectations—that is, when there is substantial sentiment bias. Skewed distributions need not be inherently more common under one set of market conditions than another. However, as shown in Chapter 6, "Market Interventions," skewed distributions may be more likely at turning points.

Not only do market conditions and sentiment influence the magnitude and duration of the market's response to a trading catalyst, but market conditions and sentiment influence the breadth of the price move. This may cause a catalyst that might otherwise affect a single commodity or security to affect the overall market. Market conditions and sentiment may also influence the direction prices move in reaction to a trading catalyst as well as how long a trading catalyst impacts market prices. In some cases, market conditions and sentiment may cause a potential trading catalyst to be ignored. In other cases, with different market conditions and sentiment levels, the same trading catalyst may exert a powerful impact on market prices.

Consider the Treasury announcement to discontinue issuance of 30-year Treasury bonds discussed previously. As noted in Footnote 2, *The Wall Street Journal* article on the announcement reports: "many Wall Street traders were betting the price of the security would drop not rise. Some had sold 30-year bonds short, borrowing and selling them." This illustrates the prevailing bearish sentiment among many market participants that there would be increased supply of the bonds as the government financed "new spending programs resulting from the Sept. 11 terrorist attacks." It also illustrates a common trading position that many market participants had on at the time. The fact that many, presumably key, market participants were short bonds meant that any catalyst that prompted a rise in Treasury bond prices could trigger a short covering rally as traders with short positions moved to limit their losses. This, in turn, would exacerbate the market's reaction to the news.[9] This illustrates how market conditions and sentiment bias can exacerbate a price move.

Although the general tone of the market may be easy to assess, the degree of market sentiment bias is more difficult to measure. Some market observers use price action as a proxy for market sentiment. This can be misleading because some of the largest jumps in prices may occur when the overall market is bearish and some of the largest declines in prices may occur when overall sentiment in the market is preponderantly bullish. An example of the latter would be the stock market crash of 1929.

Reverses can occur suddenly as well. For instance, recall the excerpt from the January 11, 2005 issue of *The Wall Street Journal* that was discussed in Chapter 1, "Introduction," and reported a bullish short-term market bias for energy.[10] At one point, crude oil futures were up almost $2 per barrel, setting a multi-week high. Yet, crude oil prices fell to close $.10 below the level of the previous day.

Simply stated, a significant price break occurred quickly in a market with a bullish short-term outlook.

It might be argued that knowledge of market conditions and sentiment bias is more important in assessing the impact of news than on scheduled economic reports and other similar announcements. In the latter case, information on consensus expectations may be available; whereas in the former case, it most often is not. Earnings announcements are another example of potential trading catalysts whose timing is often scheduled. As was stated earlier, scheduled trading catalysts allow for more precise estimates of consensus expectations. However, sometimes even a slight disappointment in earnings can lead to sharp declines in a stock's price. Consider, for example, eBay's announcement of 2004 fourth-quarter earnings as reported in the January 20, 2005 issue of the *Financial Times*.

eBay failed to live up to Wall Street expectations when it announced fourth quarter earnings yesterday, prompting a sharp reversal in its stock price in after-market trade... Investors...wipe[d] more than 11 per cent from the stock price.

eBay's latest earnings per share, at 33 cents, slipped a cent below expectations...After a stock price rally that has seen the shares soar by more than 300 per cent over the past two years, the mild shortfall brought a sharp reaction from investors. Shares were down $11.96 in after-hours trading at $91.09...[11]

The preceding example is interesting for several reasons. First, it demonstrates how even a small forecast error can have a dramatic effect on market prices. The one-cent miss in fourth-quarter earnings accounted for about 3% of earnings, but the stock price fell three times that amount. This example also illustrates the importance of the market environment on the behavior of prices. Notice how the article notes how the past sharp 300% increase in the stock price made the market for the stock vulnerable to a larger decline in the stock's price. This gives a better sense of the interrelationships between market conditions and sentiment bias.

The level of risk aversion impacts financial and commodity market prices by affecting the risk premium that market participants demand. A sudden increase in risk aversion can cause a sharp drop in financial market prices.

A fundamental belief of most traders is that market conditions recur with some frequency. And because they recur, traders may look at how the market responded to a given trading catalyst in the past under similar market conditions and sentiment bias to gauge how market prices are likely to respond this time. Another way to look at this is that the response of market prices is conditional upon market conditions and sentiment (or as economists might say, the *state of the world*). Thus, traders speculating at the end or the sudden beginning of a war might look at the reaction of financial markets the last time war began or ended. The same is true of traders trying to anticipate the impact of the first in an anticipated series of Federal Reserve interest rate cuts or hikes. As noted in Chapter 1, this is called *event time*.

When there are multiple occurrences of similar events under similar market conditions, the question naturally arises as to how much weight should be attached to past events. One approach is to take advantage of the larger sample size and use an average of past market reactions to get a measure of the market's likely reaction. Another approach is to attach greater weight to the more recent events. The latter approach is probably more commonly employed by traders. There is also some theoretical justification for it. Again, as noted in Chapter 1, the French economist and 1988 Nobel Laureate in Economics, Maurice Allais, posited a *rate of forgetfulness* in which the weight attached to past observations declines as time passes.[12]

Treasury Announcement of Potential Resumption of 30-Year Bond Issuance

The Treasury's decision to discontinue issuance of 30-year bonds in October 2001 is made more interesting by the announcement on

Wednesday, May 4, 2005 that the U.S. Treasury was *considering* whether to resume issuance of 30-year bonds. The announcement was made at about 9:00 A.M. by Assistant Treasurer Timothy Bitsberger. He noted that a final decision on whether the Treasury would resume issuance of 30-year bonds would be made in August 2005. Not surprisingly, the announcement sparked a sharp sell-off in 30-year Treasury bonds. The excitement of the day's market action was captured in the following story that was reported on Bloomberg.com on May 4, 2005.

> The 30-year U.S. Treasury bond had its biggest drop in almost two months after the government said it may resume sales...The 5 3/8 percent bond due in February 2031 fell as much as 8.5 points, or $85 per $1,000 face amount, in the minutes after the announcement as investors suddenly became concerned about more supply.
>
> The bond pared some of its losses in afternoon trading, and was down about 1 3/4 to 111 25/32 at 5:05 P.M. in New York...The yield rose 11 basis points,...to 4.59 percent...The yield reached 5.02 percent as its price tumbled to 105 soon after the 9 A.M. announcement. The plunge was the biggest fluctuation of any government debt security today.[13]

The behavior of Treasury bond prices in reaction to the announcement is both instructive and puzzling. One would expect a sharp sell-off in Treasury bond prices given the huge rally that followed the announcement 3 1/2 years earlier that Treasury bond issuance would be discontinued. Indeed, bond prices dropped a massive 8.5 points initially. This decline in Treasury bond prices was almost the same size (in absolute value terms) as the combined two-day nine-point rise in Treasury bond prices on October 31 and November 1, 2001. The initial drop in bond market prices might be attributable to the fact that many traders remembered what happened 3 1/2 years earlier when 30-year Treasury bonds were discontinued and expected the reverse to happen when the announcement was made that issuance might be resumed. Rather than happening over two days, the effect was telescoped to an immediate sharp decline. This is an example of event time. Traders look to what happened when 30-year Treasury bonds were discontinued in order to anticipate what will happen when issuance is likely resumed. The wide trading range in Treasury bond prices is depicted in Figure 2.3.

After the initial sharp decline following the announcement, Treasury bond prices rose enough to recover most of the early losses. The excerpt notes that Treasury bond prices closed down 1.75 points to close at 111. This behavior is more puzzling. The question naturally arises as to why the market's response to the Treasury announcement was so short-lived relative to what happened on October 31, 2001 and November 1, 2001. Once again, part of the difference may lie in market conditions and sentiment bias.

The dearth of liquidity that accompanied the massive price decline made transactions difficult and made it easier for bids to push prices up. Unlike the situation in 2001 where many market participants were short the long bond, there may have been a lack of trading positions that would reinforce the price decline like the short-covering trades in 2001 reinforced the price rise. To be sure, prices were at their lowest for only a relatively short time period.

It should also be noted that unlike the October 31, 2001 announcement discontinuing further issuance of 30-year Treasury bonds, the May 4, 2005 announcement was qualified. Indeed, Assistant Treasury Secretary Bitsberger indicated that a final decision on whether 30-year Treasury bond issuance would resume would be made in August 2005, opening up the possibility that long bond issuance would not be resumed. The belated realization that the re-issuance was conditional rather than unconditional could have mitigated the reason for a sharp price decline.

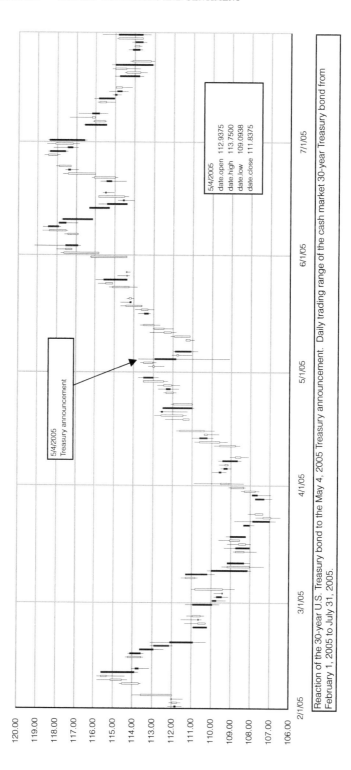

5/4/2005
Treasury announcement

5/4/2005
date.open 112.9375
date.high 113.7500
date.low   109.0938
date.close 111.8375

Reaction of the 30-year U.S. Treasury bond to the May 4, 2005 Treasury announcement. Daily trading range of the cash market 30-year Treasury bond from February 1, 2005 to July 31, 2005.

FIGURE 2.3   The Treasury reconsiders issuance of the long bond.

As was the case for the October 31, 2001 announcement, CBOT Treasury bond futures contracts moved less than the cash market Treasury bond. The behavior of Treasury bond futures prices around the announcement day is depicted in Figure 2.4. June 2005 Treasury bond futures contracts opened at 115 5/32 at 8:20 A.M. Eastern time and stood at 115 1/32 at 9:00 A.M. a few moments before the announcement. At 9:00:21 the price of the June T-bond futures contract fell suddenly by 6/32. Prices fell another 6/32 and stood at 114 21/32 at 9:00:33, and a *fast market* was designated. By 9:01:01 the contract was trading at 114 11/32. The contract traded 4/32 lower at 9:01:57. Thirty seconds later, the contract was trading 5/32 higher at 114 12/32. Another 30 seconds later, the contract was trading at 114 14/32. At 9:09:00 the contract traded at 114 6/32 and the fast market designation was lifted. The market started to break again a few minutes later and stood at 113 18/32 when it was designated a fast market for a second time at 9:20:39. The fast market designation was lifted less than 10 minutes later when the contract traded at 113 27/32. The market bounced around but generally rose throughout the day and stood at 114 22/32 at 14:59:57.

Clearly, the announcement served as a trading catalyst for the Treasury bond futures market. Equally clearly, the price action in the Treasury bond futures market paled in comparison with the price action in the cash market. The price action in Treasury bond futures was relatively short-lived. One interesting characteristic of the Treasury bond futures trading was that there were two periods of intense trading and price choppiness sufficient to warrant a fast market designation.[14] A trader who shorted the Treasury bond futures market and covered his position at 3:00 P.M. would have made 11 ticks at most, or $343.75 per contract.

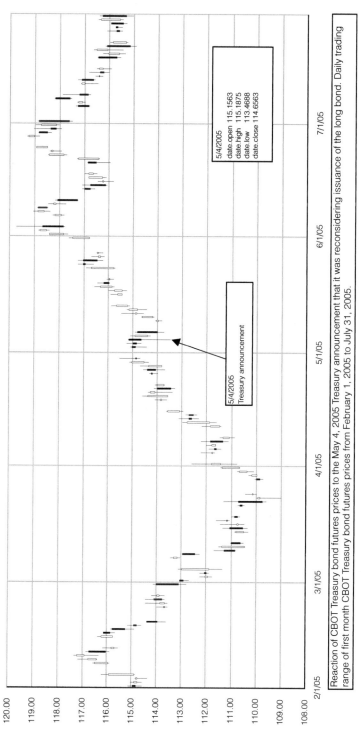

5/4/2005
date.open 115.1563
date.high 115.1875
date.low   113.4688
date.close 114.6563

5/4/2005
Treasury announcement

Reaction of CBOT Treasury bond futures prices to the May 4, 2005 Treasury announcement that it was reconsidering issuance of the long bond. Daily trading range of first month CBOT Treasury bond futures prices from February 1, 2005 to July 31, 2005.

FIGURE 2.4   Treasury bond futures prices react.

Both the initial reaction to the announcement and the duration of the impact that this trading catalyst exerted on market prices are interesting. Clearly, there was an immediate negative reaction to the announcement. Equally clearly, the reaction took some time before the full impact was felt. The first large downward drop in prices occurred at 9:00:24 when Treasury bond prices fell almost one quarter of a point instantly. The next jump occurred a moment later when prices fell another 5/32.

The price action in the cash Treasury bond market is instructive. Prices fell in the cash bond market as they had in the Treasury bond futures market. It appears that the price action in the Treasury bond futures market led that of the corresponding cash market by a few seconds. The first price break occurred at 9:00:24 when cash bonds fell by approximately 6/32 to 112 53/64. Prices held there for a few seconds before falling to 112.217 at 9:00:30. The price decline continued. The price moves accelerated less than a minute later and stood at 111.132 at 9:01:21. Three seconds later, prices suddenly fell almost three points to 108.276. Another three seconds later at 9:01:27, prices of Treasury bonds collapsed *seven whole points* and stood at 101.226. This situation lasted for almost three seconds before rising *three points* to 104.202. Prices quickly recovered.

It should be pointed out that the bid offer spread widened dramatically during the short period of time that cash market bond prices were collapsing. At one point, the bid offer spread stood at more than 4 points, or 256/64, in a market where the bid offer spread is often just 1/32 or a plus (i.e. 1/64). This is an absolutely enormous bid offer spread. In sharp contrast, the implicit bid offer spread in Treasury bond futures prices remained relatively tight throughout the immediate post-announcement period.

In addition to impacting outright trades, the Treasury's announcement had implications for yield curve trades. Specifically, the

Treasury's announcement raised concerns about potential changes in the shape of the yield curve. The prospect of additional supply at the long end was interpreted as implying a steepening yield curve. This encouraged many market participants to put on *steepening* trades (i.e., short long-maturity Treasury bonds and long shorter-maturity Treasury notes) in the belief that long-maturity bond prices will fall relative to shorter maturity notes and bonds. Indeed, the May 5, 2005 *Financial Times* reported that "the yield curve steepened sharply [after the Treasury announcement], with the gap between 10 and 30 year yields widening to 40 basis points on Tuesday."[15] This is a huge one-day move in a yield curve spread trade.

It should be noted that despite the substantial impact that both announcements exerted on Treasury bond prices, other financial markets were largely unaffected by the price action in the Treasury bond market. There were no spillover effects from the two Treasury announcements on equity prices. There was some impact on other fixed-income securities. In particular, the *on-the-run* (i.e., most recently issued and usually most actively traded) 10-year Treasury note fell about half a point soon after the news broke. However, unlike the long bond, the reaction in the 10-year Treasury note was short-lived in that prices soon stabilized at the new, somewhat lower level.

It is interesting to speculate how the Treasury bond market would have reacted under different market conditions and sentiment bias. What if the announcement to potentially resume issuance had been made in the early summer of 2004 during a period when there was a widespread belief that a strengthening U.S. economy would lead to significantly higher long-term interest rates? How would a sentiment bias toward rising long rates have affected the observed reaction? Conversely, what impact would the announcement that the Treasury was going to discontinue issuance of 30-year bonds have had if it had been made in a bullish bond market environment?

Trading Lessons

A trader's thesis as to how financial and commodity markets should respond to a given trading catalyst depends, among other things, on the market conditions and sentiment bias that prevail at that moment in time. However, there are a large number of potentially significant market conditions at any moment in time. For instance, the Fed may be pursuing an expansionary monetary policy during an economic recession, a presidential election year, and a period of dollar weakness. In such an environment, the trader has to decide which market conditions matter and which ones do not. Defining market conditions broadly facilitates comparing the present situation with similar situations in the past to guide trading decisions. Even broadly defined market conditions may result in only a few observations, making it difficult to infer the future from what happened in a similar event in the past.

One question that occurs is the weight to attach to various market conditions at any point in time. Suppose that the Federal Reserve is continuing to pursue an expansionary monetary policy during an economic expansion as it did during part of the 1990s. Several questions naturally arise. Should one give more weight to the fact that the Federal Reserve is pursuing an expansionary monetary policy or to the economic expansion? Are the weights attached to various market conditions constant or do they change over time? What would prompt a trader to change the assigned weights?

Market conditions and sentiment bias may explain why there is sometimes a strong market reaction to a catalyst even though the news is not a surprise. Consider the following example from the February 4, 2005 issue of the *Financial Times*.

> The US dollar spiked higher yesterday, although quite why it did so was less clear. Most analysts and traders cited the improving yield differential of US assets, with the European Central Bank [ECB] yesterday holding its key repo rate at

2 per cent just a day after the Federal Reserve sanctioned a 25 basis point rise to 2.5 per cent.

Yet no one should have been unduly surprised by these developments, or indeed the simultaneous clues as to the future direction of monetary policy.

The Federal Open Market Committee's universally expected increase was accompanied by a near-identical statement… proffered after December's meeting.

Likewise, the 20th straight month of inaction from the ECB came as no surprise…With such sentiment to the fore, the US dollar rose 0.6 per cent to $1.2956 to the euro…0.9 per cent to $104.64 against the yen and 0.3 per cent to $1.8794 against sterling.[16]

Although a strong reaction could occur for a zero forecast error if there is substantial dispersion in forecasts, there is no evidence that is the case here. Rather, the reason for the sharp response to an expected event most likely lies with market conditions and sentiment bias.

Part of the reason for focusing on market conditions is to anticipate how other market participants are likely to react to a given trading catalyst. The use of event time can cause traders to react earlier than they otherwise would as they try to avoid missing the trade—that is, a market reaction that took some time to complete might be telescoped into a much shorter time period as traders attempt to avoid missing the trade. This happened in the market's reaction to the Treasury's announcement that it was considering issuing 30-year Treasury bonds again.

It is possible to imagine trading catalysts that affect volume without affecting the direction of price changes or trading catalysts that affect volatility without affecting the direction of prices. For example, the prospective imposition of a transactions tax can cause market participants to advance their trading before the tax increase becomes effective. Likewise, the prospective reduction of a tax can cause volume to decrease before the tax cut becomes effective. The same is true for the elimination of fixed commissions. The "Big Bang" resulted in a sharp increase in trading volume on October 26, 1986 when fixed stock brokerage commissions were abolished in Great Britain. Similarly, the flawed U.S. presidential election of 2000 resulted in an increase in market uncertainty without arguably a corresponding impact on market prices. However, most of the time, trading catalysts that impact volume or volatility will also impact the direction of market prices.

Liquidity affects the sensitivity of market prices to various catalysts as well. Traders usually prefer to trade in liquid markets. As a result, sometimes the most liquid markets are where traders place their bets even though a trading catalyst may have a more pronounced impact on less liquid markets. Information tends to be reflected in more liquid markets first. Similarly, trading depth—the volume that one can transact without impacting a security's price—differs across markets. Other things equal, the deeper the market, the less impact that a trading catalyst may have on the price of a security.

Market conditions and sentiment bias affect the power, duration, and breadth of a trading catalyst's impact on prices and may partially explain the inconsistent market reactions to seemingly similar trading catalysts over time. Other things equal, a given trading catalyst in a tranquil or quiescent period is less likely to impact market prices as much than one in a turbulent period. Sometimes, a trading catalyst can trigger both a price move and cause a shift from a tranquil market environment to a turbulent market environment such as the Iraqi invasion of Kuwait in the summer of 1990 did to financial markets. Anything that shakes the confidence of market participants increases the risk premium traders and investors discount future cash flows with. Changes in the risk premium also exert a powerful influence on market prices.

References

Allais, Maurice. "Forgetfulness and Interest." *Journal of Money, Credit and Banking*. Vol. 4, Issue 1, February 1972, pp. 40-73.

Bahree, Bhusan, and Chip Cummins. "Energy-Price Volatility Returns Due to Output Outages, Weather." *The Wall Street Journal*, January 11, 2005, p. C5.

Balls, Andrew, Richard Beales, Joanna Chung, Jeremy Grant, and Gillian Tett. "US Treasury Might Reissue 30-Year Bonds." *Financial Times*, May 5, 2005, p. 23.

Bloomberg News (http://www.bloomberg.com), May 4, 2005.

Financial Times, May 5, 2005.

Johnson, Steve. "Greenback Makes Strong Gains." *Financial Times*, February 4, 2005, p. 26.

Keynes, John Maynard. *The General Theory of Employment, Interest and Money*. New York: Harcourt, Brace and World, 1935.

Securities and Exchange Commission. "SEC Brings Enforcement Actions Against Three Individuals, Goldman Sachs, and Massachusetts Financial Services Company Related to Trading Based on Non-Public Information About the Treasury's Decision to Cease Issuance of the 30-Year Bond." (http://www.sec.gov/news/press/2003-107.htm), September 4, 2003.

Securities and Exchange Commission. "Speech by SEC Staff: Remarks to Announce the Filing of Actions Related to Trading Based on Non-Public Information About the Treasury's Decision to Cease Issuance of the 30-Year Bond." (http://www.sec.gov/news/speech/spch090403smc.htm), September 4, 2003.

Securities and Exchange Commission. "Former Goldman Economist Youngdahl Agrees to Fraud Injunction and $240,000 Penalty in SEC Treasury Bond Insider Trading Case." (http://www.sec.gov/news/press/2003-155.htm), November 12, 2003.

Sun Tzu. *The Art of War*.

Waters, Richard. "eBay Shares Fall by 11% as Earnings Falter." *Financial Times*, January 20, 2005, p. 1.

Zuckerman, Gregory, and Michael Schroeder. "Goodbye to the 30-Year Treasury—U.S. Decides to End Its Sale; '10 Year' Reigns." *The Wall Street Journal*, November 1, 2001, p. C1.

Endnotes

[1] Sun Tzu, *The Art of War*.

[2] Gregory Zuckerman and Michael Schroeder. "Goodbye to the 30-Year Treasury Bond—U.S. Decides to End Its Sale; '10 Year' Reigns." *The Wall Street Journal*, November 1, 2001. The article notes that: "…The sharp jump for the 30-year bond came as many Wall Street traders were betting the price of the security would drop not rise. Some had sold 30-year bonds short, borrowing and selling them, hoping to buy them back at a lower price."

[3] Specifically, the contract allows delivery of noncallable Treasury bonds with maturities equal or greater than 15 years to maturity or callable Treasury bonds that aren't callable for at least 15 years. See **www.cbot.com** for more detailed information on contract specifications.

[4] According to a subsequent SEC investigation, the consultant started to inform his clients of the Treasury's impending announcement at 9:28 A.M.

[5] Securities and Exchange Commission. "SEC Brings Enforcement Actions Against Three Individuals, Goldman Sachs, and Massachusetts Financial Services Company Related to Trading Based on Non-Public Information About the Treasury's Decision to Cease Issuance of the 30-Year Bond." September 4, 2003.

[6] Securities and Exchange Commission. "Speech by SEC Staff: Remarks to Announce the Filing of Actions Related to Trading Based on Non-Public Information About the Treasury's Decision to Cease Issuance of the 30-Year Bond." September 4, 2003.

[7] As a result of the preceding insider trades, the SEC secured settlements whereby Peter Davis agreed to "disgorge $29, 598…[in consulting fees] received from Goldman Sachs and [a major money management firm] plus prejudgment interest and pay a penalty of $120,000."…Goldman Sachs agreed "to disgorge $1,742,642 in bond trading profits and prejudgment interest, and to pay a penalty of $5,000,000. In addition, Goldman Sachs [agreed] to disgorge $2,562,740 in bond futures trading profits and prejudgment interest…" The SEC also secured an approximately $900,000 settlement with a major money management firm even though the SEC subsequently dropped the charges of

insider trading against one of its fixed income portfolio managers. On November 12, 2003, the SEC announced that John M. Youngdahl, the former Senior Economist at Goldman Sachs, agreed to pay a $240,000 penalty to settle the insider trading charges.

[8] Economists refer to the set of potential future outcomes as *states of the world*. A *complete* market exists if there is a security for each member of the set of all possible states of the world. Of course, the sum of the probabilities for each state of the world would equal one.

[9] Short-covering rallies are an example of an *internal* (to the market) trading catalyst. Internal trading catalysts are discussed in Chapters 8 and 9.

[10] "Energy prices have turned volatile again, driven by the impact of production outages and unfavorable weather that have prompted traders to snap up oil and gas contracts ahead of this month's OPEC meeting, which some expect could result in further supply reductions…" *The Wall Street Journal*, January 11, 2005, p. C5.

[11] Richard Waters. "eBay shares fall by 11% as earnings falter." *Financial Times*, January 20, 2005, page 1.

[12] Maurice Allais. "Forgetfulness and Interest." *Journal of Money, Credit and Banking*, Vo. 4, Issue 1, February 1972, pp. 40-73.

[13] Bloomberg News at **www.bloomberg.com**, May 4, 2005.

[14] The designation of a fast market for an *unscheduled* trading catalyst is invariably made slightly late and the designation is invariably lifted late as it is lifted after the fast market ends. As a result, designated periods of fast markets do not completely correspond to observed periods of intense market action and price movements.

[15] Andrew Balls, Richard Beales, Joanna Chung, Jeremy Grant, and Gillian Tett. "US Treasury might reissue 30-year bonds." *Financial Times* May 5, 2005, page 23.

[16] Steve Johnson. "Greenback makes strong gains." *Financial Times*, February 4, 2005, page 26.

3

TALK ISN'T CHEAP

"Silence is golden."

—Proverb

Irrational Exuberance

On Thursday, December 5, 1996, Federal Reserve Chairman Alan Greenspan accepted the Francis Boyer Award from the American Enterprise Institute and gave an after-dinner speech. The speech, "The Challenge of Central Banking in a Democratic Society," focused largely on the history of monetary policy in the United States and the evolution of central banking. However, as both the guest of honor and the dinner participants knew, anything that the Fed chairman said would be closely scrutinized by market participants for hints on potential Fed monetary policy actions as well as his views on financial markets. Listeners found what they were looking for when Chairman Greenspan made a few brief remarks on the "interactions of asset markets and the economy" about three-quarters into his talk. To be sure, the comments were cautiously stated and rhetorical questions were raised, but the choice of words ensured that the message was clear. Although the speech was more than 4,300 words long, only two words are likely to be long remembered: "irrational exuberance." The phrase was interpreted as questioning whether the level of stock prices was too high and indicative of a financial bubble.

The reaction to Greenspan's comments was both swift and dramatic. The reaction was international in scope and also relatively short-lived. Although most markets in the U.S. were closed, markets in Asia were open along with some U.S. futures markets. Not surprisingly, equity markets around the world bore the brunt of the sell-off. Greenspan's comments echoed the belief, in some quarters, that the U.S. equity market was already in the midst of a financial bubble in 1996—especially the high-tech sector. As is often the case, trading catalysts expected to impact U.S. financial markets often have an even more pronounced effect on foreign markets. The reverse is not true for trading catalysts expected to principally impact foreign markets. U.S. markets often seemingly ignore the impact of trading catalysts on foreign markets.

On Friday, December 6, the Dow opened sharply lower and was down, at one point, about 145 points or more than 2 percent.[1] The market later rallied back to close only 56 points lower. The impact of Greenspan's comments on financial markets was short-lived.

An individual who *anticipated* Greenspan's comments and shorted an exchange traded fund or a portfolio of stocks that mirrored the Dow Jones Industrial Average at 6437.10 (the level that the Dow closed at on December 5, 1996) would have been profitable for, at most, two weeks.[2] The hapless short who kept his position open would still be underwater in July of 2006. The Nasdaq Composite Index closed at 1300.12 on December 5, 1996. An individual who shorted an exchange traded fund or a portfolio that mirrored the Nasdaq Composite Index immediately before Greenspan's comments would have been profitable until January 1997, then unprofitable until mid-March 1997, and then unprofitable after May 2, 1997. And, assuming the individual survived the multiple heart attacks that would have occurred when the Nasdaq Composite Index hit a high of 5,132.52 on March 10, 2000, the short would have been periodically profitable from July 22, 2002 to October 29, 2002. The short would be underwater after that point. The lessons are simple: Timing is everything and beware of policymakers offering investment advice. Figures 3.1 and 3.2 depict the immediate- and medium-term impact of Greenspan's comments on the Dow Jones Industrial Average and the Nasdaq Composite stock indices.

The short-lived effect of Greenspan's comments is seen also in the behavior of stock index futures prices. For instance, an examination of the (most actively traded) December 1996 S&P 500 stock index futures contract time and sales price data indicates that the S&P 500 futures hit an intraday low of 725.50 at 9:53:17 (Eastern time) Friday morning December 6, 1996 only to rally sharply higher immediately thereafter. On Monday, December 9, 1996, the Dow Jones Industrial Average closed up 82 points on no significant news erasing Friday's losses. This is a point worth emphasizing. Large moves in financial market prices sometimes occur in the apparent absence of news.

It is worth noting that the, albeit short-lived, immediate 2.5% decline in U.S. stock prices attributed to Mr. Greenspan's remarks represented a significant loss to market participants who sold at the lower prices the remarks precipitated. Put differently, 2.5% of the capitalized market value of U.S. equities evaporated for part of a day but fortunately reappeared. It is not clear what policy objective Greenspan's comments accomplished. Was it to encourage individuals to short the market in order to bring market prices back to "rational exuberance" levels, whatever that is?

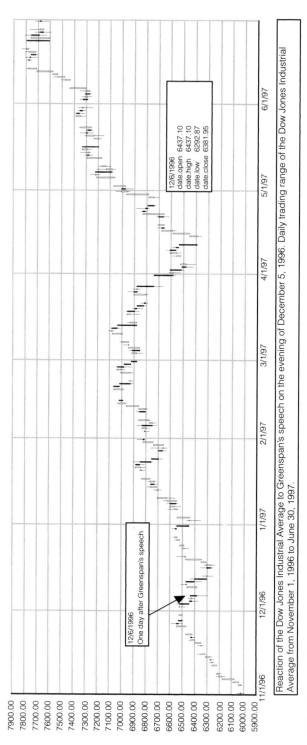

Reaction of the Dow Jones Industrial Average to Greenspan's speech on the evening of December 5, 1996. Daily trading range of the Dow Jones Industrial Average from November 1, 1996 to June 30, 1997.

FIGURE 3.1   Greenspan speaks: irrational exuberance and the DJIA.

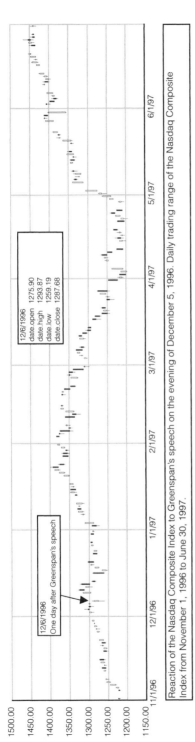

FIGURE 3.2 Greenspan speaks: irrational exuberance and the Nasdaq.

Reaction of the Nasdaq Composite Index to Greenspan's speech on the evening of December 5, 1996. Daily trading range of the Nasdaq Composite Index from November 1, 1996 to June 30, 1997.

Although the phrase "irrational exuberance" was widely reported by the media and applied to U.S. stock prices, Greenspan's exact comments are largely rhetorical in nature and very cautiously stated. It is instructive to consider exactly what Greenspan said that triggered the selloff around the globe.[3]

The December 1996 Greenspan irrational exuberance comments are interesting because of subsequent events in the U.S. stock market, particularly in the high technology and dot.com sectors. The magnitude and duration of the impact of Greenspan's remarks are similar to the financial market impact of other remarks by policymakers. It should be also be noted that despite Greenspan's "irrational exuberance" remarks and subsequent occasional comments that the stock market might be in a bubble, the Federal Reserve pursued a monetary policy over the subsequent few years that accommodated what some observers viewed, at the time, as excessive growth in U.S. stock prices. For instance, the Federal Reserve chose not to raise stock margin requirements during this time period, which would have hindered the ability of individuals to place levered bets on the stock market.

Comments by Politicians and Policymakers as Trading Catalysts

The old saying that "talk is cheap" need not apply to the comments of politicians and policymakers. When the comments of politicians and policymakers impact financial markets, talk may not be cheap for the traders and investors on the wrong side of the market whose positions are adversely affected. The financial market impact of such comments may be substantial as the preceding example detailing the market's reaction to Greenspan's irrational exuberance comments illustrate. Unfortunately, ordinary investors often foot the bill for ill-advised comments by politicians and policymakers in terms of lower prices for the assets they hold and more volatile financial markets that such comments often create.

This chapter details the impact that the comments of politicians and policymakers sometimes have on financial market prices. Such comments can be decomposed into those that are intended to impact financial markets and those that unintentionally do so. Comments can also be categorized into those that impact financial markets as intended, those that do so perversely, and those that exert no effect. Several examples are provided to illustrate the various impacts that past comments have exerted on financial market prices.

When a policymaker speaks, market participants have to determine whether the comments contain potentially market-moving news—that is, market participants must ascertain whether the comments of policymakers signal a change in policy, an impending policy action, or are inadvertent. Given that policymakers know that their comments can roil financial market prices, the prevailing bias is to treat most policymaker comments as intentional. These comments impact financial markets and often create short-term trading opportunities.

Intentional comments are viewed as signals to market participants about the preferred level of commodity or security prices, interest, or exchange rates by policymakers. However, it is not the words that pack the punch to financial markets; it is the implicit threat of a policy action by one or more large players such as the central bank or the central bank in concert with other central banks.

Traders fear that a policymaker can cause momentary large gaps between supply and demand and influence prices in the process. A classic example in this regard is intervention in the foreign exchange market to prop up a weak currency or weaken a strong currency in order to achieve some policy objective.

Although much of the power of policymaker comments derives from the implicit threat of a policy action, savvy policymakers have increasingly attempted to increase their influence by piggy-backing on market trends and internal market forces. One of the ways that policymakers can maximize their influence is by carefully timing their announcements and market operations. For example, a central bank may make an announcement on exchange rates during a period when major foreign markets are closed. Similarly, an announcement made during a pre-holiday lull in trading for the domestic market may have more impact than the same announcement made during regular trading hours. Market conditions may also play a role. Given the popularity of technical analysis among many traders, announcements made when exchange rates are near key resistance or support points may trigger a larger reaction than the announcements otherwise would due to *positive feedback trading* (i.e., trading that feeds on itself).

The speed, magnitude, and duration of pronouncements vary. In most cases, the market is very quick to respond and the markets move sharply. As noted previously, the magnitude of the response may depend upon market conditions and sentiment bias. For instance, if the market is currently trending in one direction, the announcement may accelerate the move. Any policy action that triggers positive feedback trading can have a greater impact on market prices. Knowledge of various feedback effects may affect a policymaker's choice of instrument to implement the policy action. For instance, the Bank of Japan considered using options a few years back to maximize its influence because it knew that sellers of options would dynamically or delta hedge their positions by taking an appropriate fractional corresponding position in the cash market.[4] A sharp price move that increases the value of the options increases the absolute value of delta and forces the option hedger to increase his hedge position and thereby exacerbate the price move.

One special category of pronouncements by policymakers and politicians are broken promises. These utterances attempt to reassure the public that the status quo will remain so (e.g., that a currency will not be devalued). Often, market prices increase slightly after these pronouncements. These public reassurances are followed in short order by a decision announcing the opposite of what was recently promised. Unfortunately, broken promises of this nature are distressingly frequent. However, such comments may assist traders by serving as a confirmatory signal that the current policy is no longer tenable and will be changed soon. To be sure, such pronouncements invariably occur during a period of tremendous pressure in financial markets. Put differently, market participants are voting with their wallets, and the current politicians and policymakers in power are losing. Nevertheless, the broken promises exert substantial losses on those unable to get out before the change.

Greenspan Speaks and Markets Move

There are numerous examples where the comments of the chairman of the Federal Reserve System have impacted market prices. Indeed, this chapter opens with an example of the impact of former Fed Chairman Alan Greenspan's comments on financial markets. Ten months after he uttered the words "irrational exuberance" in an after-dinner speech in Washington, Greenspan testified before the House Budget Committee on Wednesday, October 8, 1997. During the course of his remarks on the economy, Greenspan made the following comments about financial markets and the real economy:

> …The long-term outlook for the American economy presents us with, perhaps, even greater uncertainties. There can be little doubt that the American economy in the last several years has performed far better than the history of business expansions would have led us to expect. Labor markets have tightened considerably without inflation emerging as it has in the past. Encouraged by these results, *financial markets seem to have priced in an optimistic outlook*, characterized by a significant reduction in risk and an increasingly benevolent inflation process. [Emphasis added]

Thus, there would seem to be emerging constraints on potential labor input. If the recent 2 million plus annual pace of job creation were to continue, the pressures on wages and other costs of hiring large numbers of such individuals could escalate more rapidly…Thus, the performance of the labor markets this year suggests that *the economy has been on an unsustainable track*… [Emphasis added][5]

The market's reaction to Greenspan's testimony was immediate and negative. The prices of both stocks and U.S. Treasury bonds fell. The Dow Jones Industrial Average fell almost 1 percent, whereas the long bond was down 1 and 21/32 points.[6] Market participants who were long stocks or Treasury bonds suffered losses both during and after Greenspan's testimony. Although there was an initial overreaction to Greenspan's comments, the markets closed lower for the day. Unlike the market's larger reaction to Greenspan's irrational exuberance comments in December 1996, the stock and bond markets did not immediately rebound the next day and remained below where they stood before Greenspan testified for a number of days.

Other Voices at the Fed

Although attention is usually focused on the comments of the Fed chairman, other individuals at the Federal Reserve can impact financial market prices through their comments. This applies not only to the vice chairman and other members of the Federal Reserve Board of Governors, but also to the presidents of the twelve individual Federal Reserve district banks that comprise the Federal Reserve System. One consequence is that traders must monitor the comments of a number of individuals at the Federal Reserve System.

Sometimes, the remarks of a Federal Reserve president can exert a significant impact on market prices. For instance, on Wednesday,

June 1, 2005, Richard W. Fisher, the president of the Federal Reserve district bank of Dallas, Texas indicated that he thought that the Federal Reserve might stop raising short-term interest rates. Treasury note and bond prices rallied sharply in response to the remark with yields on the 10-year U.S. Treasury note falling 11 basis points.[7] The Fed typically lowers or raises short-term interest rates in a series of changes. The article also notes that Mr. Fisher's comments appear to diverge from those of other Fed officials.

The Asian Financial Crisis

The Asian Financial Crisis of 1997 and 1998 is an example of how a catalyst-induced price change in one market can become itself a trading catalyst for other markets. There are also several illustrative examples of how ill-advised comments by policymakers and politicians during the Asian Financial Crisis adversely impacted market prices. To better appreciate the impact of the comments, it is important to understand the origins and evolution of the crisis.

The devaluation of the Thai baht by the Bank of Thailand on July 2, 1997 is widely regarded as the beginning of the Asian Financial Crisis. In fact, the Asian Financial Crisis began well before then. The absence of well-developed local currency fixed income markets in Thailand and in many other parts of Asia meant that firms had to rely on local banks for borrowing short-term debt or issue longer-term foreign currency (principally dollar) denominated debt. Excessive speculation in property and stocks was accommodated by banks. The resulting bad loans weakened the banking sector. It was not just a Thai problem. The crisis had deep roots across the region. This is important to understand when one considers how the crisis seemingly spread from Thailand to other countries in the region. It also illustrates how ill-advised comments from politicians and policymakers during a crisis can have perverse results.

Problems in Thailand had arisen in 1995 when the stock market—as measured by the Stock Exchange of Thailand (SET) index—started to decline. Margin rules that required investors who bought on margin to sell if the stock was down by 15% or more from the purchase price exacerbated the decline and led to ill-advised government policies designed to support the market. Problems started to surface across the region in early 1997. For instance, Hanbo Steel, a major South Korean steel company, went bankrupt with $6 billion of debt in January 1997. This was followed by the failure of Sammi Steel, another South Korean steel producer, in March of 1997. Malaysia acted to rein in excessive speculation by restricting loans for stocks and property at the end of March 1997. An early March 1997 promise by the Thai government to buy almost $4 billion of bad property debt from financial firms made the situation worse when the action was later abandoned.

Broken Promises

Just like the onset of the Asian Financial Crisis was preceded by problems, the devaluation of the Thai baht was preceded by waves of speculative selling of the currency. One such episode occurred during May 14 and 15. This speculative attack prompted intervention by the Bank of Thailand to defend the baht. The Monetary Authority of Singapore joined in this intervention. Perhaps the surest sign that devaluation was imminent was the promise by the prime minister of Thailand on June 30, 1997 that the baht would not be devalued. Shortly after his address to the nation, the Thai baht stood at 25.15. On July 1, 1997, the Thai baht had improved to 24.52 per dollar by noon during New York trading hours.

On July 2, 1997, the Bank of Thailand instituted a *managed float*—that is, let the baht float within a given range. The managed float resulted in an almost immediate 20% devaluation against the U.S. dollar; it now took 30.18 bahts to buy one U.S. dollar. The Thai baht appeared to stabilize following the devaluation hovering around 29 baht to the U.S. dollar for several days. However, the devaluation of the Thai baht quickly put other Asian currencies under tremendous selling pressure, which prompted significant central bank intervention—that is, the devaluation of the Thai baht became a trading catalyst for other currencies in Asia that traders rushed to sell. These include the Malaysian ringgit, the Indonesian rupiah, the Philippine peso, and the Hong Kong dollar. The spread of the selling to other currencies is known as *contagion*.

The breadth and depth of the selling of the currencies led to further devaluations and, in some cases, triggered an end to central bank interventions. For instance, the Malaysian ringgit stood at approximately 2.52 to the U.S. dollar prior to the devaluation of the Thai baht on July 2 and improved to about 2.50 ringgit to the dollar after massive central bank intervention on July 8. The intervention seemed to work as the ringgit improved to 2.489 on July 10. However, the improvement apparently came at a substantial cost as the Malaysian central bank, Bank Negara, decided to stop intervening to defend the ringgit on July 14. The Monetary Authority of Singapore devalued the Singaporean dollar slightly on July 17 in a bid to stem the decline. The central bank of Indonesia widened the bands by which the rupiah could fluctuate to 12% from 8% on July 11. Less widely appreciated at the time was the tremendous pressure the Hong Kong Monetary Authority (HKMA)—the de facto central bank of the Hong Kong Special Administrative Region—was under to devalue the Hong Kong dollar by eliminating the currency board system, which pegged the Hong Kong dollar to the U.S. dollar. Speculative selling of the Hong Kong dollar also came indirectly in the form of foreign selling of Hong Kong shares, which the HKMA quelled by intervening in the equity and equity index futures markets. This episode is discussed in more detail later in the book.

From a trading perspective, central bank intervention to defend a currency that is perceived as weak often creates the opportunity for *one-sided bets*—that is, a trader who shorts a troubled currency may face relatively small losses if a central bank intervenes to maintain a fixed exchange rate but obtain large gains if the central bank does not intervene (or the intervention is not effective) and the currency breaks to a new level. The sale of a currency necessarily entails the simultaneous purchase of another one. A central bank may soon exhaust its foreign exchange reserves as it attempts to prop up its currency. The odds of a readjustment in exchange rates increases as a central bank's foreign exchange reserves dwindle. This can increase speculative pressure on the currency. It should be pointed out that central bank intervention to protect a given exchange rate is tantamount to speculation.[8]

Speculation or Fundamentals?

Not surprisingly, the charged atmosphere led some policymakers and politicians to accuse external speculators of masterminding the decline in exchange rates and creating the Asian Financial Crisis. One politician to levy such a charge was Malaysian Prime Minister Dr. Mahathir Mohamad.

On Thursday, July 24, 1997, Prime Minister Mahathir Mohamad blamed rogue speculators for the currency depreciation.[9] At the time of Dr. Mahatir's July 24 accusation, the ringgit had fallen about 5% to the U.S. dollar since the crisis began on July 2, 1997. The market largely ignored the prime minister's comments. The ringgit traded lower and broke through the 2.65 level before regaining some strength before the prime minister spoke.[10] Although the comment did not trigger a significant market reaction, it was yet another comment that, taken with other ones, may have helped to undermine the confidence of market participants in the ability of the Malaysian government to deal effectively with the crisis.

On Saturday, July 26, 1997, the Malaysian prime minister elaborated on his earlier comments on the cause of the currency crisis and directly blamed hedge fund manager George Soros.[11] He also demanded that currency trading be regulated or outlawed. The bizarre nature of the comments was made worse by the apparent anti-Semitism implicit in the accusations against George Soros. Fortunately for the Malaysian people, financial markets were closed on Saturday.

The row between Prime Minister Mahathir and George Soros soon degenerated with Dr. Mahathir calling Mr. Soros a "moron" and Mr. Soros calling Dr. Mahathir a "menace to his own people."[12] At a later date, the prime minister elaborated on the supposed reason behind Mr. Soros' alleged currency speculation—namely to punish Association of Southeast Asia Nations for admitting Burma into its membership.[13]

A Trading Pattern Emerges

A period of relative stability in exchange rates soon followed with the ringgit drifting gradually lower against the dollar during the month of August with an occasional spike. One sharp downward move on Friday, August 8, 1997 was attributed to Prime Minister Mahathir's comments on the appropriateness of the level of the ringgit and whether the central bank would intervene to support the ringgit. The market's reaction is captured in the following report by Reuters on Monday, August 11, 1997.

> The ringgit remained weak against the dollar in early Asian trading after plunging 500 points late on Friday, dealers said. The selloff was triggered by Malaysian Prime Minister Mahathir Mohamad's comments late on Friday that he was happy with the level of ringgit, despite the local unit's sharp recent falls...Mahathir also said that the authorities would not intervene to defend the ringgit. Bank Negara [Malaysia's central bank], however, was in the market earlier on Friday, selling dollar/ringgit around 2.6510, dealers said. Dealers said thin volumes and wide [bid/ask] spread would continue to exaggerate currency movements.[14]

The preceding excerpt illustrates how currency market participants started to view comments by the prime minister as a significant
trading catalyst. This invariably set the stage for other comments to
exert an impact on exchange rates. The excerpt also illustrates how
the credibility of politicians and policymakers is undermined when
market participants observe governmental actions (e.g., central bank
intervention to support the ringgit) that openly contradict stated
policy. Finally, the excerpt illustrates how market conditions—thin
volumes and wide [bid/ask] spread—can increase the size of the price
reactions.[15]

Other Voices Impact the FX Market

On Wednesday, September 24, 1997, Deutsche Bundesbank President Hans Tietmeyer's remark that a falling Deutsche mark was not
in Germany's best interest precipitated, at one point, a 2.3 pfennig
rally in the mark against the dollar in European trading. On the same
day, Mr. Eisuke Sakakibara, Japanese Vice Minister of Finance for
International Affairs, also roiled the foreign exchange market. Mr.
Sakakibara, commonly known as "Mr. Yen" for the impact his comments have on the yen, sparked a 3-yen slide in the dollar during
Tokyo trading after he indicated that the G-7 was serious about halting the rise in the value of the dollar. The dollar recovered some of its
earlier losses against the yen and Deutsche mark during New York
trading hours.[16]

The preceding episode illustrates how the comments of policymakers can impact exchange rates in the direction that policymakers
desire. It also illustrates how signals to the market can sometimes be
lost in translation. The question naturally arises as to why the comments of Messrs, Tietmeyer, and Sakakibara impacted currency markets in the direction that they desired, whereas the comments of
Prime Minister Mahathir did not. One explanation for the differential
impact is the greater resources that both the Bank of Japan and the
Deutsche Bundesbank had at their disposal. Another explanation is

that the seemingly bizarre charges against currency trading undercut Prime Minister Mahathir's credibility.

Speech Is Silver

On October 1, 1997, Prime Minister Mahathir Mohamad repeated some of his comments about negative effects of currency trading together with his call to "regulate or outlaw currency trading." This time, the financial markets reacted sharply to his comments prompting both Malaysian stocks and the foreign exchange value of the ringgit to fall. The markets reacted even though the comments were really not news—the prime minister's views on the origin of the Asian Financial Crisis and his advocacy of a prohibition on currency speculation had already been widely disseminated weeks earlier. Nevertheless, the market reacted to his comments. The impact of his comments on market prices is reflected in the following news story Reuters reported on October 1, 1997.

> Malaysian Premier Mahathir Mohamad's renewed call for a ban on currency trading pulled the floor out from under an already battered ringgit on Wednesday and fuelled hefty drops in other Southeast Asian currencies. Dealers said regional currencies…were hit by a fresh crisis of nerves as players piled into the dollar, triggering stop-loss orders in thin trade…The ringgit dropped dramatically. It fell more than four percent in less than two hours to a low of 3.4080 to the dollar. It recovered slightly to 3.3540/3605 at 0440 GMT against 3.1915/65 late on Tuesday…The Kuala Lumpur stock market was also hit, the key index falling 2.19 percent to 796.75.[17]

Rather than calming the foreign exchange market for ringgit, the effect of the prime minister's comments was perverse. Both Malaysian equity prices and the ringgit fell. Once again, the comments had the perverse effect of driving Malaysian stock prices lower and the ringgit fell more against the dollar. Moreover, selloff in the ringgit and

Malaysian equities induced by the prime minister's comments acted as a trading catalyst for other currencies in the region. Notice that while Prime Minister Mahathir's comments acted as the trading catalyst in this instance, market conditions and sentiment bias increased the strength of the market's reaction. The impact of the prime minister's remarks was huge—(the preceding excerpt notes that the ringgit "fell more than 4 percent in less than two hours"). Perhaps surprisingly, the prime minister predicted that his comments would roil the currency markets and affect adversely the foreign exchange value of the ringgit, yet he still chose to make them.[18] Not surprisingly, a number of market observers suggested that the prime minister should keep future such comments left unspoken.[19] Ironically, the comments of his deputy, Anwar Ibrahim, were credited with calming the foreign exchange market and, on one occasion, sparking a 5% rise in the ringgit against the dollar.[20]

Believers in conspiracy theories might argue that the subsequent decline in the foreign exchange value of the ringgit and the Malaysian equity market was simply more evidence that the Malaysian economy was being victimized by outside speculators. However, the more plausible scenario is simply that Malaysian nationals were trying to get their wealth out of a declining market and a declining currency. Indeed, a firm that had borrowed in dollars was seeing the real value of its debt increase and the dollar value of its ringgit-denominated assets decrease as the ringgit declined. One way to stem the increase in real liabilities was to sell ringgit immediately. The selling pressure on the ringgit led to declines in its value against the U.S. dollar and increased the pressure to exit ringgit-denominated assets. Alternatively stated, the market decline fed on itself and exacerbated the decline in the ringgit independent of foreign speculative activity.

The extent of the comment-induced decline in Malaysian equity values and the exchange rate against the dollar were substantial. The full brunt of the declines was primarily borne by Malaysian investors. The duration lasted longer, and the magnitude was certainly longer lived. The question naturally arises as to whether it is fair to blame the prime minister for the declines as other nations in the region suffered as well. Put simply, did the prime minister's comments have any effect on the market that would not have occurred anyway? The answer to that question is impossible to ascertain. However, one can infer from the substantial declines in market prices on days where the prime minister's comments were the trading catalyst that his comments exacerbated the crisis. It may well have been the case that the duration would have been shorter without them.

In retrospect, it may seem that the decline in the dollar value of many Asian currencies was swift and deep immediately after the devaluation of the Thai baht. That was not the case. Rather, the initial decline in the dollar value of various Asian currencies was fairly modest relative to the eventual decline. Put differently, the Asian Financial Crisis continued to worsen, and with it the foreign exchange value of many Asian currencies and the associated Asian stock markets.

Mr. Yen

No discussion of the impact of policymaker comments on financial market prices would be complete without mention of Mr. Eisuke Sakakibara. Mr. Sakakibara, the former Vice Minister of Finance for International Affairs in Japan, is probably the quintessential example of a policymaker whose comments often exerted a substantial impact on market prices. Indeed, during his tenure as Vice Minister of Finance, Mr. Sakakibara was known as "Mr. Yen" for the sharp impact that his comments frequently had on the dollar/yen exchange rate.[21] Mr. Sakakibara's influence owed much to his willingness to make unambiguous comments for the record in a society where much is left unsaid.

One example of the powerful influence of Mr. Sakakibara exerted on the currency market occurred on Thursday, May 8, 1997 when Mr. Sakakibara stated that the dollar could conceivably fall as much as 23 yen during the year. The comments were made at a Finance Committee meeting in the House of Councillors—a branch of the Japanese

Diet, or parliament—and were based on past average annual varia-
tions in the dollar against the yen. The dollar fell almost 2 yen from
the previous day to about 123.72.[22]

A larger move came the next day when the dollar fell almost 4
yen. Contemporary news reports that comments by Japanese Finance
Minister Hiroshi Mitsuzuka supporting a stronger yen and comments
by U.S. Fed Chairman Alan Greenspan that the Fed was unlikely to
continue to raise U.S. short-term interest rates reinforced the bearish
mood on the dollar against the yen created by Mr. Sakakibara's comments on May 8, 1997.[23] The dramatic drop in the value of the dollar
against the Japanese yen on May 9, 1997 is depicted in Figure 3.3.
Note that the impact of Mr. Sakakibara's comments on the yen
extended over two days and helped to change market sentiment from
bearish on the yen to bullish.[24]

During spring 1998, the dollar advanced against the yen. Mr.
Sakakibara would periodically talk up the yen, often indicating that a
rise in the dollar beyond a certain level was "excessive." Mr. Sakakibara's comments had the effect of temporarily halting the dollar's
rise.[25]

In general, a policymaker who rarely makes potentially market-
moving comments has more impact on financial markets when he
makes comments than a policymaker who frequently makes such
comments. Mr. Sakakibara may be an exception to that rule. Nevertheless, there are many instances where comments by Mr. Sakakibara
or other government officials were ignored by the market. Words
alone do not drive financial markets. It is the potential for government action that gives weight to the comments. Interestingly, the
Bank of Japan intervened massively to support the yen less than 10
days later. The intervention managed to cause the dollar to fall as
much as 4 yen in a single day and is discussed in more detail in Chapter 6, "Market Interventions."[26]

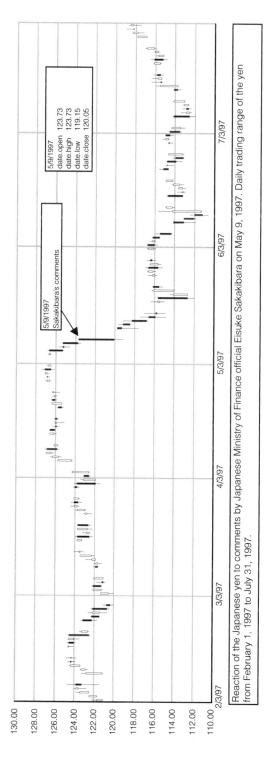

FIGURE 3.3 **Sakakibara's comments lift the yen.**

Reaction of the Japanese yen to comments by Japanese Ministry of Finance official Eisuke Sakakibara on May 9, 1997. Daily trading range of the yen from February 1, 1997 to July 31, 1997.

Lost in Translation

Not surprisingly, foreign policymakers and politicians often make comments in a language other than English. This creates the potential for their comments to get garbled in translation and cause market participants to react to things they did not say. Mistranslations probably result in greater market overreactions and subsequent corrections than would have otherwise occurred if the comment were translated correctly. Even the allegation that foreign language comments were mistranslated can impact market prices as the Tietmeyer example discussed earlier demonstrates. Similarly, even the English language comments of some foreign politicians and policymakers can be misinterpreted. Of course, the meaning of the statements of some nonnative English-language-speaking policymakers (such as Mr. Sakakibara) is often exceedingly clear.

On Monday, June 23, 1997, a comment by Prime Minister Ryutaro Hashimoto suggesting that Japan might sell some of its massive holdings of U.S. Treasury securities triggered a 1/2 point decline in the long bond, caused a decline in the value of the dollar against the yen, and exacerbated the slide of an already declining U.S. stock market. The essential reasoning was that the Japanese would no longer willingly finance their portion of the U.S. trade deficit, thus driving down the value of the dollar, Treasury bonds, and U.S. equity prices. One relevant question is whether the prime minister was simply bluffing. Would the Japanese really sell their Treasury holdings? The comment came late in the trading day and exacted a heavy price on U.S. equities and Treasury bonds. The precise quote that sparked the market actions was somewhat puzzling as reported by the radio news program *Marketplace* that same day: "So we will not succumb to the temptation to sell off Treasury bills and switch our funds to gold."[27]

The impact of the prime minister's comments was dramatic but short-lived. On Tuesday, June 24, 1997, Japanese officials said that the prime minister's comments were misconstrued. That comment was credited at the time for sparking rallies in the stock and bond markets.[28]

On Thursday, May 19, 2005, South Korean Central Bank Governor Park Seung was quoted as saying that South Korea would no longer intervene in the currency market. The comment precipitated a selloff in the U.S. dollar against the South Korean won. A short time later, the South Korean government indicated that Governor Park had been misunderstood, which precipitated a rally in the dollar.[29]

The preceding examples illustrate what might be called *translation risk*—the risk that the market has inappropriately reacted to the translated comments of a policymaker and is likely to correct itself if there is a new and better translation. Inappropriate market reactions may also occur when a nonnative English-language-speaking foreign government official makes a comment in English that is misunderstood. There are several lessons for traders. First, a trader acquiring a position in a security moving as the result of a foreign policymaker's non-English language comment may want to take a smaller position. Second, a trader may want to hold the position for a shorter time than she otherwise might do. Third, the trader may want to employ tighter stop-loss orders. Fourth, the risk that the market-moving comments of foreign policymakers may have been mistranslated creates an opportunity to play the rebound.

Trading Lessons

As was shown earlier, the comments of politicians and policymakers can substantially affect market prices, even when they are not accompanied by policy actions. Sometimes, the comments are intended to push prices in a desired direction to achieve a certain policy objective and they succeed. Sometimes, the comments are intended to push prices in a desired direction to achieve a certain policy objective and they fail to move the market—or they backfire and do the opposite.

Sometimes, policymakers and politicians simply choose the wrong words and the comments have an inadvertent impact on market prices.

Whether or not they are intended to impact financial markets, the speed, magnitude, timing, and duration of market-moving comments by policymakers vary. In most cases, the market is very quick to respond and prices move sharply. However, sometimes there is a seemingly delayed response to policymaker comments. As always, the magnitude of the response in prices also depends upon market conditions and sentiment bias. A policymaker's comment may have a far stronger impact on market prices in an environment where the market is currently trending in a given direction or in periods when liquidity is limited, such as holidays. Similarly, comments that are likely to push prices enough to set off stop-loss orders or trigger other types of positive feedback trading exacerbate the eventual price move. Policymakers have shown that they understand these relationships and often carefully time their comments for periods when trading volumes are light and liquidity is limited. Indeed, Mr. Sakakibara has stated that intervention is most effective when market sentiment is changing.[30]

The duration of the effect of policymaker comments on market prices is usually relatively short-lived and confined to a part of a single trading day. Sometimes, the effect is transitory with prices returning to where they stood before the comments were made. Other times, the duration of the effect may last longer. Note, however, that government action need not accompany or immediately follow a policymaker's comments.

Ultimately, it is not the words of policymakers and politicians per se, but rather the prospect of action that influences market prices. For instance, the Bank of Japan has repeatedly intervened in the currency market in an attempt to influence the value of the dollar/yen exchange rate. Consequently, when Mr. Sakakibara spoke, currency traders had to assess whether Mr. Sakakibara's comments signaled likely central bank intervention.

Sometimes, comments are not intended to impact market prices but do—usually adversely. These are frequently off-the-cuff comments that often show a profound ignorance of market behavior. Unfortunately, there are numerous examples in this regard. For instance, the euro was under pressure soon after it was introduced in January 1999. On Thursday, May 31, 1999, then European Central Bank (ECB) President Wim Duisenberg indicated that the ECB was unlikely to intervene in support of the euro. The subsequent sell-off of the euro against the dollar was attributed to his remarks.

What lessons can one learn from the impact that the remarks of policymakers and politicians sometimes have on financial markets?

1. The principal consequence of policymaker comments on financial markets is to create excess volatility. Such volatility harms traders and investors who happen to be on the wrong side of the market. For them, policymaker *talk isn't cheap.*

2. Although it is difficult to trade off of many policymaker remarks because they are unscheduled, it may be possible to trade off of any anticipated correction. It may also be possible to bet on the likely market impact of policymaker comments for certain scheduled events such as congressional testimony by the chairman of the Federal Reserve.

3. The duration of market impact is often shorter for inadvertent policymaker comments than comments intended to communicate current policy views to market participants.

4. Traders need to assess the likelihood that the words spoken will be backed up by policy actions. If the remarks are unlikely to be backed up by policy actions, the impact should be smaller and the duration much shorter.

5. The deliberate comments of policymakers may reverse a trend as occurred with the Japanese yen in May 1997 following the comments of Mr. Eisuke Sakakibara on May 8, 1997.

The market is larger than any single individual, including government officials and central bankers. The danger for policymakers is to confuse the short-term impact on financial market prices precipitated by the remarks of public officials with long-term control of market prices. Policymakers should carefully weigh potentially market-moving comments before making them. There is a consequence for impacting market prices. Such talk isn't cheap.

References

Associated Press and Dow Jones Newswire. "Malaysia Ringgit/Late-2 Central Bks Powerless, Says Dealer." July 24, 1997.

Brancaccio, David. *Marketplace*. Monday, June 24, 1997.

Brancaccio, David. *Marketplace*. Monday, June 23, 1997.

Bransten, Lisa. "Markets Expect Calm to Follow Friday Price Scare." *Financial Times*, December 9, 1996, p. 1.

Desai, Sonali. "FOCUS-Asian Currencies Pare Losses on Ringgit Rise." Reuters Friday, December 5, 1997.

Dow Jones Newswire. "Malaysia Mahathir Scolds U.S. Allowing Soros's Speculation." August 22, 1997.

Greenspan, Alan. "Economic and Budgetary Outlook." Testimony before the Committee on the Budget, U.S. House of Representatives, October 8, 1997 (http://www.federalreserve.gov/boarddocs/testimony/1997/19971008.htm).

Greenspan, Alan. "The Challenge of Central Banking in a Democratic Society." Remarks at the Annual Dinner and Francis Boyer Lecture of The American Enterprise Institute for Public Policy Research, Washington, DC, December 5, 1996 (http://www.federalreserve.gov/BoardDocs/speeches/1996/19961205.htm).

Ip, Greg, and Thomas Sims. "Bond Yields Plunge amid Falling Rates World-Wide." *The Wall Street Journal*, June 2, 2005.

Jiji Press English News Service. "Intervention Effective at Shift in Market Sentiment." September 1, 1998.

Jiji Press English News Service. "Sakakibara Comment Sends Dlr Below 124 Yen in Tokyo." May 8, 1997.

Karmen, Craig. "More 'Distorted' Comments Roil Markets." *The Wall Street Journal,* May 20, 2005.

Kazmin, Amy. "Thai Ex-Banker Told to Repay Pounds 2.5bn." *Financial Times*, June 1, 2005.

Mainichi Daily News. "Dollar Likely to Remain Bearish." May 11, 1997.

Reuters News. "Ringgit Plunges After Fresh Remarks by Mahathir." October 1, 1997.

Reuters. "Dollar Capped in Tokyo by Sakakibara's Remarks." April 1, 1998.

Reuters. "Asian Exotics—Mahathir Pulls Plug on Regionals." October 1, 1997.

Reuters. "Focus-PM Comments Shake Malaysia Ringgit, Stocks." October 1, 1997.

Reuters. "Ringgit Remains Weak after Selloff." August 11, 1997.

Reuters. "Malaysia's Mahathir Attacks Currency Traders Again." September 30, 1997.

Reuters. "German, Japanese Comments Blast Dollar Lower." September 24, 1997.

Reuters. "U.S. Defends Soros, Unaware of Conspiracy on Currency." July 27, 1997.

Zielenziger, Michael. "Currency War: The Moron vs. the Menace." *The Advertiser*, September 23, 1997.

Endnotes

[1] Lisa Bransten. "Markets Expect Calm to Follow Friday Price Scare." *Financial Times*, December 9, 1996, p. 1.

[2] *Shorting* refers to selling a security that one does not own. Essentially, one borrows a security, sells it, and hopes to be able to profit by buying back the security at a lower price before repaying the security.

[3] The relevant text of Greenspan's comments follow:

> Clearly, sustained low inflation implies less uncertainty about the future, and lower risk premiums imply higher prices of stocks and other earning assets. We can see that in the inverse relationship exhibited by price/earnings ratios and the rate of inflation in the past. But how do we know when irrational exuberance has unduly escalated asset values, which then become subject to unexpected and prolonged contractions as they have in Japan over the past decade? And how do we factor that assessment into monetary policy? We as central bankers need not be concerned if a collapsing financial asset bubble does not threaten to impair the real economy, its production, jobs, and price stability. Indeed, the sharp stock market break of 1987 had few negative consequences for the economy. But we should not underestimate or become complacent about the complexity of the interactions of asset markets and the economy. Thus, evaluating shifts in balance sheets generally, and in asset prices particularly, must be an integral part of the development of monetary policy.

Alan Greenspan. "The Challenge of Central Banking in a Democratic Society." Remarks at the Annual Dinner and Francis Boyer Lecture of The American Enterprise Institute for Public Policy Research, Washington, D.C. (http://www.federalreserve.gov/BoardDocs/speeches/1996/19961205.htm), December 5, 1996.

[4] *Delta* is a measure of how the price of an option changes as the price of the underlying security changes. The value of delta can range from 0 to 1 in the case of calls (options to buy) or between 0 and -1 in the case of puts (options to sell). The absolute value of delta is akin to the probability that the option would be exercised. The delta is sometimes referred to as the *hedge ratio*.

[5] Alan Greenspan. "Economic and Budgetary Outlook." Testimony Before the Committee on the Budget, U.S. House of Representatives (http://www.federalreserve.gov/boarddocs/testimony/1997/19971008.htm), October 8, 1997.

[6] David Brancaccio. *Marketplace*. October 8, 1997.

[7] Greg Ip and G. Thomas Sims. "Bond Yields Plunge Amid Falling Rates World-Wide." *The Wall Street Journal*, June 2, 2005.

[8] Central bank attempts to defend indefensible exchange rates are akin to speculation. The June 1, 2005 issue of the *Financial Times* reported that Mr. Marakanond Rerngchai, the former governor of the central bank of Thailand was ordered by a Thai court to repay 186 billion baht expended in the failed effort to defend the fixed exchange rate of the baht prior to the Asian Financial Crisis.

Amy Kazmin. "Thai Ex-Banker Told to Repay Pounds 2.5bn." Financial Times, June 1, 2005, p. 9.

[9] On July 24, 1997, the Associated Press and Dow Jones News reported Malaysian Prime Minister Mahathir Mohamad as contending that there was a "well-planned effort to undermine the economies of all Asian countries by destabilizing their currencies...Our economic fundamentals are good, yet anyone with a few billion dollars can destroy all the progress that we have made." Associated Press and Dow Jones Newswire. "Malaysia Ringgit/Late-2 Central Bks Powerless, Says Dealer." July 24, 1997.

[10] Associated Press and Dow Jones Newswire. "Malaysia Ringgit/Late-2 Central Bks Powerless, Says Dealer." July 24, 1997.

[11] Reuters reported the following on July 27, 1997: "...On Saturday, after a week of calling currency speculators 'rogues,' 'robbers' and 'brigands,' Mahathir said: 'Today I am confirming that George Soros was the man that I was talking about.' Mahathir also accused Soros of using his financial clout to try to block Burma's admission to ASEAN." It should be noted here that George Soros is probably most famous as the man who broke the Bank of England during the currency crisis of 1992. What is less well-known is that the Malaysian central bank, Bank Negara, lost several billion dollars during this same period when it bet on the pound against George Soros.

[12] Michael Zielenziger. "Currency War: The Moron vs. the Menace." *The Advertiser*, September 23, 1997.

[13] Dow Jones Newswire. "Malaysia Mahathir Scolds U.S. Allowing Soros's Speculation." August 22, 1997.

[14] Reuters, "Ringgit Remains Weak After Selloff." Monday, August 11, 1997.

[15] It is also possible that the threat of the prohibition of currency trading may have accelerated the decline of the ringgit as those with long ringgit positions feared increased difficulty in getting out of ringgit-denominated positions.

[16] Reuters. "German, Japanese Comments Blast Dollar Lower." September 24, 1997. The article also notes that Hans Tietmeyer's comments may have been mistranslated from German into English.

[17] Reuters. "Focus-PM Comments Shake Malaysia Ringgit, Stocks." October 1, 1997.

[18] Reuters. "Malaysia's Mahathir Attacks Currency Traders Again." September 30, 1997.

[19] Reuters News. "Ringgit Plunges After Fresh Remarks by Mahathir." October 1, 1997.

[20] Sonali Desai. "FOCUS-Asian Currencies Pare Losses on Ringgit Rise." Friday, December 5, 1997.

[21] Mr. Sakakibara left the position of vice minister on Thursday, July 8, 1999 and was replaced by Mr. Haruhiko Kuroda.

[22] Jiji Press English News Service. "Sakakibara Comment Sends Dlr Below 124 Yen in Tokyo." May 8, 1997.

[23] *Mainichi Daily News.* "Dollar Likely to Remain Bearish." May 11, 1997.

[24] The *Mainichi Daily News* reported on May 11, 1997:

> The U.S. dollar is likely to remain bearish against the yen in Tokyo this week as the recent Japanese government stance in favor of a stronger yen is expected to continue affecting the market. Speculation that a gap in interest rates between Japan and the United States could narrow is also expected to step up dollar-selling moves on the market. With a rapid depreciation of the dollar in New York on Friday, currency dealers [said] the trend of the strong dollar may have ended.

[25] Reuters. "Dollar Capped in Tokyo by Sakakibara's Remarks." April 1, 1998.

[26] Reuters. "Dollar Battered by Aggressive BOJ Action in Tokyo." April 10, 1998.

[27] David Brancaccio. *Marketplace.* June 23, 1997.

[28] David Brancaccio. *Marketplace.* June 24, 1997.

[29] Craig Karmen. "More 'Distorted' Comments Roil Markets." *The Wall Street Journal,* May 20, 2005.

[30] Jiji Press English News Service. "Intervention Effective at Shift in Market Sentiment." September 1, 1998.

4

GEOPOLITICAL EVENTS

"In the field of observation, chance favors only the prepared mind."

—Louis Pasteur

War with Iraq

At approximately, 5:30 A.M. Baghdad time, on Thursday, March 20, 2003, *Operation Iraqi Freedom* began when coalition forces invaded Iraq.[1] The invasion occurred approximately 90 minutes after a 48-hour ultimatum expired from U.S. President George W. Bush that Iraqi President Saddam Hussein and his sons Uday and Qusay leave Iraq.[2] Saddam Hussein did not leave Iraq. The resultant war was relatively brief. The U.S.-led coalition easily dominated Iraqi armed forces on the battlefield, suffered minimal casualties, and achieved most of its military objectives in a matter of days and total victory within three weeks.[3]

Although the invasion began on March 20, financial markets had started to deliver their assessment of the outcome before hostilities began. On Thursday, March 13, 2003, almost a week before hostilities began and days before President Bush issued his ultimatum to Saddam Hussein, U.S. stock prices and the U.S. dollar suddenly surged while gold and bond prices fell. The sudden rally in stock prices and the foreign exchange value of the dollar was made even more dramatic coming, as it did, against a backdrop of bearish market sentiment. The Dow Jones Industrial Average rose 269.68 points, or 3.57%, whereas the Nasdaq rose almost 4.8%. Some observers dismissed the rally in stock prices as a dead cat bounce in a bear market. It was not.

The sharp moves in commodity and financial markets are depicted in Figures 4.1 to 4.4.

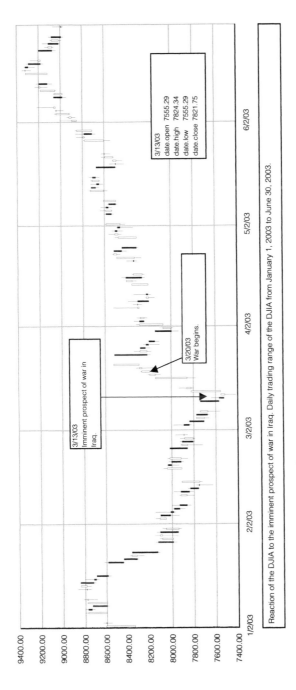

FIGURE 4.1   Stocks rally as war approaches.

Reaction of the DJIA to the imminent prospect of war in Iraq. Daily trading range of the DJIA from January 1, 2003 to June 30, 2003.

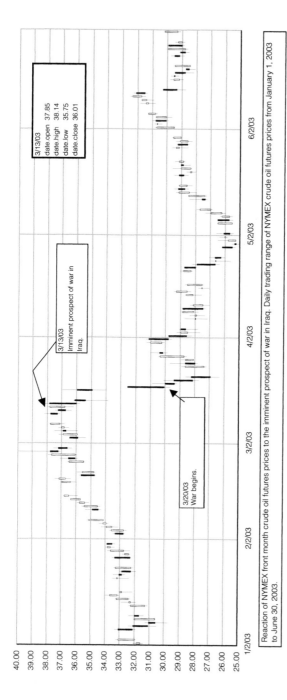

FIGURE 4.2 Crude oil prices fall.

Reaction of NYMEX front month crude oil futures prices to the imminent prospect of war in Iraq. Daily trading range of NYMEX crude oil futures prices from January 1, 2003 to June 30, 2003.

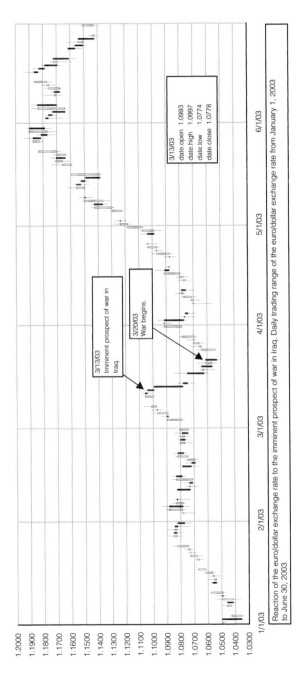

Reaction of the euro/dollar exchange rate to the imminent prospect of war in Iraq. Daily trading range of the euro/dollar exchange rate from January 1, 2003 to June 30, 2003.

FIGURE 4.3   The euro falls against the dollar.

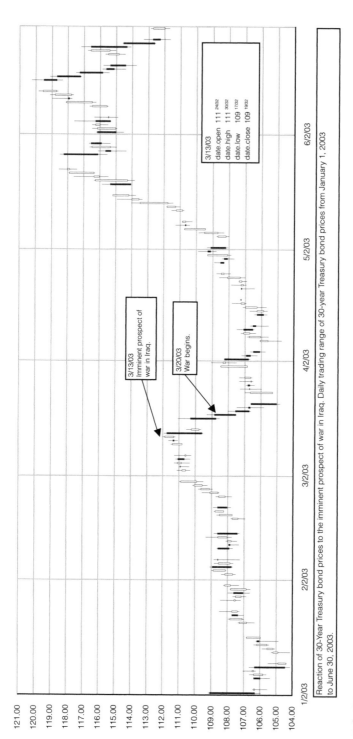

3/13/03
date.open 111 24/32
date.high 111 30/32
date.low   109 17/32
date.close 109 19/32

3/13/03
Imminent prospect of
war in Iraq.

3/20/03
War begins.

Reaction of 30-Year Treasury bond prices to the imminent prospect of war in Iraq. Daily trading range of 30-year Treasury bond prices from January 1, 2003 to June 30, 2003.

FIGURE 4.4   Treasury bond futures prices fall.

They are also captured in the following excerpt from Reuters that was disseminated at 7:53 P.M. (New York time) on Thursday, March 13, 2003.

> Stocks rallied everywhere but Japan on Thursday and the dollar climbed, while U.S. bonds and gold prices fell on hopes that any war with Iraq might be short—or perhaps avoided through diplomacy.
>
> …Wall Street's surge proved to be contagious, and Tokyo's Nikkei was up 1.92 percent or 151 points at 8,019.59 in early Friday morning trading…On Thursday, the dollar jumped after television network CNN reported during Asian trading hours that Iraqi officials may have begun secret negotiations to surrender.
>
> Bond prices tanked in the U.S. Treasury market's worst selloff in three months. Gold hit a three-month low.
>
> In New York, crude oil futures plummeted almost $2 a barrel, a drop of about 5 percent, on news that the United Nations Security Council may delay until next week a vote on a U.S. and British resolution to authorize war against Iraq.[4]

As is sometimes the case with trading catalysts, the appropriate interpretation of the reason for the price moves is controversial. Did stocks rally on the prospect of a short war or did they rally in the belief that war could be averted or delayed? The preceding excerpts suggest that it could be either. Other commentators also explicitly recognized the conflicting reasons for the sharp moves in commodity and financial market prices.[5] Some news reports took a more narrow view and argued that the market rallied in the belief that war with Iraq could be avoided or delayed.[6]

Factors internal to the market helped fuel the rally. In this case, the stock market rally was exacerbated by short-covering.[7] Although it is possible that the market reacted to the potential for the war to be averted, it seems more likely that the market anticipated that a war would break out soon and that coalition forces would win a quick and decisive victory. The reason is as follows.

At the time, it was commonly believed by many market participants that there was a $4 to $5 per barrel *war premium* in the price of oil. This meant that a quick resolution of the conflict could trigger a steep decline in oil prices. In addition, many observers believed that uncertainty about whether there would be a second war with Iraq acted as a drag on the economy. The trading thesis that likely prevailed was that the war would be short and military success would precipitate a sharp decline in oil prices and enhance the prospects for U.S. economic growth.[8]

The market's reaction to the prospect of a short war with Iraq also illustrates the influence of past events in guiding the market's likely response to current events. The early and easy success of coalition forces in the 1991 Gulf War triggered a massive market reaction as detailed in the following excerpt from *The Wall Street Journal Europe* on Thursday, January 18, 1991.

> Stocks in the U.S. rocketed 4.6% in euphoric trading, pushing the Dow Jones Industrial Average 114.60 points higher to 2623.51, the second-biggest point gain ever. Oil and gold prices plunged in a stunning reversal to their initial run-up when the war erupted. Crude for February delivery plummeted a record $10.56 a barrel to $21.44; February gold dived $30.10 an ounce to $374.40.

> The dollar skidded as the apparent success of air attacks on Iraq led traders to believe the gulf war will be short...U.S. Treasurys rose on the early news from the Mideast. The 30-year bond was quoted Thursday at 106 2-32, up 2 11-32...London stock prices surged 2.4%...Share prices jumped throughout the Asian-Pacific region...In Tokyo, the Nikkei stock average increased 4.5%...[9]

The market's reaction to the success of coalition forces in the 1991 Gulf War provided traders with a road map of how the market would likely react to the second Iraq war if it occurred. The imposition of sanctions on the Iraqi regime after the Gulf War ended meant that the Iraqi military was less prepared than it was before the Gulf War even if the sanctions were only partially effective. This meant that if a second war began with Iraq it would also likely be short with minimal losses on the coalition side. After the prospect of war became certain, the only question was when it would begin. Traders did not want to miss the likely moves in the market by waiting until the war actually started. This illustrates the market's tendency to telescope, or shorten, its reaction time to current events when the reaction is largely based on how the market responded to similar events in the past. If the market reacted the day after the Gulf War started in 1991, it is not surprising that the market reacted as soon as a second war with Iraq became a virtual certainty. As shown in Chapter 2, "Market Conditions and Sentiment," a similar phenomenon occurred in May 2005 in the steep and immediate reaction of Treasury bond prices to the announcement that the Treasury Department was considering issuing 30-year Treasury bonds again. The combined two-day rally of almost 9 points that occurred on October 31 and November 1, 2001 was telescoped to an almost immediate 8.5 point decline in long bond prices a few minutes after the May 4, 2005 announcement that the Treasury was considering reissuing 30-year bonds.

In order to appreciate the market's behavior on March 13, 2003, it is important to understand the significance of geopolitical factors as trading catalysts in the run-up to the second war with Iraq. The prospect of a second war between Saddam Hussein's Iraq and the U.S. and its allies jumped after the September 11, 2001 terrorist attacks on the United States with unsubstantiated claims of Iraqi involvement in promoting terrorist actions against the U.S. It jumped further with faulty intelligence that suggested that Iraq possessed weapons of mass destruction. The almost 18-month period after the September 11, 2001 terrorist attacks until the war began on March 20, 2003 was a period in which geopolitical events frequently roiled financial markets. During this period, even speeches in the United Nations or the passage of resolutions by the United Nations Security Council could impact world markets. Not surprisingly, commodity and financial markets were subjected to periodic bouts of volatility as the prospect of war increased or decreased.

It is instructive to examine the price action of several key commodity and financial markets over the months preceding the second war with Iraq. Interestingly, the markets did not move in unison. For example, gold—which is often viewed as a safe haven in times of trouble—peaked in January almost two months before the surprise stock market rally of March 13. Similarly, the Japanese yen had reached a similar level to where it traded on March 13 in late February 2003 before selling off and rallying again. Crude oil was on a steady uptrend from November 2002 when it traded around $24 per barrel. Although the prelude to the second Iraq war was the dominant factor in the markets during late 2002 and early 2003, other factors specific to each market were also important. For instance, crude oil prices were pushed up by oil-worker labor disputes in Venezuela. The behavior of the various markets after the war started is equally interesting as prices bounced around in reaction to press reports of military actions and Iraqi resistance.

Geopolitical Events as Trading Catalysts

Politics and finance intersect in the impact that the actions of governments and electorates have on financial markets. The reaction of financial markets to various political events around the world creates new trading opportunities and exposes traders to another type of risk—*geopolitical risk*. Traders are not interested in politics, per se, but rather the impact that various political actions or their prospects have on market prices and volatility. Geopolitical events are another source of trading catalysts.

Geopolitical events may take a variety of types ranging from non-violent to violent. Wars, revolutions, coups d'etat, assassinations, and terrorist actions are examples of the violent types of geopolitical events. Such events often exert a profound impact on financial market prices. The events leading up to the Iraq war in March 2003 exemplify the impact of geopolitical risk on financial markets.

Financial markets have long responded to the outcomes of the individual battles that wars are comprised of. For instance, during the Napoleonic wars, information from the battles affected the value of government "stock" (i.e., British government debt), also known as *gilts*. It is said that the London branch of the Rothschild family made a fortune when it found out that Lord Nelson had won the Battle of Waterloo. The use of carrier pigeons gave the Rothschilds a technological and informational edge over their rivals. Their rivals knew that the Rothschilds possessed an informational edge and the Rothschilds knew that their rivals knew that they had an informational edge. It was readily apparent that news of Lord Nelson's victory would spark a huge rally in gilt prices. Consequently, it is alleged that when Nathan Rothschild found out that Lord Nelson had won the battle of Waterloo, he promptly sold gilts knowing that other traders would believe that the information Rothschild possessed (presumably about the outcome of the battle of Waterloo) was negative for gilts. This, in turn, sparked panic selling of gilts. Rothschild then was able to buy even more bonds for a fraction of what he would have had to pay moments earlier.

Nonviolent types of geopolitical events can also exert a substantial impact on financial market prices. As was mentioned in Chapter 1, "Introduction," the assassination of President John F. Kennedy on Friday, November 22, 1963 precipitated a sharp drop in stock prices and the early closure of the New York Stock Exchange. The market remained closed on Monday, November 25 but experienced a massive rally when it reopened on Tuesday, November 26.[10] Examples of nonviolent types of geopolitical events include: elections, expropriations, and changes in tax rates or regulatory policy. The outcomes of elections may pose a real or imagined threat to the economy and, hence asset prices, likewise, the outcomes of referenda. In addition to affecting the level of market prices, geopolitical risk may affect the volatility of financial markets. Increased volatility makes options more expensive and may adversely affect liquidity if trading volume falls substantially as a result. Geopolitical events may also change the prevailing market sentiment as well as the economic outlook.

Individuals who have a talent in anticipating the outcome of elections and referenda or in discerning the likely course of political events may have a trading edge provided they are also able to assess correctly the likely market reaction to those political events. Such a trading edge may be valuable episodically, perhaps only a few times a year. This requires that traders trading off of their comparative geopolitical expertise limit their trading accordingly. It may also require that such traders assume larger position sizes when they put on a trade than they might otherwise do if they were trading more frequently.

The Arrest of Mikhail Khodorkovsky

On Saturday, October 25, 2003, Mikhail Khodorkovsky, head of the Russian oil company Yukos and the wealthiest man in Russia, was arrested by Russian police in Novosibirsk, Siberia. Khodorkovsky was subsequently charged with fraud and tax evasion. Despite the prediction by Deputy Prime Minister and Finance Minister Alexei Kudrin that there would be no significant market reaction to Khodorkovsky's arrest, the Russian stock market plummeted and the rouble fell sharply when the market opened on Monday, October 27.[11] The principal index of the Russian market, the Russian Trading System (RTS), was down over 14% before bouncing back to close down just over

10%.[12] Not surprisingly, Yukos shares were more severely affected, at one point losing more than 20% of their value before closing down over 15%.[13]

The arrest of Khodorkovsky was seen (correctly or not) as politically motivated and a form of retribution by the government. (Khodorkovsky had financed opposition to Russian President Vladimir Putin.) Traders had to assess whether Khodorkovsky's arrest meant a return to old ways of doing business in Russia. They also had to determine which markets would be affected and the likely magnitude of the impact. Although there was little reason to suspect that Khodorkovsky's arrest would impact markets in the developed world, it could adversely affect other emerging markets by affecting foreign investors' appetite for risk. It did not. The impact of the arrest was limited to Russian financial markets and did not impact foreign markets.

A trader did not have to have prior knowledge of Khodorkovsky's arrest to make money from its impact on financial market prices. The large drop in Russian stock prices on Monday, October 27, 2003 created the potential for a rebound. Part of the rebound came on Monday when stock prices bounced off their lows of down almost 14% to close down over 10.6%. Russian financial markets recovered somewhat more with a 2.5% bounce in the RTS index on Tuesday, October 28, 2003.

Elections

The surprise outcomes of elections and referenda sometimes serve as trading catalysts, inducing a significant change in market prices. Because both elections and referenda are scheduled political events, information about consensus expectations is frequently available through opinion polls. This tends to reduce the number of surprise outcomes but probably increases the market impact of any surprise. It should be noted that survey results from opinion polls may fluctuate more than actual consensus expectations. This means that opinion polls are often less reliable than market assessments.

May 2004 Indian Parliamentary Election

Indian parliamentary elections (which occur in stages) were held between April 20, 2004 and May 10, 2004. The surprise loss of Indian Prime Minister Atal Behari Vajpayee's Bharatiya Janata Party (BJP) and the *presumptive* election of Congress Party leader Sonia Gandhi as prime minister prompted a sharp selloff in Indian equities.[14] The selloff in Indian stock prices started with exit poll results and climaxed in a 16.62% decline in Indian share prices on Monday, May 17, 2004 before rallying to close down only 11.14% after "powerful state-run financial institutions" were instructed to buy shares.[15] Put differently, the market capitalization of Indian stocks fell by $40 billion on May 17. It is important to emphasize that there was ample time for traders who believed that the new government was bad for the market to put on a significant short-equity position. Indeed, the market was down around 6% the previous week after news of the election results first broke. Not only did the market continue to decline a week after the news was out but the magnitude of the decline increased.

Once again, the market reaction was exacerbated by market participants who were forced to sell stock bought on margins—that is, the external trading catalyst (the likely election of Sonia Gandhi as prime minister) was less important than the internal trading catalyst (margin calls and the positive feedback trading it induced). In other words, lower prices resulted in more margin calls, which in turn pushed stock prices even lower. The sharp decline in stock prices occurred despite two trading halts that temporarily suspended trading after the overall market was down 10% and again when the overall market was down 15%. This is described in the May 18, 2004 issue of the Business Standard.

...The dramatic collapse in the Bombay Stock Exchange (BSE) Sensex today [Monday] had its origins in Friday's 330-point decline that triggered huge margin calls on brokers and investors. This, in turn, forced them to sell heavily to raise cash, setting the stage for a hugely negative start today. The Sensex opened 100-150 points below Friday's close, which made the subsequent 842-point intra-day crash and two trading stoppages a self-fulfilling trend...

In today's trading, there was no hint of panic till the Sensex fell 200 points, but around this point cascading margin calls forced speculators and big investors to keep selling in order to raise cash. ...With margins as high as 80 per cent being called for, the market saw only sellers most of the time...[16]

Selling as the result of margin calls explains part of the magnitude of the decline in Indian stock prices. Not surprisingly, foreign institutional investors were blamed for instigating much of the selling.[17] (However, no evidence of market manipulation was reported by the Securities and Exchange Board of India—the governmental regulatory agency—in a subsequent investigation.)[18] The delayed reaction to the Indian parliamentary elections was largely localized with limited impact on foreign markets. It should be noted that there was a significant intraday bounce as the market went from being down 16.6% to closing down 11% after large domestic institutional buy orders came to the market.

The concern of market participants supposedly centered on the selection of Sonia Gandhi as prime minister and uncertainty over the economic policies that the Congress Party would pursue with its left-wing coalition partners. The decision by Sonia Gandhi not to seek the position of prime minister coupled with the selection of Manmohan Singh—a respected former finance minister in a previous Congress government—as the new prime minister served as a trading catalyst. News of Manmohan Singh's selection as prime minister designate precipitated an 8.5% rally in Indian stock prices.[19] The magnitude of the rally also reflected the likely overreaction the previous day due to margin sales.

Knowing the likely source of selling pressure in any break allows traders to ascertain whether a price decline is overdone—that is, traders need to be able to assess the potential for positive feedback trading from margin calls, stop-loss orders, technical analysis, short-covering, or other sources. In turn, this allows traders to position themselves for the potential subsequent rebound in market prices and assess the potential magnitude of the rebound in prices.

The Brazilian Presidential Election of 2002

The prospect of the election of Luiz Inacio Lula da Silva as president of Brazil in October 2002 sparked periodic declines in the Brazilian stock market, Brazilian government bonds, and the foreign exchange value of the real, Brazil's currency unit, as the odds of Lula's election increased. For instance, a weekend poll indicating a significant rise in Lula's support sparked a 3.5% decline in the Brazilian stock market, a 5% decline in the key Brazilian government bond, and a 4.8% decline in the value of the real against the dollar on Monday, September 23, 2002.[20]

Perhaps a more dramatic effect of the 2002 Brazilian presidential election campaign was the impact on the bond market. The spread of Brazilian government dollar-denominated debt over comparable maturity U.S. Treasury debt is a measure of country risk. In the run-up to the election of Mr. Lula da Silva as president of Brazil, the spread of Brazilian dollar-denominated C bonds over comparable maturity U.S. Treasury bonds widened to 2436 basis points on Friday, September 27, 2002.[21]

This is a tremendously wide spread, or put differently, a substantial increase in Brazil risk. To put it in perspective, 2400 basis points means that if 10-year U.S. Treasury notes were yielding 6%, 10-year dollar-denominated Brazilian debt would be yielding 30%. Although the spread was at its widest shortly before the first round of the presidential election, it should be noted that the increase in the spread over its normal level took place over a period of several months.

Not surprisingly, the yield spread widened as the probability of Lula's election as president increased. However, this is only part of the story. To be sure, the level of the spread conveys the sense of panic that existed among some participants in the Brazilian bond market over Lula's likely election as Brazil's president; but it also conveys the impact of other factors. Factors internal to the market also played a significant role in the widening of the spread. In particular, the spread increased as the result of hedging activities of sellers of credit protection of Brazilian dollar-denominated C bonds.[22] This is yet another illustration of the importance of understanding the likely behavior of market participants. Dealers who sell protection against credit risk want to hedge their position, especially if prices start to move against them. In this case, dealers who had sold protection against the risk that Brazil would default protected themselves by selling Brazilian C bonds that they did not own. The rush to hedge by dealers pushed Brazilian C bond prices sharply lower, which encouraged more dealers to hedge themselves by shorting the Brazilian C bond, and in turn, exacerbated the downward move in bond price and increase in yield. The hedging activity by dealers can create yield distortion among bonds with seemingly similar risks.[23]

1992 Maastricht Treaty Referendum

The Treaty of Maastricht (also known as the Treaty on European Union) was agreed upon by European Community governments on February 7, 1992.[24] The purpose of the treaty was to promote economic integration by establishing a European Monetary Union (EMU). The treaty required ratification by all European Community member governments. On June 2, 1992, Danish voters were given the opportunity to vote for or against the Maastricht treaty in a referendum. In a surprise result, Danish voters rejected the treaty by a vote of 50.7% to 49.3%.

The outcome plunged the European Community into crisis mode. The outcome of the Danish vote, coupled with the prospect of a French referendum on the same issue, impacted financial markets with most European stock markets closing lower.[25] Besides impacting stock prices, the outcome of the Danish referendum also sparked a rise in the dollar against both the Danish krone and the German mark.[26] In addition, the outcome of the referendum prompted many European bonds (especially European Currency Unit (ECU) denominated bonds) to fall, whereas German mark denominated bonds rose.[27]

At first glance, the duration of the market impact of the Danish rejection of the Maastricht seems relatively limited as the dollar fell against the German mark and stock prices recovered on Thursday, June 4, 1992.[28] However, the real impact of the Danish vote was to change sentiment about the viability of the European Monetary Union. In fact, it might be argued that the result of the Danish referendum was to set in motion a wave of bets against the EMU, which ultimately resulted in the Black Wednesday, September 16, 1992 currency realignment when the Bank of England was forced to withdraw from the EMU and let the pound sterling float.

Finally, it should be noted that Danish voters eventually approved the Maastricht treaty. After receiving a number of rights to opt out of certain provisions of the treaty, voters in Denmark approved the Maastricht treaty by a vote of 56.7% to 43.3% on May 18, 1993.

2005 European Union Constitution Referenda

On October 29, 2004, the treaty establishing a European Union Constitution (or, more simply, the *European Constitution*) was signed by all 25 European Union (EU) member governments. The idea was to replace a set of existing treaties with a single treaty among EU member states, change relative voting powers, clarify individual rights, and simplify decision making. Implementation of the treaty required formal ratification of all the member states—some of whose governments decided to put ratification of the proposed treaty to a vote among their citizens. France was one such government. The Netherlands was another. Although citizens were restricted to voting yes or no, the European Constitution referenda became vehicles by which dissatisfaction with the policies of the government in power or the European Union could be expressed.

The growing prospect of a French no vote acted as a catalyst in driving down the foreign exchange value of the euro against the dollar and changing market sentiment as contemporary news reports suggest.[29]

On Sunday, May 29, 2005, French citizens rejected the proposed European Constitution by a vote of almost 55% to 45%. The election results, despite being widely expected, acted as a trading catalyst on financial markets. The euro fell in response to the news on Monday, May 30, 2005 and again on Tuesday, May 31, 2005 for a total of 2.2%.[30] This is depicted in Figure 4.5.

On June 1, 2005, Dutch voters rejected the European Constitution by almost 62% to 38%. The result of these two back-to-back rejections of the European Constitution was to cast doubt on the eventual ratification of the treaty, but more importantly, on the vitality of the European Union itself. The euro fell an additional cent against the dollar on news of the defeat of the proposed treaty by Dutch voters.[31]

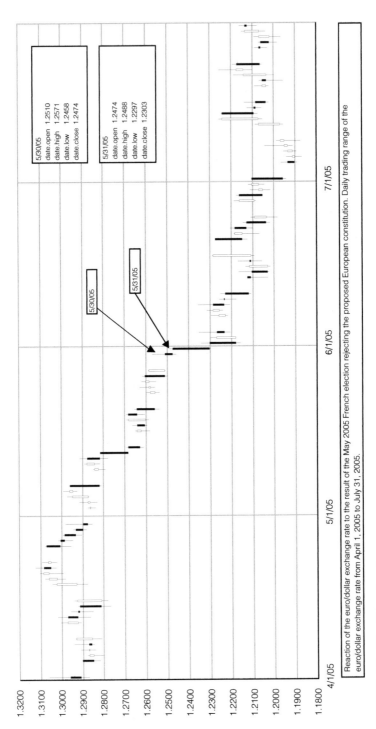

FIGURE 4.5   The French vote no.

Reaction of the euro/dollar exchange rate to the result of the May 2005 French election rejecting the proposed European constitution. Daily trading range of the euro/dollar exchange rate from April 1, 2005 to July 31, 2005.

Two points should be kept in mind. First, the referenda results accorded with expectations. Yet, there was a substantial market reaction to what was expected. Second, the effect was relatively long-lived contrary to what the theory of market efficiency would suggest. The former effect can be explained, in part, by the existence of dispersion around consensus expectations. This meant that even a situation where there was no apparent forecast error would surprise some market participants and lead to further appreciation of the dollar against the euro. However, the latter effect (i.e., the delayed reaction to the news of the French referendum results) is not easily reconciled with the notion of informational market efficiency.

It should also be emphasized that traders did not wait until the vote before placing their bets—nor was the foreign exchange market the only place to wager on the outcome of the referenda. In anticipation of a majority of French and Dutch citizens voting no, many speculators sold government bonds of EU member countries—whose economies are perceived to be weaker—and bought the bonds of EU member countries whose economies are considered stronger.[32]

Such spread-widening trades had a fair amount of risk associated with them. These risks arise as the result of leverage as much as from a bet on the election outcomes. The probability of a no vote in France varied substantially over the month before the vote on Sunday, May 29. This volatility in expectations of the election outcome was reflected in the market price of a contract on the outcome of the referendum.

For instance, on May 2, 2005, Tradesports.com, an online betting site offering opportunities to wager on various events, reported a bid price of 49.3 and an ask price of 51.3 for the contract that French voters would approve the EU constitutional treaty. (The price of the contract varied between 0 and 100. A price of 100 corresponded to absolute certainty that French voters would approve the treaty, whereas a price of 0 corresponded to absolute certainty that French voters would reject the treaty.) The Tradesports.com Web site also showed that the price of a yes vote outcome on the EU constitution referendum steadily increased from a contract low of 38.6 on April 28 to 50 on May 2. Put differently, the prices of the EU constitutional treaty contract on the Tradesports.com Web site suggested that the probability of French approval of the constitutional treaty was increasing.

Volatility in consensus expectations creates more opportunities for traders to profit from a correct position as well as increases the risk of any position taken. Increased volatility in consensus expectations also impacts how a rational trader would trade this event. Namely, a trader would take a smaller position in the *spread widening* or *spread narrowing* trade in the eurozone bond market.

Traders looking at the prospect of the French or Dutch referenda serving as trading catalysts would have likely looked at the reaction of the financial markets to the rejection of the Treaty of Maastricht by Danish voters in the summer of 1992. Even though the subject of the two referenda differed, the background situations had some similarities.

Terrorist Actions

Although terrorist acts against U.S. interests outside the United States have increased in recent years, terrorist acts on U.S. soil have fortunately been limited. The market impact of terrorist acts on U.S. soil has been mixed. Both the February 26, 1993 World Trade Center bombing and the April 19, 1995 Oklahoma City bombing had little apparent effect on U.S. financial markets as measured by the behavior of the Dow Jones Industrial Average. In fact, the DJIA rose slightly on both days. In contrast, the September 11, 2001 terrorist attacks on the World Trade Center, the Pentagon, and United Airlines flight 93 had a dramatic negative impact on financial markets.

Terrorist acts are more common outside the United States. The financial market impact of such acts has also been mixed. Although such acts have impacted local or regional markets, there has often been no appreciable impact on U.S. financial markets. There have been a number of significant terrorist actions around the world. This section considers only a few terrorist actions and assesses their financial market impact. This is not meant to diminish the tragic loss in human lives from the numerous terrorist actions not considered, such as the March 20, 1995 Sarin poison gas attacks on the Tokyo subway system; the October 12, 2002 bombing of a bar in Bali; the September 1-3, 2004 terrorist seizure of a school in Beslan, Russia; or the seemingly countless terrorist acts in parts of the Middle East.

The question naturally arises as to why one should consider terrorist actions as trading catalysts. Surely, only those with foreknowledge of the terrorist acts would be able to profit from trading off of terrorist acts. Indeed, an unusual surge in the volume of put options on airline and property insurance company stocks led some observers to openly question whether some traders had advance knowledge of the terror attacks on September 11, 2001.[33] Subsequent investigation, however, did not support such allegations.

Terrorist acts may be as unpredictable as earthquakes. However, the market's response to such actions may be entirely predictable. It is in that response that trading opportunities and risks may arise. Trading opportunities and risks may also arise with presumed terrorist actions. For instance, the crash of American Airlines flight number 587 to Puerto Rico outside John F. Kennedy international airport at 9:17 a.m. shortly after takeoff on November 12, 2001 immediately raised fears of another terror attack. This sparked a temporary selloff in stock prices with the Dow Jones Industrial Average plummeting almost 200 points before rebounding to close down 53.63 points. Not surprisingly, airline and travel industry stocks were especially hard hit by the news.[34]

September 11, 2001

At approximately 8:45 A.M. on Tuesday, September 11, 2001, a hijacked passenger airplane intentionally crashed into the north tower of the World Trade Center complex in New York City. Less than 18 minutes later, a second hijacked airplane intentionally crashed into the south tower of the World Trade Center complex. When the second collision occurred, it was immediately apparent that the first crash was not an accident but a terrorist attack. The crashes not only tore large holes into the buildings but also started fires. Less than two hours later, both the south and north towers of the World Trade Center collapsed. At approximately 9:43 A.M., a third hijacked passenger airplane crashed into the Pentagon, igniting a fire and causing part of the building to collapse 27 minutes later. At about the same instant in time, a fourth hijacked airplane crashed in the fields of rural Pennsylvania when passengers—alerted to the terrorist attacks in New York and Washington—resisted the hijackers.[35] More than 3,000 innocent people were killed in the terror attacks.

U.S. equity markets had not opened when the terrorist attacks occurred in New York and did not open until Monday, September 17, so it is not possible to get an immediate read of the U.S. stock market's assessment of the impact of the terrorist attacks. The electronically traded e-mini S&P 500 stock index futures contract traded on the Chicago Mercantile Exchange was open. The larger pit-traded S&P 500 stock index futures market was not open at the time of the attacks and did not reopen until Monday, September 17. Eurodollar futures traded at the Chicago Mercantile Exchange, and Treasury note and bond futures traded on the Chicago Board of Trade were open at the time of the attacks but closed shortly thereafter. Both markets reacted sharply.[36] Currency futures markets at the Chicago Mercantile Exchange were also open at the time of the terrorist attacks but closed shortly thereafter.

The currency market was open at the time of the attacks. Figure 4.6 depicts the reaction of the Swiss franc—a traditional safe haven in times of crisis—to the terrorist actions in the United States. Consistent with the safe haven trading thesis, Figure 4.6 shows that the value of the Swiss franc rose against the dollar (i.e., it took fewer Swiss francs to buy a dollar). Many European markets were also open at the time of the terrorist attacks. The following report from Agence France Press notes that European stock prices fell sharply.

> …Stock prices dived in response to the attacks—the German stock market plunging 9.1 percent, Paris falling 5.74 percent and London shedding 3.0 percent. Trading on the New York stock exchange was suspended. The euro meanwhile firmed in response to the crisis while oil prices jumped nearly two dollars in London…[37]

The U.S. stock market reopened on Monday, September 17 and gave its assessment of the financial impact of the terrorist attacks of September 11. The Dow Jones Industrial Average closed at 8,920.70, down 7.07% for the day, whereas the Nasdaq Composite index closed at 1579.28, or down 6.85% for the day. This break occurred despite a 50-basis point cut in the Federal funds rate by the Federal Reserve prior to the stock market's reopening. Not surprisingly, travel industry stocks were hard hit, whereas defense and security company stocks rose.[38]

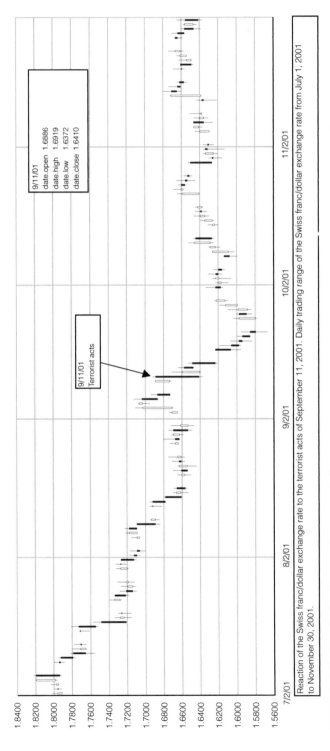

9/11/01
date.open   1.6886
date.high   1.6919
date.low   1.6372
date.close 1.6410

9/11/01
Terrorist acts

1.8400
1.8200
1.8000
1.7800
1.7600
1.7400
1.7200
1.7000
1.6800
1.6600
1.6400
1.6200
1.6000
1.5800
1.5600

7/2/01   8/2/01   9/2/01   10/2/01   11/2/01

Reaction of the Swiss franc/dollar exchange rate to the terrorist acts of September 11, 2001. Daily trading range of the Swiss franc/dollar exchange rate from July 1, 2001 to November 30, 2001.

FIGURE 4.6   The Swiss franc acts as a safe haven.

The financial market's response to the terrorist attacks had several components. First, there was a *flight to safety* as stocks fell, bonds and gold rose, and the dollar fell against the euro and the Swiss franc. Second, oil prices rose in the belief that the supply of oil may be more uncertain. Third, there was a belief that the terrorist actions would spark a recession, which is often viewed as positive for bonds and negative for stocks. (Note that a recession would probably result in a decline in oil consumption, which is inconsistent with the observed rise in oil prices.) Fourth, airlines, hotels, and other travel industry stocks were hard hit (due to a perceived drop in travel) along with property and casualty insurance companies (due to a perceived increase in payouts associated with the World Trade Center destruction). Fifth, security and defense stocks rose in the belief that such companies would benefit from increased business following the terrorist attacks. It should be noted that the various components that comprised the market's reaction to the terrorist acts lasted for different lengths of time. The flight to safety response was much shorter-lived than the assessment that travel industry stocks would be hard hit in the aftermath of September 11, 2001.

Madrid Train Bombings, March 11, 2004

On Thursday morning, March 11, 2004, a series of bombs exploded on trains in Madrid, Spain killing 191 innocent people during the morning rush hour. The bombs were placed on four different trains and were intended to go off simultaneously when all of the trains were in the station. Had the bombs exploded simultaneously in the train station, thousands of people may have been killed. Fortunately, they did not. Bomb explosions occurred from 7:39 to 7:42 A.M., Madrid time. The bombs were the work of terrorists affiliated with the al-Qaeda terrorist group. The terror group demanded the withdrawal of Spanish armed forces from Iraq.

The timing of the bombings—three days before a Spanish general election—ultimately claimed another victim as Mariano Rajoy (incumbent prime minister and President Jose Maria Aznar's choice to succeed him as prime minister) was defeated in his election bid by Jose Luis Rodriguez Zapatero. Newly elected Prime Minister Zapatero announced his decision to withdraw Spanish armed forces from Iraq a few days later.

Spanish stocks fell 2.2% in response to both the terrorist attacks and lower U.S. stock prices the day before.[39] The financial impact of the Madrid train bombings was not limited to the Spanish stock market. Rather, a number of foreign markets were also affected, as the following excerpt from a column by Brian Blackstone in Dow Jones Newswires on March 11, 2004 makes clear.

> ...Rush-hour bomb blasts in Madrid train stations...[sent] equity markets plummeting and boost[ed] safe-haven demand for government securities. Demand waned as reports linked the attacks to Basque separatist group ETA and not international terrorists.

> The yield on the benchmark 10-year Treasury note fell as low as 3.67% on the news, and remained near 3.70% in early afternoon trade despite encouraging [economic] reports...The 10-year German bund...fell two basis points to 3.90%, and Japan's 10-year note fell four basis points in yield to 1.285%.

> The dollar...fell slightly versus the euro and more notably against the Swiss franc...The price of gold languished, even though it's also traditionally viewed as a safe harbor..., but analysts say market fundamental factors are weighing more on the yellow metal than the events in Madrid.[40]

As the preceding excerpt notes, U.S. Treasury bonds, German bonds, and Japanese government bonds were all impacted by the terrorist attack. The terrorist action served as a trading catalyst boosting the demand for "safe haven" assets. However, the report also notes at least one puzzling reaction: namely, gold "languished," even though it is regarded as a safe haven investment. The apparent rationale for gold's *non-response* (i.e., other fundamental factors were pushing down the price of gold) highlights the importance of understanding the factors driving each market.

By design, the terrorist bombing in Madrid was intended to affect the election result. The reaction to the vote on Monday, March 15, 2004 was even steeper than the initial reaction to the terrorist bombings. Indeed, the change in stock prices on Monday was a combination of a reaction to the election and the terrorist attack. The Spanish IBEX stock index fell in excess of 4%.[41]

Uncertainty associated with the terrorist attack in Madrid and the election outcome impacted other markets. The U.S. stock market closed down 1.34% as measured by the Dow Jones Industrial Average and down 1.43% as measured by the S&P 500 stock index. Nasdaq closed down 2.9%. Separating the reaction to the election outcome from the reaction to additional information on the probable cause of the Madrid train bombing is not possible. However, it is likely that U.S. stock prices reacted more to the additional information about the Madrid train bombing than the election of Zapatero if the general lack of U.S. stock market reaction to past foreign elections is any guide. Yet another explanation is that market participants assumed that the election of Zapatero would be seen as a capitulation to terrorists and, thus, evidence that terrorism is effective. This, in turn, would increase terrorism around the world. In any event, whatever the relative impact on market prices, both events represent geopolitical risk and adversely impacted financial markets.

Terror in London, July 7, 2005

At approximately 8:52 A.M. London time on Thursday, July 7, 2005, the first in a series of explosions occurred in the London underground subway system. This was followed some minutes later by an explosion on a bus. More than 56 people died from the terror attacks, including some of the suicide bombers. The London terror attacks had an immediate impact on financial markets as reported in *USA Today* on July 8, 2005.

> ...On a hectic Thursday: Europe's Dow Jones Stoxx 600 Index had the biggest loss since August. The benchmark fell 1.8% to 274.69 after losing as much as 4.2%. Travel related stocks, including British Airways, led the decline along with insurers. In New York, both the Dow Jones Industrial Average and the Standard & Poor's 500 index lost about 1% before recovering lost ground. By late afternoon, the Dow was down 8.06 points at 12,262.12...The Nasdaq Composite index was up 0.93 at 2069.58. Treasuries rose, sending the benchmark 10-year note's yield as low as 3.93%, before a later retreat sent the yield back above 4%.[42]

Once again, markets followed a pattern similar to the response to previous terrorist actions—sharp price declines followed by partial recoveries. One difference is that the reaction to the London bombings was shorter lived.

Impeachment of South Korean President Roh Moo-hyun

On Thursday morning, March 11, 2004, South Korean President Roh Moo-hyun was impeached from office for violating an electoral law prohibiting government officials from trying to influence the outcome of elections. The South Korean Parliament determined that the president had violated the law when he stated on February 25, 2004 that he would support the Uri political party "within the limits of the law" in the April 15, 2004 parliamentary elections. The president's refusal to apologize for his comment led opposition political parties to demand and force his impeachment (subject to review by the Korean

Constitutional Court). The reaction in Korean financial markets, which were open at the time, was swift and sharp. The Korean won fell against the dollar; the yield on three-year Korean government securities fell sharply, and the Korean stock market fell as much as 5.5% before rallying to close down only 2.5%.[43]

A March 12, 2004 story from Yonhap News Agency indicated that market participants expected the financial market impact of the impeachment to be short-lived.

> The South Korean parliament's impeachment of the country's president rattled its financial markets Friday. The Korean won plunged 11.80 to the dollar to end at 1,180.80, while the nation's key bond yield fell .04 percentage point to 4.57 percent...Dealers said the unprecedented move caused the won to tumble against the greenback, but its descent was limited on rumors the government intervened to prop up the local currency. However, they predicted the flap over the impeachment crisis may soon die down...Analysts said the parliamentary vote to impeach President Roh was the main reason for the tumble in share prices on the main bourse. An overnight fall in U.S. stock prices was also responsible.[44]

The preceding excerpts indicate how political actions can impact financial market prices. The apparent trading thesis triggered by the impeachment was a *flight to safety*. Korean investors sold stocks and bought Korean bonds and U.S. dollars. The magnitude of the overreaction in the Korean bond and stock markets is interesting. As noted earlier, the yield on the three-year South Korean Treasury note was down, at one point, 10 basis points yet (according to the Yonhap News Agency excerpt) closed down only 3 basis points. Similarly, as noted, the stock market was down 5.5% at one point during the trading session but closed down only 2.5%. Put differently, there was a substantial snapback rally after the initial selloff in stocks and a substantial break in the three-year Treasury note price after the initial rally. These are violent price moves within the larger price move. The principal lesson for a trader trading on the initial news of the impeachment is twofold: have a short trading horizon and reduce your position size.

Coup d'Etat: The Gorbachev Ouster

In the early morning hours of Monday, August 19, 1991, forces loyal to hardliners in the Communist Party of the Soviet Union staged a coup d'etat. President Mikhail Gorbachev was put under virtual house arrest and special Red Army tank units were sent to Moscow. A six-month state of emergency was imposed. The resistance of thousands of ordinary Soviet citizens, Moscow Mayor Boris Yeltsin, international pressure, and basic blunders by the coup leaders caused the coup to collapse and Mikhail Gorbachev was restored to power on August 21. The coup exerted tremendous pressure on financial markets and caused a flight to safety.

News that Gorbachev had been ousted and placed under house arrest while vacationing in the Crimea created pandemonium in financial markets. Markets in Asia, Australia, and New Zealand were open when the news broke. The basic trading thesis was a flight to safety. The dollar rose against the various European currencies. The price of gold rose and equity prices plummeted. The situation and market outlook remained dire when European markets opened a few hours later. At one point, the Israeli stock market was down over 10%. The impact of the news on equity prices started to diminish as time passed. By the time the U.S. market opened, there was only a little more information. The Dow Jones Industrial Average opened down and fell over 100 points during the early part of the trading day and closed down almost 70 points in terms of the Dow Jones Industrial Average, a far lower response than in many other equity markets around the world. Some of the power of the Gorbachev ouster as a trading catalyst is captured in the following news report by *The Wall Street Journal* on Tuesday, August 20, 1991.

> ...Bond prices ended slightly lower after an early surge. The Dow Jones industrials dropped 69.99 points, or 2.4%, to 2898.03 in heavy trading. Over-the-counter stocks lost 2.9%. Shares fell more sharply on markets elsewhere, with prices plunging 5.95% in Tokyo, 9.4% in Frankfurt and 3.1% in London.
>
> The...damage [to the economy] so far seems psychological. Petroleum prices shot up on fears of a disruption in the flow of Soviet oil. Crude futures rose $1.17 to $22.47 a barrel. Grain prices in the U.S., meanwhile, plummeted amid concern that the U.S. will lose its biggest corn and soybean meal customer. Precious metals surged in Tokyo and Europe but retreated in New York as their "safe haven" appeal gave way to worries that the Soviets may increase sales of gold and platinum.[45]

The return of Mikhail Gorbachev to power on August 21, 1991 acted as a trading catalyst for financial markets as well. Market participants fled their safe haven investments and returned to equities, prompting U.S. stocks to soar over 3% and the dollar to fall.[46]

Did the market's reaction to the news of Gorbachev's ouster and reinstatement really make sense?[47] The Soviet Union was a military superpower given its possession of nuclear weapons and the means to deliver them. At the same time, it was an economic basket case. President Mikhail Gorbachev's attempts to increase personal freedoms through a policy of *glasnost*—political openness—and reform the economic system via a policy of *perestroika*—restructuring—only succeeded in bringing lingering resentments against the Soviet Communist Party and government to the surface without providing increased economic output.

The Gorbachev attempted coup teaches an important trading lesson—namely, that the initial reaction to such an episode that foreign stock markets may be more sensitive to geopolitical factors than the U.S. stock market. Although there was time for more information to get out, it is not clear that the U.S. market was responding to the eventual failure of the coup as to other factors. The motivation for panic selling even if Gorbachev was overthrown is also unclear. There is opportunity in panic situations. Note, though, that the reasoning behind a trading catalyst need not make sense.

Although Gorbachev was restored to power, his remaining tenure in office was short-lived. By the end of 1991, the Soviet Union collapsed after 74 years of existence. The Cold War was over.

Trading Lessons

There are numerous factors that drive markets. This chapter illustrates how geopolitical events may serve as trading catalysts for significant price moves in financial markets. One recurrent lesson in this book is that traders learn from past market reactions to similar events. The sharp rally in stock prices and fall in crude oil prices prior to the invasion of Iraq in March 2003 can be attributed, in part, to traders anticipating a stock market rally and break in crude oil prices when war became certain, because that is what happened during the last Gulf War when stock prices surged on January 17, 1991 and crude oil plummeted. Past market reactions also influence traders' perceptions of the relationship among prices to certain events and the trading theses traders develop—that is, traders may have more than one trading thesis about how a given trading catalyst should affect market prices. For example, a terrorist act may induce a flight to safety as bond prices are bid up and stocks are sold. It may also adversely affect firms in the travel industry or the property and casualty insurance industry. Some of the effects may be relatively fleeting, whereas other effects are longer lived. Sometimes, the implications of the various trading theses conflict with one another. The duration of trading catalyst-induced effects is as important to traders as the magnitude of such effects.

Another lesson is that there may be delayed reactions to political events. And the delayed reactions to political events may be larger in magnitude than the initial reaction. This was seen in the delayed reaction to the Indian parliamentary elections of 2004 when prices fell almost 17% intraday on May 17, 2004 before closing down 11%. The reaction of Indian stock prices on May 17, 2004 also demonstrates that market prices routinely overreact to geopolitical events. This was also apparent in the bond market reaction to the probable election of Luiz Inacio Lula da Silva as president of Brazil when the spread widened to over 2400 basis points over comparable maturity Treasury bonds on September 27, 2003. This tendency to overreact may sometimes be due to factors internal to the market. In any event, the tendency for market prices to overreact to trading catalysts creates potential opportunities for traders. Less apparent but no less important is the tendency of markets to not always move in sync in response to news. This is less apparent within an asset class, like stocks, but more apparent across differing asset classes. All in all, geopolitical events create risks and opportunities for traders and give those individuals who are better able to anticipate or discern the probable course of political events—and the likely market reaction—an edge in trading.

References

Agence France Press. "Russian Stock Market Plummets After Oil Tycoon's Arrest." October 27, 2003.

Agence France Press. "Indian Stocks Plunge on Investor Fears about New Government." May 17, 2004.

Associated Press Newswires. "South Korean Stocks Plunge, Dollar Rallies After Unprecedented Presidential Impeachment." March 12, 2004.

Bilefsky, Dan. "Dutch Rejection of Charter Sparks Larger EU Fears." *The Wall Street Journal*, June 2, 2005, p. A3.

Blackstone, Brian. "Global Yield: Spain Bombings Another Blow to Euro Zone." Dow Jones Newswire, March 11, 2004.

Brancaccio, David. *Marketplace*. Thursday, March 13, 2003.

Brown, John Dennis. *101 Years on Wall Street*. Englewood Cliffs, New Jersey: Prentice Hall, 1991.

Business Standard. "FIIs Making Market Jumpy: Left; Absolving Themselves of Any Blame for Monday's Bloodbath." May 18, 2004.

Business Standard. "Huge Margin Calls Triggered Free Fall; Do Not Blame It All on the Left." May 18, 2004.

CNN.com. "September 11: Chronology of Terror." Posted 12:27 P.M. EDT, September 12, 2001 (www.cnn.com).

Dennis, Neil. "Spectre of French No Casts Pall over Euro." *Financial Times*, May 28/29, 2005, p. 11.

Dizard, John. "Global Investing—The Long and Short of Brazilian Betting." *Financial Times*, September 6, 2002.

Dizard, John. "Global Investing—Playing Spread Poker with Europe's Bonds." *Financial Times*, May 2, 2005.

Dow Jones International News. "Europe, US Investigate Suspicious Pre-Attack Trades-Report." 10:46 A.M., September 16, 2001.

Dow Jones Newswires. "India Sensex Ends Up Provisional 8.6% at 4893.64." May 18, 2004.

Duclaux, Denise. "U.S. Stocks Drop, Security Fears Plague Wall Street." Reuters. 12:51 P.M., March 15, 2004.

The Economist. "India's Stockmarket, Contumacious Fetishism." May 28, 2005, pp. 76-77.

Heller, Jeffrey. "European Stock Markets Recover from EC Shock." Reuters, June 4, 1992.

Hesse, Baldwin. "Markets Nosedive, Rebound on News of Blasts." *USA Today*, July 8, 2005, p. 7A.

Karp, Jonathan. "Candidate's Gains Pummel Brazilian Currency." *The Wall Street Journal*, September 24, 2002.

O'Brien, Robert. "US Stocks Mixed at Close; Dow Transports Off 2%." *Dow Jones Newswires*, November 12, 2001.

Plummer, Robert. "Recovering from Disaster: Exchanges Reopen Against Incredible Conditions." Futures Industry Association, October/November 2001 (http://www.futuresindustry.org/fimagazi-1929.asp?a=727).

Prime-Tass Economic News Agency. "Kudrin Says Khodorkovsky Arrest Won't Have Major Market Impact." October 27, 2003.

Reuters. "Global Markets—Stocks, Dollar Soar—Bonds, Gold Sink." March 13, 2003.

Reuters. "Spanish Stocks—Factors to Watch on March 12." 2:03 A.M. March 12, 2004.

Reuters. "U.S. Stocks Plummet, Dow Posts Largest Point Loss." 4:30 P.M. EDT, September 17, 2001.

Schneider, Susan. "Emerging Debt-Brazil Climbs after Currency Bounces Higher." Reuters, September 30, 2002.

Simms, G. Thomas and Justin Lahart. "Currency Investors' Vote on the Euro: Down 2.4% in Two Days." *The Wall Street Journal*, June 1, 2005, p. C1.

Torday, Peter. "Maastricht Move Hits Bond Markets." *The Independent*, June 4, 1992.

USA Today. "U.S.S.R. Crises and the Dow." August 21, 1991.

The Wall Street Journal. "Danes' Rejection of EC Treaty Depresses Stocks in London and Other Big Bourses Across Europe—A Wall Street Journal News Roundup." June 4, 1995.

The Wall Street Journal Europe. "What's News, Business and Finance." August 20, 1991.

Wells, Rob. "Stocks Stage Dramatic Rally on Failure of Soviet Coup." Associated Press, August 21, 1991.

White House (http://:www.whitehouse.gov/news/releases/2003/03/ 2003).

Whitney, Glenn, and Douglas R. Sease. "Dollar Jumps as Danes Vote Against Treaty." *The Wall Street Journal Europe*, June 3, 1992.

Yonhap News Agency, Yonhap English News. "Presidential Impeachment Jolts Financial Markets." March 12, 2004.

Zuckerman, Gregory. "Stocks Record Biggest Rally in Five Months— Industrials Rise 269.68 Points, As Nasdaq Climbs Into the Black; Technology, Insurers Lead Surge." *The Wall Street Journal*, Friday, March 14, 2003.

Endnotes

[1] The original name, *Operation Infinite Justice*, was changed to *Operation Iraqi Freedom* in deference to Muslim sensibilities that only Allah can dispense infinite justice. Other key members of the Coalition, such as Australia and the United Kingdom, assigned different names to their invasion operations.

[2] President Bush addressed the nation from 8:01 P.M. to 8:15 P.M. EST on Monday, March 17, 2003. Relevant passages of his address follow (http://:www. whitehouse.gov/news/releases/2003/03/2003):

> Today, no nation can possibly claim that Iraq has disarmed. And it will not disarm so long as Saddam Hussein holds power. For the last four-and-a-half months, the United States and our allies have worked within the Security Council to enforce that Council's long-standing demands. Yet, some permanent members of the Security Council have publicly announced they will veto any resolution that compels the disarmament of Iraq. These governments share our assessment of the danger, but not our resolve to meet it. Many nations, however, do have the resolve and fortitude to act against this threat to peace, and a broad coalition is now gathering to enforce the just demands of the world. The United Nations Security Council has not lived up to its responsibilities, so we will rise to ours.

> In recent days, some governments in the Middle East have been doing
> their part. They have delivered public and private messages urging the
> dictator to leave Iraq, so that disarmament can proceed peacefully. He
> has thus far refused. All the decades of deceit and cruelty have now
> reached an end. Saddam Hussein and his sons must leave Iraq within 48
> hours. Their refusal to do so will result in military conflict, commenced
> at a time of our choosing. For their own safety, all foreign nationals—
> including journalists and inspectors—should leave Iraq immediately.

[3] Winning the peace, however, proved to be more problematic as strategic errors by coalition military policymakers and a series of missteps by the Coalition Provisional Authority and its predecessor organization, the Office for Reconstruction and Humanitarian Assistance, allowed a nascent insurgency to develop and grow.

[4] Reuters. "Global Markets—Stocks, Dollar Soar—Bonds, Gold Sink." March 13, 2003.

[5] David Brancaccio. *Marketplace*. Thursday, March 13, 2003.

[6] Gregory Zuckerman. "Stocks Record Biggest Rally in Five Months—Industrials Rise 269.68 Points, As Nasdaq Climbs Into the Black; Technology, Insurers Lead Surge." *The Wall Street Journal*, Friday, March 14, 2003.

[7] Ibid.

[8] Reuters. "Global Markets—Stocks, Dollar Soar—Bonds, Gold Sink." March 13, 2003.

[9] *The Wall Street Journal Europe*. "What's News, Business and Finance." January 18, 1991.

[10] John Dennis Brown states: "At the reopening Tuesday, it was quickly apparent that Wall Street's Camelot would continue under Lyndon Baines Johnson's banner; a buyers' panic swept prices steeply higher in the third largest gain in history…" Brown, John Dennis. *101 Years on Wall Street*. Englewood Cliffs, New Jersey: Prentice Hall 1991, p. 86.

[11] The Prime-Tass Economic News Agency reported on Monday, October 27, 2003:

> Russian markets are unlikely to tumble following the arrest of Mikhail
> Khodorkovsky, CEO of Russia's largest oil company Yukos, Deputy
> Prime Minister and Finance Minister Alexei Kudrin told reporters Mon-
> day…"I hope that the court system will guarantee a transparent and
> objective examination of this case," Kudrin said. "So I don't think the
> market will react in any significant way."

Prime-Tass Economic News Agency. "Kudrin Says Khodorkovsky Arrest Won't Have Major Market Impact." October 27, 2003.

[12] Agence France Press. "Russian Stock Market Plummets After Oil Tycoon's Arrest." October 27, 2003.

[13] Agence France Press. "Russian Stock Market Plummets After Oil Tycoon's Arrest." October 27, 2003.

[14] The Congress Party won a plurality of parliamentary seats but needed the support of minor parties to form a new government and elect a prime minister.

[15] Agence France Press. "Indian Stocks Plunge on Investor Fears About New Government." May 17, 2004.

[16] *Business Standard*. "Huge Margin Calls Triggered Free Fall; Do Not Blame It All on the Left." May 18, 2004.

[17] *Business Standard*. "FIIs Making Market Jumpy: Left ; Absolving Themselves of Any Blame for Monday's Bloodbath." May 18, 2004.

[18] The May 28, 2005 issue of *The Economist* reports that although UBS Securities was punished by the Securities and Exchange Board of India for "obstructing the investigation," no evidence was found of market manipulation by it, or any other foreign firms, during the May 17, 2004 selloff in Indian stock prices.

[19] Dow Jones Newswires. "India Sensex Ends Up Provisional 8.6% At 4893.64." May 18, 2004.

[20] Jonathan Karp. "Candidate's Gains Pummel Brazilian Currency." *The Wall Street Journal*, September 24, 2002.

[21] Susan Schneider. "Emerging Debt – Brazil Climbs After Currency Bounces Higher." September 30, 2002.

[22] John Dizard. "Global Investing – The Long and Short of Brazilian Betting." *Financial Times*, September 6, 2002.

[23] For example, John Dizard of the *Financial Times* reported on September 6, 2002 that the then approximately 1750 basis point spread of the dollar denominated Brazilian C bond over comparable U.S. Treasury securities "… is a significant spread over Colombia (8.13 per cent over Treasuries), for example, or Peru (9.13 per cent over Treasuries)." John Dizard. "Global Investing – The Long and Short of Brazilian Betting." *Financial Times*, September 6, 2002.

[24] The ultimate adoption of the Treaty of Maastricht resulted in the European Community becoming the European Union on November 1, 1993.

[25] *The Wall Street Journal*. "Danes' Rejection of EC Treaty Depresses Stocks in London and Other Big Bourses Across Europe—A Wall Street Journal News Roundup." June 4, 1995.

[26] Glenn Whitney and Douglas R. Sease. "Dollar Jumps as Danes Vote Against Treaty," *The Wall Street Journal Europe*, June 3, 1992.

[27] Peter Torday. "Maastricht Move Hits Bond Markets." *The Independent*, June 4, 1992.

[28] Jeffrey Heller. "European Stock Markets Recover from EC Shock." June 4, 1992.

[29] Neil Dennis. "Spectre of French No Casts Pall over Euro." *Financial Times*, May 28/29, 2005, p. 11.

[30] G. Thomas Simms and Justin Lahart. "Currency Investors' Vote on the Euro: Down 2.4% in Two Days." *The Wall Street Journal*, June 1, 2005, p. C1.

[31] Dan Bilefsky. "Dutch Rejection of Charter Sparks Larger EU Fears." *The Wall Street Journal*, June 2, 2005, p. A3.

[32] John Dizard. "Global Investing—Playing Spread Poker with Europe's Bonds." *Financial Times*, May 2, 2005.

[33] Dow Jones International News. "Europe, US Investigate Suspicious Pre-Attack Trades-Report." 10:46 A.M. September 16, 2001.

[34] Robert O'Brien. "US Stocks Mixed At Close; Dow Transports Off 2%." *Dow Jones Newswires*, November 12, 2001.

[35] CNN.com. "September 11: Chronology of Terror." Posted 12:27 P.M. EDT, September 12, 2001 (www.cnn.com).

[36] In an article describing how U.S. futures exchanges were affected by September 11 terrorist attacks, Robert Plummer reports: "Traders said there were some 'wild' moves in Eurodollars and bond trading on Tuesday before those markets were shut down shortly after the disaster." Robert Plummer. "Recovering from Disaster: Exchanges Reopen Against Incredible Conditions," Futures Industry Association, October/November 2001 (http://www.futuresindustry.org/fimagazi-1929.asp?a=727).

[37] Agence France Press. "Shares Crash, Oil Rises as World Reels in Horror at US Attacks." September 11, 2001.

[38] Reuters. "U.S. Stocks Plummet, Dow Posts Largest Point Loss." 4:30 P.M. EDT, September 17, 2001.

[39] Reuters. "Spanish Stocks—Factors to Watch on March 12," 2:03 A.M. March 12, 2004.

[40] Brian Blackstone. "Global Yield: Spain Bombings Another Blow to Euro Zone." Dow Jones Newswire, March 11, 2004.

[41] Denise Duclaux. "U.S. Stocks Drop, Security Fears Plague Wall Street." Reuters. 12:51 P.M., March 15, 2004.

[42] Baldwin Hesse. "Markets Nosedive, Rebound on News of Blasts." *USA Today* July 8, 2005, p. 7A.

[43] Associated Press Newswires. "South Korean Stocks Plunge, Dollar Rallies After Unprecedented Presidential Impeachment." March 12, 2004.

[44] Yonhap News Agency, Yonhap English News. "Presidential Impeachment Jolts Financial Markets." March 12, 2004.

[45] *The Wall Street Journal*. "What's News, Business and Finance." August 20, 1991.

[46] Rob Wells. Associated Press. "Stocks Stage Dramatic Rally on Failure of Soviet Coup." August 21, 1991.

[47] *USA Today* on August 21, 1991 noted that the stock market reaction to news of the Gorbachev ouster was over three times the percentage reaction that the Dow Jones Industrial Average had news of the ouster of former Soviet Premier Nikita Khrushchev in 1964.

5

WEATHER AND NATURAL DISASTERS

"A merchant's happiness hangs upon chance, winds, and waves."

—Japanese proverb

A Tale of Two Natural Disasters

Shortly before 8:00 A.M. (local time) on Sunday, December 26, 2004, a magnitude 9.0 earthquake occurred off the west coast of the island of Sumatra in the Indian Ocean.[1] The powerful earthquake induced a tsunami that quickly spread across the Indian Ocean. The Boxing Day tsunami killed tens of thousands of people from Aceh, Indonesia to Phuket, Thailand; to Tamil Nadu, India to Sri Lanka; to the coasts of Somali and Kenya in Africa; and caused billions of dollars in property damages.

Financial markets were closed when the earthquake and subsequent tsunami occurred. This gave market participants time to assess the impact of the tsunami's damage and consider the implications for financial market prices. Although the tsunami caused tremendous damage and suffering, the tsunami did not wreak similar havoc on financial markets. Indeed, although equity markets in Thailand, Indonesia, and India fell somewhat in the wake of the disaster, the impact on world financial markets was minimal. This was the case even though the death toll continued to escalate rapidly in the days that followed and the full extent of the disaster was substantially worse than initial accounts indicated.

The financial market reaction to the Boxing Day tsunami of 2004 stands in sharp contrast to the reaction that occurred when a magnitude 6.9 earthquake struck 20 kilometers southwest of Kobe, Japan at 5:46 A.M. on Tuesday, January 17, 1995.[2] Despite rigid building codes designed to minimize structural damage and deaths from earthquakes, thousands of buildings were destroyed by the quake and subsequent fires and more than 5,500 people were killed.[3] Tens of billions of dollars in property damages resulted.[4] In this case, as with other potential trading catalysts, market participants must assess which markets would be impacted, the direction of the impact, as well as the magnitude and duration of the anticipated price move. Again, these assessments come in the form of *trading theses*, which rationalize and motivate prospective trades. Sometimes, the theses are simple. Sometimes, the theses are complex. The trading theses are invariably *partial economic equilibrium* arguments. Even if the trading theses are correct, traders must assess the appropriate magnitude, duration, and timing of the expected reaction.

Perhaps surprisingly, there was not an immediate response to the Kobe earthquake in world financial markets. Judging from contemporaneous news reports and the market reaction, it appears that an obvious and very simple trading thesis motivated market participants immediately after the earthquake and likely went along the following lines.

Japanese firms with assets in Kobe and Japanese property and casualty insurance companies with significant Kobe exposure will suffer substantial losses, so the stock prices of those firms should fall. Similarly, the stock prices of companies likely to be engaged in the reconstruction efforts should rise.

Another trading thesis probably went along the following lines: Japan will rebuild Kobe. The Japanese government will pay for rebuilding infrastructure in Kobe. Private individuals and firms will pay (via insurance payouts) for reconstructing damaged private property. In either case, the cost will be immense. The cost of reconstruction will be financed by selling Japanese holdings of foreign assets and reneging on an earlier pledge by the government to cut taxes. This will cause the yen to rise against other currencies.

The prospect of rebuilding Kobe acted as a trading catalyst for base metals, as detailed in this report from the Inter Press Service on Friday, January 20, 1995:

> Base metal prices earlier this week rallied as realization that the…Kobe earthquake in Japan would mean more construction for rebuilding and hence increased demand for steel, copper, nickel and aluminum. Adding to the reconstruction was the disruption to metals production in Japan and the possibility of shortages. The main beneficiary was nickel—used in the production of stainless steel—where three-months traded to four-and-a-half year highs…Copper and aluminum…also advanced, trading to their highest levels for over five and four years respectively. Private estimates suggest, however, that additional requirements from Japan will not be greatly significant, except perhaps for lead and zinc, which will be affected by the damage to Sumitomo's plant in Harima.[5]

Notice that the presumed trading thesis is simple—the reconstruction of Kobe will require base metals which will drive up their prices holding supply constant. The excerpt notes that the metals all rallied on the news of Kobe's earthquake. Notice also that the excerpt suggests that the rally is not fully justified in that "additional requirements [for base metals] will not be greatly significant." This illustrates how financial and commodity markets may respond to a trading catalyst using a widely shared trading thesis even when a significant market reaction is not justified.

Although the share prices of selected individual firms rose or fell depending upon their perceived exposure to the Kobe earthquake, the initial reaction of the overall stock market to news of the Kobe earthquake was fairly limited. However, as days passed, the Kobe earthquake became a powerful trading catalyst that affected not only the Japanese stock market but also European stock markets—with London's Financial Times-Stock Exchange (FTSE) 100 stock index falling 1.3%, Frankfurt's Deutscher Aktienindex (DAX) index falling 1.4%, and Paris' Cotation Assisteé en Continu (CAC) stock index falling 2.2%.[6] The overall Japanese stock market reacted to news of the Kobe earthquake with a significant delay, as shown in Figure 5.1 and as described in this excerpt from an article that appeared in the *Guardian* newswire on Tuesday, January 24, 1995.

> Share prices in Tokyo crashed by more than 5 per cent yesterday in delayed reaction to the Hanshin [Kobe] earthquake and immediately sent European stock markets into a spin. But the slide was eventually halted after Wall Street showed only limited losses in response to the jitters elsewhere.
>
> Tokyo stocks plummeted by more than 1,000 points, 5.6 per cent, yesterday…as worries spread about the damage from last week's earthquake and the failure of the government to produce a reconstruction plan.
>
> …[T]he Nikkei index…[closed] at 17,785.49…In the week since the earthquake, the market has lost more than 1500 points, although the fall was slow at first because Tokyo was unaffected and brokers and economists in the capital failed to realize the extent of the damage.[7]

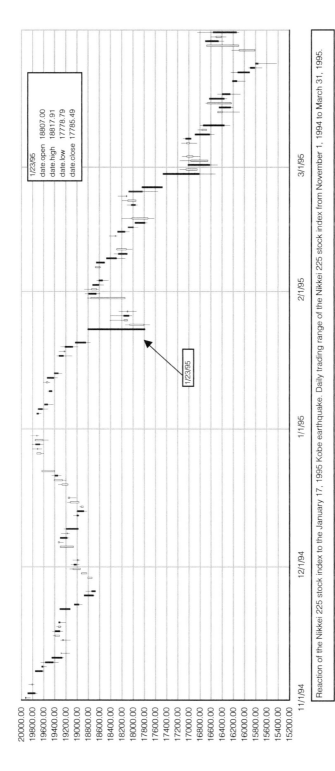

Reaction of the Nikkei 225 stock index to the January 17, 1995 Kobe earthquake. Daily trading range of the Nikkei 225 stock index from November 1, 1994 to March 31, 1995.

FIGURE 5.1   The Nikkei finally reacts to the Kobe earthquake.

The preceding excerpt details the significant impact that the earthquake-induced decline in Japanese stock prices had on foreign equity markets. The reason foreign equity markets should be significantly affected by the Kobe earthquake, however, is not clear. Notice that the excerpt provides a seemingly plausible but unlikely explanation for the delayed reaction, namely that "worries spread about the damage from last week's earthquake and the failure of the government to produce a reconstruction plan."

Earthquakes are measured on a logarithmic scale such that the power of an earthquake increases by a factor of 10 for every one-point increase in magnitude. The destructive power of the earthquake-induced Boxing Day tsunami was immense and eventually claimed 283,106 lives.[8] Only three earthquakes in the world in the preceding 100 years had a greater magnitude.[9] The destructive power of the Kobe earthquake was considerably less than that of the Boxing Day 2004 earthquake and tsunami, yet the market reaction was considerably different. There was a substantial, albeit delayed, reaction to the Kobe earthquake but virtually no reaction to the Boxing Day tsunami. Why the differential reaction?

Clearly, where an earthquake occurs matters. Equally clearly, news of the Kobe earthquake was well-known to market participants. Yet, there was a delayed reaction in the financial markets to the news of the earthquake. Two questions naturally arise. First, why didn't market participants react earlier to the news? Second, was the market's reaction to the news appropriate given the magnitude of the price changes?

Other observers have also commented on the delayed reaction of the Japanese stock market and the reaction of other financial markets to the Kobe earthquake. Yale University Professor Robert Shiller, author of the book *Irrational Exuberance* argues:

> The best interpretation of the effects of the Kobe earthquake on the stock markets of the world is that news coverage of the earthquake, and of the accompanying stock market declines,

engaged the attention of investors, prompting a cascade of changes that brought to the fore some more pessimistic factors...

As the main source of public information about the stock market's performance, the media will continue to have a tangible impact on the playing out of significant market events. On a day-to-day basis, a large part of the media's coverage is snake oil. Then, the price level is firmly in the hands of investors with better sources of information. But in media-defined watershed periods, many people look to the media as their advisor of last resort. Market analysts should not underestimate the media's power to shape public attention.[10]

Essentially, Professor Shiller argues that saturation media coverage is principally responsible for the market's large and delayed reaction to news of the Kobe earthquake. Although this is an interesting conjecture, it does not explain why other media-saturated events like the coverage of the Boxing Day tsunami did not have a similar effect on market prices. There is a natural human desire to impose order on seeming chaos. However, market reactions do not have to make sense. Perhaps a more convincing explanation of both the delayed response to the news and the appropriateness of the market's reaction is that trading is a game where the "rules" change but the objective (i.e., to make money) remains constant.

What are the lessons for traders from the market reaction (or lack thereof) to these two natural disasters? One lesson is that the size of the humanitarian disaster is not a good measure of the likely reaction of financial markets. Rightly or wrongly, it matters greatly where the disaster occurs. Large death tolls associated with earthquakes in China on July 7, 1976 where more than 255,000 people perished; western Iran on June 20, 1990 where more than 40,000 people died; southeastern Iran on December 26, 2003 where 26,200 people died; India on January 26, 2001 where 20,023 people died; or Turkey on August 17, 1999 where 17,118 lives were lost were not associated with significant reactions in world financial markets.[11] From a financial market perspective, these natural disasters were essentially non-events despite the tremendous human suffering and loss of life the disasters inflicted. To be sure, part of the explanation for the seeming dearth of response of global financial markets to these events lies in the comparatively low money value of what was destroyed. Yet another lesson and important part of the explanation lies in the tenuous reasoning that underlies the assumption that global markets should be affected by local disasters. There is little reason to believe that global markets should be affected by many of these events despite the reaction to the Kobe earthquake. The differential reaction of financial markets to these two humanitarian disasters illustrates the fickle response of financial markets to news of natural disasters and serves as yet another lesson. A third lesson is that the market's response can be delayed and can increase rather than diminish as time passes.

A final lesson is that there may be numerous opportunities to trade off of events that are well-known to market participants. A minute is a lifetime in the world of trading—that is, it is more than enough time to enter or exit a position in many markets. Indeed, often only a few seconds are needed to enter or exit a trading position.

Natural Disasters as Trading Catalysts

Natural disasters can take many forms including earthquakes, tsunamis, hurricanes, tornadoes, fires, pandemics, epidemics, volcanic eruptions, landslides, droughts, and floods, among others. The localized nature of many natural disasters means that the market impact is often, but not always, localized as well. Sometimes, the market's reaction to a natural disaster is limited to impacting the stock price of specific companies whose fortunes are adversely or favorably impacted. For instance, in the run-up to and aftermath of a hurricane, building supply and home repair firms like Lowe's or Home

Depot often experience a discernible increase in their stock price, presumably based on the trading thesis that such firms will experience greater sales as consumers attempt to repair damaged homes.

Some natural disasters, like earthquakes, are inherently difficult, if not impossible, to predict. Other natural disasters may be more readily predictable, but the extent of the likely destruction is not. From a trading perspective, it is far more important to be able to predict the likely market response and its timing to a natural disaster than to be able to predict the occurrence of the natural disaster itself. As shown earlier, the market reaction to natural disasters can vary substantially.

Natural disaster trading catalysts that affect a number of markets may do so *sequentially* rather than *simultaneously*. Moreover, as is the case for other trading catalysts, the market reaction sometimes increases as time passes. Once again, this gives rise to potential trading opportunities after the news is out. It should be emphasized, however, that such impacts may be relatively short-lived. This risk means that traders should adjust their trading position size and trading horizon accordingly.

The questions about the role of natural disaster trading catalysts are similar to those of other trading catalysts—namely, which markets will be affected and when? How long will the reaction last? Will the reaction increase or decrease in intensity and magnitude as time passes? If the reaction increases in intensity and magnitude as time passes, will that be due to an increase in estimated damages from the disaster or something else?

Contamination of the Food Supply: Mad Cow Disease

Diseases that affect plants and animals raised for human consumption directly or indirectly can also act as trading catalysts. For instance, on Tuesday, May 20, 2003, Canadian authorities announced that a Canadian cow had been diagnosed with bovine spongiform encephalopathy (BSE), or mad cow disease.[12] This led the United States Department of Agriculture to impose a ban on the importation of Canadian cattle and certain meat products. Canada is a large exporter of beef and the United States is one of its largest customers. Once again, traders must assess which markets will be affected, as well as the direction, magnitude, and duration of the impact. The market's response to the announcement provides a fascinating illustration of how the discovery of a dreaded disease in beef cattle can serve as a trading catalyst and impact a number of markets. It also provides an insight into the relationships traders perceive. Figure 5.2 depicts the reaction of Chicago Mercantile Exchange (CME) live cattle futures contract prices to news of the discovery of a Canadian cow with mad cow disease. Other markets were also impacted. The Canadian dollar initially fell against the U.S. dollar before ending the trading day three quarters of a cent higher. At one point, McDonald's stock fell 8%.[13]

It is interesting to consider the implicit trading theses market participants were operating under. Figure 5.3 depicts the reaction of the price of McDonald's stock to news of the discovery of BSE in a Canadian cow. Presumably, the stock prices of McDonald's and other (burger-oriented) fast-food restaurants fell because of concerns that U.S. beef consumption would drop substantially as a result of the discovery of mad cow disease in a Canadian cow. (Whether 8% is an appropriate amount is questionable.) The overall stock market—as measured by the Dow Jones Industrial Average—did not move much that day with the index closing at 8491.36, down 2.03 points from the previous day. The presumed reasoning for the report to affect the Canadian dollar is likely the following.

Canadian beef exports are likely to decline as foreign governments ban the importation of Canadian beef after the Canadian government's confirmation of the diagnosis of a Canadian cow with mad cow disease. These restrictions are likely to last for an unknown length of time leading to fewer exports of Canadian beef and less demand for the Canadian dollar. Lower demand for the Canadian dollar would cause its foreign exchange value to fall.

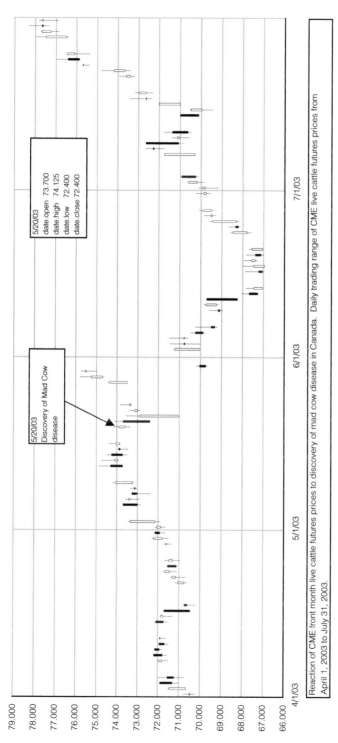

FIGURE 5.2 Mad cow disease and cattle futures prices.

Reaction of CME front month live cattle futures prices to discovery of mad cow disease in Canada. Daily trading range of CME live cattle futures prices from April 1, 2003 to July 31, 2003.

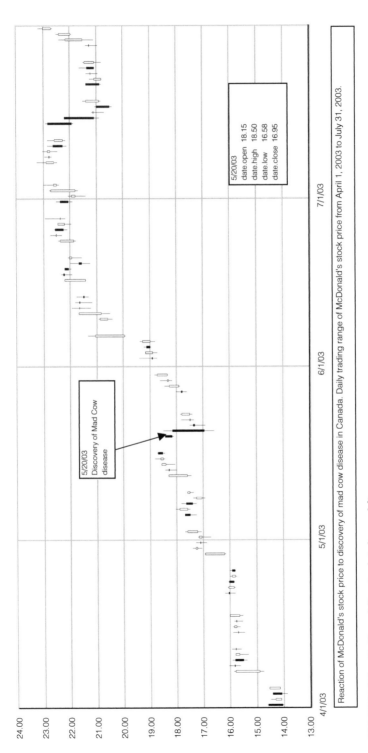

FIGURE 5.3   McDonald's stock takes a hit.

Reaction of McDonald's stock price to discovery of mad cow disease in Canada. Daily trading range of McDonald's stock price from April 1, 2003 to July 31, 2003.

Once again, traders must assess the magnitude and the duration of any impact. Although the Canadian dollar fell initially, the impact of the discovery of mad cow disease on the foreign exchange market was short-lived and the *loonie*—the slang term traders use for the Canadian dollar—closed higher on the day. This was not the case for McDonald's stock even though Canada was *not* a major beef supplier to McDonald's restaurants.

One problem with most contemporary news accounts is that insufficient attention is paid to the timing of market responses. Moreover, the impact of a trading catalyst on minor markets is often ignored. Fortunately, a fascinating academic study by Professors Yiuman Tse and James Hackard examined this particular episode and a related subsequent diagnosis of a U.S. cow with mad cow disease in the U.S. in detail.[14] Professors Tse and Hackard paid particularly close attention to the sequencing of the response of various markets to the news.

As Professors Tse and Hackard point out, information on the prospective announcement reached live cattle futures traders at 11:10 A.M., or more than an hour *before* Canadian authorities made their announcement at 12:15 P.M. The source of the advance information was a newsletter on the cattle industry e-mailed to subscribers. However, there is reason to believe that the information was disseminated even earlier to some traders as live cattle futures prices plunged to their daily limit at 10:48 A.M. and the decline was attributed to the news about mad cow disease in a Canadian cow. The decline in live cattle futures prices appears to suggest the probable trading thesis that beef consumption in the U.S. would fall sharply in the wake of the announcement.

This episode also highlights the difficulty of trying to determine the correct interpretation to assign to a given piece of news. An alternative interpretation of the announcement is that the discovery of BSE in foreign cattle would adversely affect the supply of *foreign* (i.e., Canadian) beef thus aiding U.S. beef prices, which the live cattle futures contract tracks. Indeed, Professors Tse and Hackard observe that live cattle futures prices rose later in the week in part for this reason.

The impact of the announcement extended beyond the live cattle futures market and impacted a number of other commodity futures markets. These include feeder cattle futures, pork belly futures, and lean hog futures, all traded on the CME; and soybean futures, soybean meal futures, corn and wheat futures, traded on the Chicago Board of Trade (CBOT). One interesting finding that Professors Tse and Hackard report is that the timing of the price moves was not simultaneous. The selloff in feeder cattle continued for 14 minutes *after* the selloff in live cattle futures ends because the price limit for feeder cattle was not reached until then. Traders apparently hypothesized that pork consumption would rise as beef consumption fell and bid up the price of lean hog futures and pork belly futures contracts. Professors Tse and Hackard report that lean hog futures prices initially rose following the news and that the high of the day for lean hogs occurred at 11:39 A.M. However, lean hog futures prices subsequently fell and closed lower for the day. Pork belly futures rallied after the news on mad cow disease came out and reached a high at the same time as lean hog futures prices did; but unlike lean hog futures, contracts managed to close up for the day.

Grain futures prices were also affected by the news of the discovery of a Canadian cow with mad cow disease. Grain futures prices rose in response to the news but at different times. Corn and wheat futures seemed to have reacted at 11:16 A.M., whereas soybean and soybean meal futures didn't rally until the 12:15 P.M. announcement. All of the grains gave up some of their gains (i.e., they overreacted) and closed higher for the day except for corn, which closed unchanged. Professors Tse and Hackard suggest that the differential reaction between corn and the other grains "…is indicative of herd behavior on the part of corn futures traders being sucked along by the momentum of the other grain traders."[15]

Professors Tse and Hackard also report that the stock prices of the various burger-oriented fast-food companies reacted to the news at different times, ranging from 11:37 A.M. to 11:43 A.M. They argue: "The lag between livestock futures, grain futures, and stock price movements indicates a spillover effect from the futures market to the stock market, which is consistent with cascading information and herd behavior as defined in the relevant literature."[16]

After surveying the information, the empirical evidence on the reaction of these and other markets to news of the discovery of a Canadian cow with mad cow disease, Professors Tse and Hackard conclude the following.

> We find that related livestock and grain futures and stock prices do not quickly and accurately process information, but follow a pattern of herd behavior. This behavior is evidenced by the uncertainty about the impact of the announcement on the value of certain securities, and the composition of information entering the markets immediately following the initial announcement. These uncertainties are the aspects of herd behavior that Avery and Zemsky (1998) cite as the conditions necessary for herd behavior to lead to mispricing.[17]

The differential reactions that the Tse and Hackard article document are commonly observed in commodity and financial markets to *unscheduled* news. This creates opportunities for traders who did not foresee the occurrence of the trading catalyst but discern quickly the likely interpretation most traders will assign to a given catalyst. Even so, there is still considerable risk that the effect may be transitory.

Potential Epidemics and Pandemics: SARS

Contagious human diseases represent another type of natural disaster that can become a trading catalyst. The scale of such disasters is often compounded by political decisions to minimize the extent of the problem or conceal the existence of the problem. Such attempts also increase the power of such diseases to act as a trading catalyst and increase the breadth of assets affected. One example in this regard is the identification of a strain of atypical pneumonia, later named *severe acute respiratory syndrome*, or SARS, in early 2003.

The disease may have originated in Guangdong province in southern China. The disease had a number of pneumonia-like symptoms and was called *atypical pneumonia*. SARS first came to public attention on February 10, 2003 when Chinese authorities in the province of Guangdong in southern China announced that 305 people had become sick from a pneumonia-like illness and five people had died from it. Additional information about the disease became slowly available. However, there were plenty of disconcerting rumors about the magnitude and severity of the problem.

The disease later spread to Hong Kong when a doctor who had treated patients with SARS visited Hong Kong. Several individuals with whom the doctor had come into contact contracted the disease. A number of medical personnel in Hong Kong later contracted the disease (sometimes with fatal results) when treating patients with SARS.

Diseases transmitted through the air pose a special risk in that they may be more easily contracted than water-borne diseases. The ease of international air travel—and with it a means of transmitting the virus to new populations in distant lands—heightened concerns about the spread of SARS. The discovery of SARS cases in Singapore, Canada, and elsewhere in mainland China reinforced the view of the ease of transmission of this potentially deadly disease.

The relatively high fatality rate associated with the disease and the threat of an epidemic or global pandemic increased fears further. Reports that the disease was being understated by health authorities in China added to concerns. The spread of the disease to Canada also increased concern about the impact of the disease. Yet, for whatever reason, these concerns were not immediately reflected in financial market prices.

It should be mentioned that SARS broke out during a period when many market participants focused on the potential of an imminent second U.S. war with Iraq. The war broke out in mid-March with the invasion of Iraq by coalition forces.

Unlike some natural disasters, SARS was not a one-off event. Moreover, it was a new disease whose cause was initially unknown but had a high mortality rate. Like other natural disasters, estimates of the damage that SARS had on the economy were periodically revised. This meant that market participants had far greater information on the impact of SARS on the economy as time progressed. On Monday, March 31, 2003, the Hong Kong stock market fell 2.58%.[18]

Fear of the impact of SARS also affected the currency market by causing the one-year forward premium to widen significantly.[19] The premium got even larger in a few days' time when it rose to an intraday high of 360-370 points and closed at 348-358.[20] The forward premium, in this instance, can be viewed as a market measure of the probability that the Hong Kong dollar will be devalued. SARS started to cast a pall over the broader equity market rather than just individual sectors. Concern over the effects of SARS started to affect other Asian currencies, stock, and fixed income markets.[21] The outlook of the impact of SARS also started to evolve and a new trading thesis took root.[22]

Weather Conditions

Weather plays a major role in determining agricultural futures prices. Indeed, in many cases, weather is arguably the most important fundamental economic factor determining agricultural commodity prices. Traders who have access to consistently more accurate weather forecasts or obtain information on changes in weather conditions before others have a decided advantage over other less well-informed traders. For this reason, many agricultural commodity traders employ the services of private weather forecasters.

There are many examples where price changes in grain futures contracts are attributed to the effects of changes in weather on grain production. The basic idea is that changes in supply (i.e., production) will cause changes in prices in the opposite direction, holding demand constant.

Given the central role that weather conditions play in determining agricultural output, it seems that weather would be the dominant factor in determining the price of an agricultural commodity. That notion is incorrect, however.

Most commodities are grown over a fairly large area and exposed to many different weather systems. This makes it difficult to assess the influence of weather on commodity prices. In an interesting and provocative study that was published in 1984, Professor Richard Roll of the University of California Los Angeles (UCLA) examined the influence of weather on frozen concentrated orange juice futures prices. At the time of the study, orange juice futures prices were determined based on orange production in central Florida. This represented a fairly limited area from a weather perspective. Roll found that changes in weather conditions accounted for only a small fraction of the total variation in frozen concentrated orange juice futures prices. Put differently, most of the variation in orange juice futures prices was not explained by weather news or other fundamental economic factors. This suggests that there are other, potential *non-fundamental* factors driving orange juice futures prices, and by extension, the prices of other agricultural commodities.

A drought is another natural disaster and weather condition that can act as a trading catalyst. The United States Geological Service provides several definitions of a drought including meteorological, agricultural, and hydrologic, among others.[23] Financial market participants typically focus on the agricultural definition of a drought as a period where agricultural output is perceived as being potentially affected by insufficient precipitation. In practice, this may mean that market participants confuse a period of low rainfall with a drought. Droughts, by definition, span a period of time rather than occur at a single point in time. This makes documenting their impact as trading catalysts more difficult.

However, *perceived droughts* still serve as trading catalysts directly or indirectly. For instance, during the spring of 1988, below average rainfall led to concern that there was a "drought" in the U.S. Midwest agricultural heartland. This led to higher grain futures prices. Higher grain futures prices were interpreted by many market participants as a harbinger of higher rates of future inflation. Higher inflation meant higher nominal interest rates and lower bond prices. As a result, bond futures prices became temporarily linked to grain futures prices. This became known as the *beans over bonds spread*, or BOB spread. This also illustrates how price changes induced by an external trading catalyst in one market can become an internal trading catalyst for another market. It should be pointed out that the perceived relationship between beans and bonds was short-lived.

There is a famous story that may be more apocryphal than true that relates how, during a perceived drought in the Midwest one year, the sight of a sudden rainfall sparked a selloff in grain futures prices on the Chicago Board of Trade. The selloff ended and the rally resumed when traders found out that although it was raining in Chicago, it was not raining in grain producing areas.

In a related vein, poor crop production in one part of the world may trigger demand for similar crops elsewhere. For instance, the poor output of Soviet agriculture in the 1970s led to massive purchases of U.S. grain in the 1970s with an attendant huge impact on grain spot and futures prices. Of course, chronic low Soviet grain output was as much related to the flawed system of production known as communism as it was to weather conditions in the Soviet Union.

In addition to agricultural commodities, weather conditions can affect the demand for energy to heat buildings in the winter or cool buildings in the summer. Weather conditions can also affect supply by affecting production. An example of how weather can act as a trading catalyst for energy prices is illustrated in the following excerpt from an article by Masood Farivar about Tropical Storm Arlene that appeared in the Friday, June 10, 2005 issue of *The Wall Street Journal.*

> ...[July NYMEX] Crude [oil] futures...shot $1.74 higher to $54.28 a barrel...[due to] Tropical Storm Arlene...The storm is expected to pass with little damage to production, but coming at a time when global capacity is stretched...had a psychological impact on prices.

> ...Hurricane Ivan last September cost the industry some $3.5 billion. "The hangover from the damage done by Ivan is still on everybody's mind," said John Kilduff, senior vice president of risk management at brokerage Fimat Futures in New York. "We're still in that mode where any bullish news is tremendously bullish even if it is slight."

> But natural gas futures, typically more sensitive to severe weather patterns...rose only slightly. July [NYMEX] natural gas futures...settled...up 4.5 cents...[T]raders...said there was little concern about the storm's potential impact.[24]

Several points are of interest here. First, note the large reaction to weather news by crude oil futures market participants, even though most analysts didn't expect any significant impact on oil production. Second, notice that natural gas futures prices did not rise much in reaction to the same piece of news, even though natural gas production is arguably more sensitive to weather conditions. The preceding example illustrates how critical it is to determine which market would be most impacted by a trading catalyst and the magnitude of the impact. A trader who bought a natural gas futures contract in response to the news of Tropical Storm Arlene would not have performed as well as a trader who bought crude oil futures. Third, notice that the prospect of significant production damage that arose during September 2004 with Hurricane Ivan is one of the driving factors here. This is yet another example of how past reactions can guide the market's response to new trading catalysts. Fourth, the excerpt illustrates how sentiment—in this case, bullish sentiment—in the market can exacerbate the impact of any news consistent with the sentiment.

The relevant question is whether the magnitude of the reaction was appropriate. Should crude oil prices really rise by 3% on storm warnings when most observers do not expect that Tropical Storm Arlene will impact crude oil production? The reaction of crude oil prices to the news is even more puzzling when one considers that the impact is not limited to crude oil for July delivery. Crude oil for August 2005 delivery rose by $1.72 per barrel, whereas crude oil for September 2005, October 2005, or November 2005 delivery rose by $1.63, $1.56, and $1.55 per barrel, respectively. Should November 2005 crude oil rise by $1.55 per barrel because of a tropical storm in mid-June 2005 that is *not* expected to affect production?[25] To be sure, futures prices are linked across maturity, but truly short-term factors should not drive long-term prices.

The impact of weather conditions on crude oil, natural gas, and gasoline prices was demonstrated to the public in the sharp price increases in the preceding commodities when Hurricane Katrina made landfall in August 2005. Figure 5.4 depicts the reaction of crude oil futures prices to Tropical Storm Arlene in June 2005 and Hurricane Katrina in August 2005.

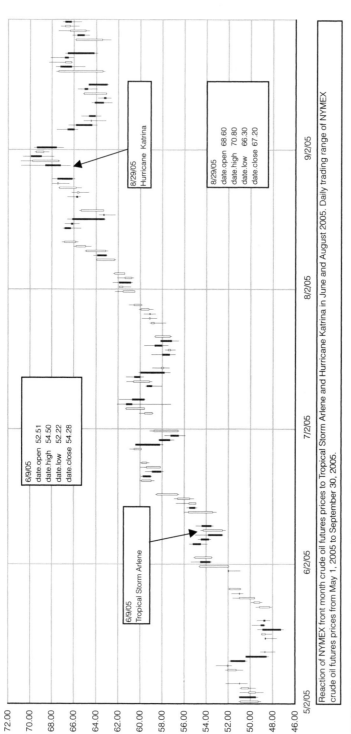

FIGURE 5.4   Crude oil prices and the weather.

Reaction of NYMEX front month crude oil futures prices to Tropical Storm Arlene and Hurricane Katrina in June and August 2005. Daily trading range of NYMEX crude oil futures prices from May 1, 2005 to September 30, 2005.

Other Natural Disasters

The impact of natural disasters on market prices can be broad or fairly narrow. Some examples follow.

Hurricane Andrew and Prepayment Speed

Sometimes, natural disasters impact a specialized market. For instance, in the wake of Hurricane Andrew, which hit the Miami area in 1992, mortgage traders saw an opportunity in selling pools of high-yielding mortgages from the Miami area in the belief that the mortgages on many damaged homes would be prepaid. The high interest rates on these mortgages meant that prior to the arrival of Hurricane Andrew these mortgage-backed securities were selling at a *premium* (i.e., above par). However, they would be redeemed early at *par*. The opportunity in this case was to sell premium bonds that were going to become par bonds very, very soon. In this case, the hurricane damage affected the prepayment speed of mortgages underlying mortgage-backed securities and acted as a trading catalyst.[26] In this instance, the potential for market overreaction was limited because traders knew that the bonds could not fall below par.

The Chicago Flood

Most floods are classic examples of natural disasters. Sometimes, a flood is the result of, or exacerbated by, the flawed actions or inaction of man. The resultant disaster is a combination of a natural and man-made disaster. Such an example occurred on April 13, 1992 when old freight and coal tunnels connecting buildings in downtown Chicago flooded as the result of bureaucratic inaction. In its own way, the flood became a trading catalyst, although not in the way one might expect. The flooding of an old system of underground railway tunnels that carried coal to office buildings in the loop caused the closure of both the CME and the CBOT. The closure of the CBOT's Treasury note and bond futures markets meant that cash market bond dealers were not easily able to transfer their risks to other market participants. As a consequence, the bid offer spread widened. This effect (i.e., a widening of the bid offer spread) has been observed in other instances where the futures market has been closed while the corresponding cash market was open.

The San Francisco Earthquake

The delayed market response to the Kobe earthquake is reminiscent of the U.S. equity market's reaction to the San Francisco earthquake. At about 5:12 A.M. on April 18, 1906, San Francisco was awoken by a magnitude 7.8 earthquake. The San Francisco earthquake and the subsequent fires it engendered resulted in tremendous damage to the city of San Francisco and significant loss of life.[27] In his book *101 Years on Wall Street*, John Dennis Brown notes that news of the earthquake did not initially impact the U.S. stock market but was the principal precipitant of a subsequent selloff that, over the course of a couple of months, drove the Dow down by 17%. Part of the reason for the protracted decline was the need of property and casualty insurance companies to sell stock to pay insurance claims arising from the earthquake.[28]

It is difficult to determine what fraction of the 17% decline in stock prices over the two-month period was due to the San Francisco earthquake. The important point is simply that the earthquake was regarded at the time as a trading catalyst for part of the decline.

Trading Lessons

Many natural disasters are inherently unpredictable. What are the trading lessons when natural disasters and changes in weather conditions act as trading catalysts?

First, a trader need not be able to accurately forecast weather conditions or natural disasters to trade profitably off of them. This is because market reactions are often delayed. The temporal delay may be a matter of a few minutes or several days. Not all markets will respond to the same trading catalyst simultaneously. Second, differential reactions of similar commodities to the same catalyst occur with some frequency. This makes it important for traders to anticipate which markets will be most sensitive to a trading catalyst. Third, the severity of a natural disaster is not necessarily a good proxy for its potential importance to market participants. The great influenza pandemic of 1918-1919 wreaked enormous damage and was responsible for the deaths of more than 600,000 people in the United States and between 20 and 30 million people worldwide. However, the market reaction to the Spanish flu was muted. The deadliest or most destructive natural disasters need not exert the greatest impact on financial markets. Consequently, it is more important for traders to predict which commodities will react to a given trading catalyst, as well as the direction, timing, and magnitude of the likely reaction than to be able to forecast when a trading catalyst will occur as the result of a natural disaster or weather conditions.

As always, forecasting the likely reaction of market prices to trading catalysts requires an understanding of the likely interpretations that other traders will assign to various events—that is, what are the likely trading theses other market participants will adopt? Many of the trading theses are partial equilibrium models that assume fixed supply in the case of a demand shock or fixed demand in the case of a supply shock. These theses frequently overstate the actual impact of a natural disaster on market prices. Of course, this means that there may be trading opportunities created in any overreaction of market prices. Traders must know the current state of market conditions and sentiment bias as market conditions and market sentiment bias may exacerbate (or diminish) any price moves trading catalysts induce. Finally, besides serving as trading catalysts, weather conditions and natural disasters may become trading vehicles in themselves.

The introduction of weather derivatives and specialized online betting services allows individuals to trade on weather conditions. So far, these new vehicles have enjoyed only limited success in the marketplace.

References

Agence France Press. "HK Shares Lower on Concerns Over Iraq War, SARS." March 31, 1995.

Bary, Andrew. "Trading Points." *Barron's*, August 31, 1992, p. 39.

Brown, John Dennis. *101 Years on Wall Street: An Investor's Almanac*. Englewood Cliffs, New Jersey: Prentice Hall, 1991.

Dow Jones Newswires. "HK Dlr Mkts Late: HK Dlr Forwards Continue to Surge on SARS." April 25, 2003.

Dow Jones Newswires. "1-Yr HK$ Forward Premium to Spot Hits 5-Mo High on SARS." April 21, 2003.

Farivar, Masood. "Oil Prices Surge as Tropical Storm Approaches Gulf." *The Wall Street Journal*, June 10, 2005, p. C4.

Haavardsrud, Paul and Peter Morton. "Fast-food Stocks Plummet: McDonald's Shares Down 8%; U.S. Temporarily Bans Import of Canadian Cattle, Sheep and Goats." *National Post*, May 21, 2003.

Rafferty, Kevin and Mark Milner. "European Markets in Spin from Fall-Out of Kobe Earthquake." *The Guardian*, January 24, 1995.

Roll, R. "Orange Juice and the Weather," *American Economic Review*. 74, December 1984, pp. 861-80.

Shiller, Robert. "Exuberant Reporting: Media and Misinformation in the Markets." *Media*, Vol. 23, (1) Spring 2001.

Somerville, Paul. "Kobe Earthquake: An Urban Disaster." *Eos*, Vol. 76, No. 6, February 7, 1995, pp. 49-51.

Spicer, Andi. "Commodities-Metals: Kobe Earthquake Disaster Boosts Market Demand." Inter Press Service, January 20, 1995.

Torchia, Andrew. "Asian Markets Decline on Fears about SARS—Stock Prices, Currencies and Interest Rates Drop." *The Asian Wall Street Journal*, April 28, 2003.

Tse, Yiuman and James Hackard. "Holy Mad Cow! Facts or (Mis)perceptions: A Clinical Study." *Journal of Futures Markets*, Vol. 26, No. 4, April 2006, pp. 315-341.

United States Geological Service. Earthquake Hazards Program Web site. (http://72.14.207.104/search?q=cache:1JaDBj_xDCUJ:neic.usgs.gov/neis/eqlists/eqsmajr.htm).

United States Geological Service Web site. (http://md.water.usgs.gov/drought/define.html).

The Wall Street Journal, June 10, 2005, p. B6.

Endnotes

[1] The earthquake occurred at 7:58:53 local time at the epicenter, or 00:58:53 Universal Time. It originated when the India tectonic plate slipped below the Burma tectonic plate along 1,200 kilometers of the boundary between the two plates. According to the U.S. Geological Service, the megathrust earthquake lifted the sea floor by several meters. Subsequent estimates of the magnitude of the quake range from 9.0 to 9.3.

[2] The earthquake is also called the Great Hanshin, South Hyogo, and the Hyogo-ken Nanbu earthquake. The Kobe earthquake is sometimes referred to as having magnitude 6.9 and sometimes referred to as having magnitude 7.2. The latter number is the Japan Meteorological Agency assigned magnitude, whereas the former number is the moment magnitude. (The former commonly used measure of the force of an earthquake, the Richter scale, is no longer used.)

[3] Damages from earthquakes can be categorized into direct and secondary effects. *Direct effects* refer to the damages resulting from the rupture of the earth near or alongside the fault line (e.g., a landslide), whereas *secondary effects* refer to damages induced from the seismic waves coming from the earthquake. As with most earthquakes, the principal damage comes from the secondary effects (seismic waves) rather than the direct effects. The economic damage of an earthquake depends not only on the destructive power of an earthquake and proximity to the epicenter but also on how people live. Earthquake-resistant buildings help to minimize the death toll associated with earthquakes. Most of the buildings that were destroyed in Kobe were built before 1981 under weaker building codes.

[4] Perhaps the most famous casualty of the Kobe earthquake was Barings Bank. The trading positions that rogue trader Nick Leeson had built up started to unravel after the Kobe earthquake.

[5] Andi Spicer. "Commodities-Metals: Kobe Earthquake Disaster Boosts Market Demand." Inter Press Service, January 20, 1995.

[6] Kevin Rafferty and Mark Milner. "European Markets in Spin from Fall-Out of Kobe Earthquake." *The Guardian*, January 24, 1995.

[7] Kevin Rafferty and Mark Milner. "European Markets in Spin from Fall-Out of Kobe Earthquake." The Guardian, January 24, 1995.

[8] Information obtained from the United States Geological Service, Earthquake Hazards Program Web site: http://earthquake.usgs.gov/.

[9] The most powerful recorded earthquake of the twentieth century was a magnitude 9.5 earthquake in Chile on May 22, 1960 that killed 4,000 to 5,000 people. This is followed by a magnitude 9.2 earthquake in Prince William Sound in Alaska in 1964 and a magnitude 9.1 earthquake that occurred in Alaska in 1957.

[10] Robert Shiller. "Exuberant Reporting: Media and Misinformation in the Markets." *Media*, Vol. 23, (1) Spring 2001.

[11] Because estimated death tolls from earthquakes often vary considerably from source to source, this book uses estimated death tolls reported by the United States Geological Service, Earthquake Hazards Program Web site.

[12] There is some evidence that a rare human disease, variant Creutzfeldt-Jakob, is contracted from consuming beef from cattle infected with mad cow disease.

[13] Paul Haavardsrud and Peter Morton. "Fast-Food Stocks Plummet: McDonald's Shares Down 8%; U.S. Temporarily Bans Import of Canadian Cattle, Sheep and Goats." *National Post*, May 21, 2003.

[14] Yiuman Tse and James Hackard. "Holy Mad Cow! Facts or (Mis)perceptions: A Clinical Study." *Journal of Futures Markets*, Vol. 26, No. 4, April 2006, pp. 315-341.

[15] Yiuman Tse and James Hackard. "Holy Mad Cow! Facts or (Mis)perceptions: A Clinical Study." *Journal of Futures Markets*, Vol. 26, No. 4, April 2006, pp. 315-341.

[16] Yiuman Tse and James Hackard. "Holy Mad Cow! Facts or (Mis)perceptions: A Clinical Study." *Journal of Futures Markets*, Vol. 26, No. 4, April 2006, pp. 315-341.

[17] Yiuman Tse and James Hackard. "Holy Mad Cow! Facts or (Mis)perceptions: A Clinical Study." *Journal of Futures Markets*, Vol. 26, No. 4, April 2006, pp. 315-341.

[18] Agence France Press. "HK Shares Lower on Concerns Over Iraq War, SARS." March 31, 1995.

[19] Dow Jones Newswires. "1-Yr HK$ Forward Premium To Spot Hits 5-Mo High on SARS." April 21, 2003.

[20] Dow Jones Newswires. "HK Dlr Mkts Late: HK Dlr Forwards Continue to Surge on SARS." April 25, 2003.

[21] Andrew Torchia. "Asian Markets Decline on Fears about SARS—Stock Prices, Currencies and Interest Rates Drop." *The Asian Wall Street Journal*, April 28, 2003, p. M2.

[22] Andrew Torchia. "Asian Markets Decline on Fears about SARS—Stock Prices, Currencies and Interest Rates Drop." *The Asian Wall Street Journal*, April 28, 2003, p. M2. The article notes: "Bonds were bought ... as investors bet that SARS would force central banks to keep interest rates very low...."

[23] United States Geological Service Web site: http://md.water.usgs.gov/drought/define.html.

[24] Masood Farivar. "Oil Prices Surge as Tropical Storm Approaches Gulf." *The Wall Street Journal*, June 10, 2005, p. C4.

[25] *The Wall Street Journal*. June 10, 2005, p. B6.

[26] Andrew Bary. "Trading Points." *Barron's*, August 31, 1992, p. 39.

[27] The earthquake is popularly known as the San Francisco earthquake, even though it covered a distance of more than 430 kilometers. The United States Geological Service estimates the loss of life at around 3,000 people. Information about the quake can be found at http://72.14.207.104/search?q=cache:X_S4pAl02IcJ:quake.wr.usgs.gov/info/1906/+san+francisco+earthquake+of+1906&hl=en.

[28] John Dennis Brown. *101 Years on Wall Street: An Investor's Almanac*. Englewood Cliffs, New Jersey: Prentice Hall, 1991, p. 33.

6

MARKET
INTERVENTIONS

"The causes of events are ever more interesting than the events themselves."

—Cicero

A Tale of Two Market Interventions

On Friday, September 22, 2000, traders witnessed two major market interventions. One was intended to increase the foreign exchange value of the euro. The other was intended to decrease the price of oil. One was the result of collective action by a group of central banks. The other was a unilateral action by the U.S. government. One intervention came as a surprise to market participants. The other intervention was widely anticipated before it was announced. Both the actual intervention in the currency market and the anticipated intervention in the oil market impacted prices and volatility significantly. Yet, judged from a longer-term perspective, only one intervention was ultimately successful.

Central Banks Defend the Euro

Around 12:15 P.M. London time on Friday, September 22, 2000, the European Central Bank (ECB) together with the Federal Reserve, the Bank of Canada, and the Bank of Japan suddenly bought billions of euros in a coordinated move intended to drive up the foreign exchange value of the euro.[1] This was followed by two additional rounds of euro purchases by the central banks. The coordinated intervention by the group of central banks took the foreign exchange (FX) market by surprise. The effect was immediate and dramatic. The euro quickly rose by over two cents against the U.S. dollar and triggered a rally on some European stock markets.[2] However, the effect of the intervention on the value of the euro was also short-lived.

The market impact of the coordinated intervention is depicted in Figure 6.1 and captured in the following excerpt from an article that appeared in *The Times* on Saturday, September 23, 2000.

> ...Although the single currency leapt close to 90 cents against the dollar soon after banks began buying euros just after midday, it later fell back to around 88 cents—only modestly above its value before the intervention began, but still well above the record low of 84.43 cents hit on Wednesday...
>
> Yesterday's action caught markets on the back foot in the wake of persistent speculation that the US was unwilling to take part in a coordinated rescue attempt...The banks are already estimated to have spent between $6 billion (£4.1billion) and $8 billion in three rounds of intervention yesterday, with the European Central Bank spending as much as $4 billion.[3]

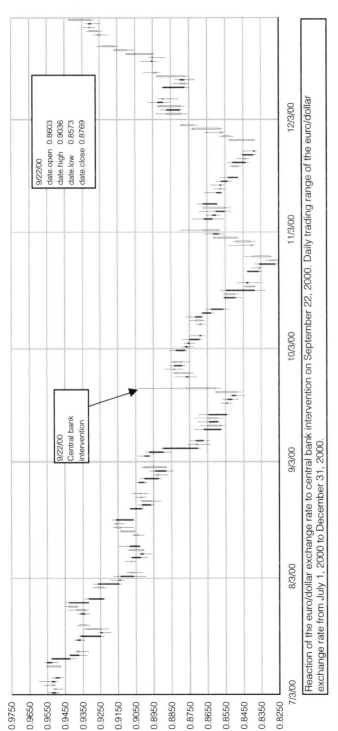

FIGURE 6.1   Central banks defend the euro.

Reaction of the euro/dollar exchange rate to central bank intervention on September 22, 2000. Daily trading range of the euro/dollar exchange rate from July 1, 2000 to December 31, 2000.

The decision to intervene jointly to defend the euro was driven by persistent weakness in the euro and fears of what a weak euro might mean for economic growth. The euro, the common currency unit for most European Community member states, had basically been in a steady downtrend since its introduction on January 1, 1999. Ill-advised comments by Wim Duisenberg, president of the European Central Bank, and other officials from various European governments since its introduction buffeted the currency and exacerbated its decline. By Wednesday, September 20, 2000, the euro had fallen almost 28% below its initial exchange rate of € = $1.17. The prospect of further declines in the euro prompted the central banks to collectively intervene to halt the slide.

Some observers attributed much of the power of the coordinated central bank intervention to the fact that the Federal Reserve participated in it.[4] The participation of the U.S. Federal Reserve was surprising because the Clinton Administration was openly pursuing a strong dollar policy at the time. It was also surprising because the U.S. was in the midst of a presidential election campaign. Indeed, some market observers argued that concern that the Federal Reserve would not participate in a joint intervention to support the euro during the U.S. presidential campaign led to sharp declines in the euro prior to the joint intervention. Put differently, many traders believed that it was safe to bet against the euro because the U.S. would not intervene in the FX markets to support the euro and previous ECB interventions had proven largely ineffective.

Contemporary news accounts indicated that the central banks would be happy if the euro stayed above 87 U.S. cents.[5] The question naturally arises as to whether the coordinated central bank action was successful. The answer depends upon the time frame one uses to evaluate the market impact. In the very short-run, the answer is yes. However, over a marginally longer period of time, such as a day, the answer is no. As the excerpt notes, there was an immediate upward boost in the value of the euro following the successive rounds of intervention that largely disappeared by the end of the trading day. The euro resumed its downward slide against the U.S. dollar in subsequent trading days and reached an all-time low against the dollar of $0.823 on October 26, 2000—significantly below the desired minimum of $0.87.

The Bank for International Settlements estimates that over $1.9 trillion of foreign currency trades every business day, based on results from an April 2004 survey.[6] Most of the trading volume is concentrated in a handful of currencies. Even the largest central banks typically do only a small fraction of that total in a currency market intervention. In this case, the excerpt notes that the ECB spent $4 billion trying to prop up the euro that day and the other central banks spent an additional $2 to $4 billion.

This raises a more fundamental question: Namely, why should central bank intervention to support a currency be successful at all given the large size of the foreign exchange market? The answer is that central bank interventions create short-term risks for market participants. To increase their impact, central banks often concentrate their interventions during market periods where liquidity is low and trading volume is low, such as around holidays or weekends. Academic studies have shown that trading volume follows a U-shaped pattern in many markets with significantly greater volume at the open and close of trading. Sometimes, the central bank or central banks can magnify the impact of a market intervention by triggering a price move that causes traders to cover their losing positions. This reinforces the central bank's actions and exacerbates the move in prices. Enlisting the support of key central banks can also have an impact as shown in the opening example with the participation of the Federal Reserve. The midday London time of the intervention allowed the central banks to influence trading in both London and New York—two of the three principal centers of foreign exchange trading.

Tapping the Strategic Petroleum Reserve

In the late afternoon (Washington, D.C. time) on the same Friday, the Clinton Administration announced a swap of 30 million barrels of oil from the Strategic Petroleum Reserve (SPR). The objective was to drive the price of crude oil down by flooding the oil market with "new" supply. The hope was that the action would trigger a decline in crude oil prices and a decrease in the price of heating oil and other key petroleum derivative products. Although the move was announced after the market closed, speculation that the administration would announce a swap drove crude oil futures prices down 4% earlier in the day. The price action is captured in the following excerpt, from an article by Katherine Spector, that appeared in *The Oil Daily* on September 25, 2000.

> Talk that the Clinton administration was preparing to release US strategic reserves onto the market...sent the crude complex down further Friday after a week of volatility. November light, sweet crude on the New York Mercantile Exchange (Nymex) plunged $1.32, settling at $32.68/barrel.
>
> Trade was somewhat tumultuous throughout the week, with the October contract reaching as high as $37.80 Wednesday before expiring at $37.20. But where the October contract went out with a bang, November came in with a fizzle, losing $1.24 on Thursday, its first day as the front-month contract. Friday's decline leaves November crude $2.56 below its $35.24/bbl debut...
>
> Products tumbled with crude, with October heating oil losing 4.41¢ to settle at 95.48¢/gallon, down a stunning 7.81¢ for the week.[7]

The Clinton Administration's decision was driven by rising crude oil and heating oil prices. Crude oil prices reached a 10-year high in the fall of 2000. Adding to the pressure on crude oil prices was a flare-up in tensions between Iraq and Kuwait. On Monday, September 18, 2000, New York Mercantile Exchange West Texas Intermediate crude oil futures closed almost a dollar higher on renewed tensions between Iraq and Kuwait.[8]

Basically, Iraq accused Kuwait of stealing 350,000 barrels of oil a day from Iraqi fields bordering Kuwait. Iraq had a powerful weapon in its arsenal of threats to achieve its objectives. Iraq's weapon was not military but economic—the threatened withdrawal of its 2.3 million barrels per day oil production from the export market during a time when other Organization of Oil Exporting Countries could not make up the slack.

On Thursday, September 21, 2000, U.S. Vice President (and Democratic presidential candidate) Al Gore reacted to higher crude oil prices by proposing a program where oil from the SPR would be lent to, or *swapped*, with private oil companies. Under his plan, the oil would be swapped at rates determined in a series of five or six auctions of five million barrels each. The borrowed oil would be repaid with interest (i.e., additional oil) at a future date when the price of oil was presumably cheaper. At the time, the U.S. government had an estimated 570 million barrels of crude oil in the SPR.[9]

The Gore campaign released the vice president's proposal to tap the SPR to the news media in the early morning of Thursday, September 21, 2000 before a scheduled campaign event later in the day (and before trading in oil futures opened on the NYMEX).[10] Not surprisingly, the oil futures market sold off on uncertainty over whether Gore's proposal would be implemented by the Clinton Administration. Coming in the midst of the 2000 presidential election campaign, the decision was also, not surprisingly, criticized as a calculated political move by the Republican presidential candidate Texas Governor George W. Bush and some market observers. The oil futures market sold off even more on Friday as it became apparent that the Gore proposal would be implemented. The reaction to the anticipated Clinton Administration decision to tap the SPR is depicted in Figure 6.2.

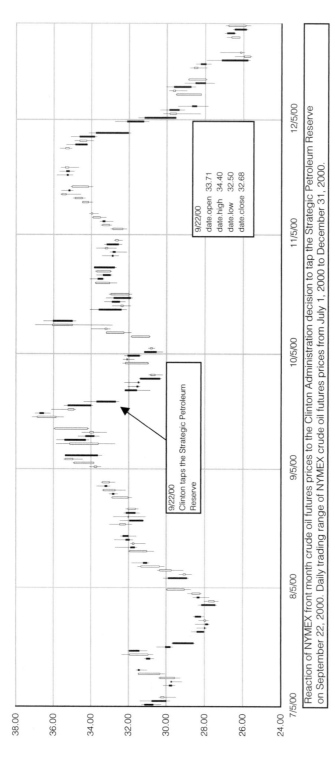

9/22/00
Clinton taps the Strategic Petroleum
Reserve

9/22/00	
date.open	33.71
date.high	34.40
date.low	32.50
date.close	32.68

Reaction of NYMEX front month crude oil futures prices to the Clinton Administration decision to tap the Strategic Petroleum Reserve on September 22, 2000. Daily trading range of NYMEX crude oil futures prices from July 1, 2000 to December 31, 2000.

FIGURE 6.2   The U.S. taps the Strategic Petroleum Reserve.

The market's reaction to the Clinton Administration's decision to tap the SPR via an oil swap also illustrates how market prices may rise due to one trading catalyst—in this case, geopolitical factors in the Middle East—and fall due to another trading catalyst—in this case, tapping the SPR—even though the factors that sparked the initial rally (e.g., tensions in the Middle East) remained. To be sure, the price rally was due to the possibility of supply disruptions (i.e., Iraq refusing to export crude oil) and the price break was due to the possibility of additional supply coming to market (i.e., from the SPR). However, the price impact on heating oil is not as easily explained given the view at the time that heating oil production suffered not from a lack of oil but a lack of heating oil refinery capacity.[11]

Recall that the official announcement of the oil swap came late Friday afternoon after the oil futures market had closed in the U.S. However, the desired effect was achieved before then as speculation on the impending announcement had already pushed crude oil futures prices down. This gave the Clinton Administration an opportunity to test the potential market reaction to the swap proposal by issuing it in the form of a *trial balloon*. The success of the oil swap stems, in part, from the fact that if the market had not reacted to it the proposal would probably never have been implemented. The success also stems, in part, from the fact that the surprise potential from tapping into the SPR was larger than it otherwise would have been precisely because many oil market participants believed that the Clinton Administration would not tap into the SPR during a presidential election campaign.

Market Interventions as Trading Catalysts

Market manipulation is illegal in most countries except when it is done by the government or the central bank. However, the ability of even the wealthiest central bank or government to maintain a price different from the market price for an extended period of time is limited. Moreover, attempts to do so often consume substantial resources and usually result in wealth transfers from the public to speculators. The inevitable adjustment to the market price is usually sharp and quick. The economic dislocations that follow the adjustment can be substantial.

Attempts by central banks or governments to maintain a non-market price or exchange rate create short-term risks for traders betting on a change. A sudden large move triggered by a central bank or government intervention may be exacerbated by traders trying to cut their losses short. As noted in Chapter 3, "Talk Isn't Cheap," the attempts by governments and central banks to maintain a nonmarket price or exchange rate also create *one-sided bets*. The bets are one-sided in that the potential changes on either side of the current price or exchange rate are not symmetric. Simply put, traders face smaller potential downside losses than potential upside profits.

For instance, consider an example where the exchange rate for a currency has been artificially set above the market exchange rate. If the central bank is able to maintain the artificially high exchange rate, the trader who shorted the currency faces the prospect of losses if the currency rises above the rate that the currency was sold at as well as any *cost of carry*. The cost of carry is simply the interest that would have been earned had the funds been invested in a default-free security denominated in that same currency over the length of time the trade is open. In many cases, the principal potential loss is the cost of carry. In a low interest rate environment, the cost of carry can be relatively low for small short-term trades. Alternatively, if the central bank is unable to maintain the current artificially high exchange rate and the government devalues the currency, the trader faces the prospect of profits substantially in excess of the potential losses.

Attempts by central banks to maintain a nonmarket exchange rate not only create one-sided bets but also provide speculators the opportunity to do *size* (i.e., take a larger position) when taking the other side of the trade. This encourages speculative attacks on a currency in certain environments—that is, the central bank may be able to maintain the mispriced exchange rate in normal times but not in a crisis environment. The crisis may be set off by a trading catalyst. It is important to emphasize that speculative attacks need not be coordinated conspiracies but are often the logical outcome when confidence is lacking that the central bank will be able to maintain a nonmarket exchange rate.

The inclination to intervene in the foreign exchange market differs across nations. Compared with many other countries, the United States rarely intervenes to support its currency or assist in supporting other currencies (i.e., weaken the U.S. dollar). The basic philosophy is that free markets should determine exchange rates. The opening example in this chapter is one exception. Another exception is discussed in the following excerpt from *Marketplace*, a financial news radio program, that aired on June 17, 1998.

> ...[T]he Federal Reserve Bank of New York began buying two maybe three billion dollars worth of yen in an effort to prop up the ailing Japanese currency. This was the first intervention in the currency markets by U.S. central bankers since 1995...and for today, at least, the effort worked with the dollar falling about 6.5 yen during the course of the New York trading day. The stock market liked...the action...and the Dow Jones Industrial Average rose 164 points...[or] 1.9 percent.[12]

The excerpt provides another demonstration of how a central bank intervention can have a substantial short-term impact on market prices—the dollar fell by 6.5 yen. It also illustrates how intervention-induced price changes in one market—the foreign exchange market—can impact price changes in another market—the stock market.

In contrast, the Bank of Japan has frequently intervened to keep its currency within a desired range. Sometimes, this has involved selling yen and buying dollars. Other times, it has involved selling dollars and buying yen. These interventions have often sparked large changes in the dollar/yen exchange rate.[13] The Bank of Japan has expended enormous sums of money trying to maintain its desired exchange rate. By one estimate, the Bank of Japan spent $182 billion during 2003 and another $100 billion during January and February of 2004 trying to maintain the yen within a desired trading range.[14]

In many instances, devaluations are preceded by denials that they will occur. This happened in Thailand shortly before the devaluation of the Thai baht on July 2, 1997, as noted in Chapter 3. It has happened elsewhere as well. For example, a sharp collapse in crude oil prices in the early 1980s put substantial downward pressure on the Mexican peso. Mexican President Jose Lopez Portillo famously pledged to "defend the peso like a dog" before abruptly devaluing the peso by almost 42% in February 1982.[15]

The common practice of politicians and policymakers denying a potential action before doing it extends beyond currency devaluations. There seems to be an implicit belief among many politicians and policymakers that the market is fooled by denials of the obvious. It usually is not. For instance, although Russia devalued its currency and defaulted on its debt on August 17, 1998, fears of a default hit financial markets days earlier as the following excerpt from an August 11, 1998 Reuters news story suggests.

> Russian officials insisted on Tuesday that economic reforms would not be derailed despite a precipitous fall in financial markets...Prices for Russian government debt fell so low, traders said the market was pricing in a risk that either the rouble would collapse or Russia would fail to repay its creditors on time.
>
> But Deputy Prime Minister Viktor Khristenko told a news conference he saw no such risk. "The question of a Russian default has not even been posed," he said...
>
> The Russian stock market has tumbled since last October on the heels of Asian markets...The benchmark RTSI-Interfax

share index ended down 9.11 percent at 109.90, a level not seen since May 1996, while yields on long-dated government debt soared to around 130-140 percent from Monday's close at around 90-110 percent.[16]

Just as denials by policymakers of prospective actions often lack credibility in the marketplace, so do announcements that appear to be an indirect implementation of some policy action that has been denied. For instance, on August 12, 1998, a Russian government announcement that it would carefully review purchases of foreign exchange nipped a nascent stock market rally in the bud and precipitated a 1.5% decline in stock prices when the announcement was interpreted by many traders as a precursor to making the rouble inconvertible. The announcement increased fears among traders of a rouble devaluation and default on Russian government debt.[17] On August 13, 1998, the Russian equity and debt markets plunged.

Defending the Indefensible

A classic example of a one-sided bet occurred during the September 1992 European monetary crisis when speculators accelerated the Bank of England's decision to withdraw from the European Exchange Rate Mechanism (ERM) and allow the pound sterling to adjust to a new lower exchange rate against the German mark. Some background information on the crisis is instructive.

Before the euro was introduced in 1999, member nations of the European Community experimented with a system of largely fixed exchange rates among the currencies of participating member nations. The objective of the European Monetary System was to reduce volatility in exchange rates among European Community member currencies. The principal feature of the European Monetary

System was the ERM, in which currencies were pegged to the European Currency Unit, or ECU, (a unit of account) and allowed to fluctuate within a narrow band of 2.25% up or down.[18] Governments could borrow funds from other central banks (most importantly, the Deutsche Bundesbank) to maintain the exchange rate within a narrow band. After some initial resistance, the British government joined the European Monetary System and ERM in 1990 when the pound sterling had a relatively high exchange rate to the German mark. The pound sterling entered the ERM at an exchange rate of DM2.9. This was an unsustainably high exchange rate. It was also an invitation for a speculative attack on the pound sterling at some point given the right trading catalyst.

The creation of the European Union appeared certain when the Treaty of Maastricht was concluded. It required the approval of the parliaments of all 12 member nations of the European Community. The Danish and British governments requested permission to hold referenda so that citizens of their respective countries could vote on whether the proposed treaty should be ratified. On June 2, 1992, the Danish electorate narrowly rejected the Treaty of Maastricht. French President François Mitterand decided that the French would also have an opportunity to vote on whether the treaty should be ratified, and a referendum was scheduled for Sunday, September 20, 1992.[19] The Danish rejection of the Treaty of Maastricht (discussed in Chapter 4, "Geopolitical Events") was a geopolitical event that served as a trading catalyst that (along with uncertainty over whether French voters would approve the treaty) cast doubt on the prospects of a successful European Union and likely encouraged speculative attacks on the currencies of various European Community members.

A full-fledged currency crisis emerged by early September 1992. Central banks of affected countries responded by raising interest rates. The Bank of Sweden announced a target short-term interest rate of 500% in a vain attempt to slow selling of the Swedish krona. This was soon abandoned. The Italian lira came under attack and was devalued 7% on Sunday, September 13, 1992. The Spanish peseta came under attack. The pound sterling came under attack. The decline in the pound sterling accelerated on Monday, September 14, 1992. On September 16, 1992, the Bank of England raised short-term interest rates from 10% to 12% and later to 15%, even though the U.K. economy was arguably in a recession. The interest rate hikes failed. The Bank of England threw in the towel and withdrew from the ERM, effectively letting the pound sterling float. The Bank of Italy withdrew the lira from the ERM and decided to let it float. The Spanish central bank devalued the peseta by 5%. The collapse of the pound sterling is depicted in Figure 6.3.

George Soros is justly famous as the trader who broke the Bank of England on Black Wednesday. Various news reports suggest that Mr. Soros' hedge fund (whose principal trader was Stanley Drucken-miller) made over $1 billion overnight from shorting the pound sterling during the crisis. George Soros indicated, in a later interview, that the Bank of England's decision to raise interest rates during a recession to discourage speculation was a signal that it was unable to defend the pound sterling and would have to exit from the ERM.[20] This gave him the confidence to have his hedge fund put on an extremely large short sterling position. During the same interview, Mr. Soros was asked whether he had assumed too much risk by taking such a large position if the Bank of England was able to maintain the exchange rate and the trade went against him. He replied that he had not because it was a one-sided bet, or as he characterized, it was an "uneven bet" where the potential losses were minimal and the potential gains were enormous.[21]

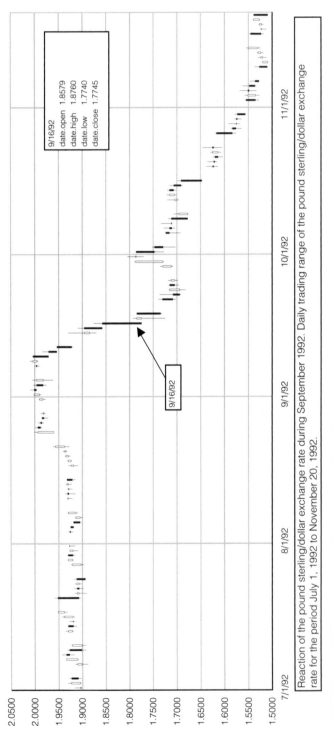

FIGURE 6.3   Calling a one-sided bet on pound sterling.

Although much attention has focused on the enormous trading profits that Mr. Soros' hedge fund and other currency speculators made that day, considerably less attention has been directed toward the total amount of losses that were incurred by the Bank of England in defending the indefensible exchange rate level. The Bank of England spent nearly £15 billion defending the exchange rate.[22] Of course, not all £15 billion was lost. The *Financial Times* reported later that the Bank of England lost £3.3 billion from the misguided operations. At recent exchange rates, this translates into a $6.1 billion loss.[23] Approximately one-fourth of the loss was attributed to outright trading losses with the balance attributed to lost appreciation of foreign reserves expended to defend the pound sterling.

Total central bank losses were larger because the Bank of England received substantial assistance from at least one other central bank during the crisis—Bank Negara Malaysia. Subsequent news accounts indicated that the central bank of Malaysia lost almost 10 billion ringgit, or about $4 billion, at the time defending the pound sterling. *The Asian Wall Street Journal* reported that Bank Negara lost another 5.7 billion ringgit in 1993 from other currency speculation.[24] Another way of looking at it is that the Bank of England and Bank Negara Malaysia were engaged in currency speculation that resulted in a wealth transfer of billions of dollars from average citizens of those two nations to the foreign exchange trading community. It also highlights the considerable losses that central banks can incur when they attempt to manipulate the market.

Speculative attacks occurred on other currencies during this period as well. After the Bank of England stopped trying to defend the pound sterling, a speculative attack was launched on the French franc. This one proved unsuccessful as the Banque de France (together with the Deutsche Bundesbank) was able to maintain the French currency within the bands established by the ERM. The key factor in the success of the French effort to maintain the exchange rate was the active support of the Deutsche Bundesbank.[25] Some observers contend that the support of the Deutsche Bundesbank was lacking when the Bank of England attempted to maintain the pound sterling exchange rate.

The Hong Kong Monetary Authority Intervenes in the Stock Market

A recurrent theme in this book is that trading is a game. As a game, trading strategies do not exist in a vacuum but are dependent upon the expected behavior of other market participants as well as institutional factors that may affect the trading process. The rewards from trading can be enormous. This creates a powerful incentive to anticipate correctly how prices will behave under various circumstances. In most cases, traders are simply trying to anticipate price changes and are unable to influence price changes by their actions taken alone. However, the potential for enormous trading profits also creates a powerful incentive for *some* market participants to attempt to *engineer* the desired price change by manipulating markets. The resultant trading strategies may be simple or complex, but the effects on market prices and volatility can be substantial.

Central banks are sometimes forced to intervene in unusual ways to fight attempts at market manipulation. One of the more unusual market interventions was the decision of the Hong Kong Monetary Authority (HKMA)—the de facto central bank of the Hong Kong Special Autonomous Region of the People's Republic of China—to buy stocks and stock index futures during August 1998.

The decision of the HKMA is interesting for several reasons.

1. Central banks rarely intervene directly in the stock or stock index futures markets.

2. The intervention was a response to traders who were attempting to profit from a complex strategy that involved selling Hong Kong stock index futures and later selling previously borrowed Hong Kong dollars from the swap market in an attempt to drive interbank interest rates up and stock prices down.

3. The intervention attempted to exploit the mechanical nature of Hong Kong's currency board monetary system.

4. The size of the intervention was immense.[26]

5. The actions of the HKMA were ultimately successful and the HKMA earned a substantial profit on the securities they acquired.

6. The intervention by the HKMA may have distorted the relationship between stock index and stock index futures prices and left apparent unexploited arbitrage profit opportunities for some time following the intervention.

To appreciate the decision of the HKMA to intervene in the stock and stock index futures market, it is important to understand how a currency board operates and what happened in previous speculative attacks on the Hong Kong dollar. First, a *currency board* is simply a monetary system in which changes in the local currency are tied to changes in central bank holdings of a foreign currency at a fixed exchange rate. Hong Kong utilizes a currency board to maintain a largely fixed exchange rate with the U.S. dollar. At the time of the crisis, the exchange rate was US$1 = HK$7.8. A currency board sharply limits discretion by the central bank. Instead, the currency board responds passively to changes in capital flows. For instance, additional Hong Kong dollars can only be issued if foreign reserves are increased by an equivalent amount (at the fixed exchange rate). Conversely, the conversion of Hong Kong dollars into U.S. dollars reduces the amount of Hong Kong dollars outstanding by the fixed exchange rate. Interbank interest rates (the Hong Kong equivalent of the Fed funds rate) are a function of the total balance of funds held by the Hong Kong clearing banks at the HKMA. The lack of reserve requirements and the efficiency of the Hong Kong banking system mean that the amount is normally relatively low. Interbank interest rates rise when the aggregate balance falls and fall when the aggregate balance rises. The sudden dumping of a large amount of Hong Kong dollars will reduce the aggregate balance and raise the interbank interest rate sharply.

Second, soon after the Asian Financial Crisis began with the devaluation of the Thai baht on July 2, 1997, the Hong Kong dollar came under a series of speculative attacks. The attacks increased during October 1997. Although the fixed exchange rate link between the Hong Kong dollar and the U.S. dollar remained unchanged throughout the repeated speculative attacks, the adjustment to the attacks— higher short-term interbank interest rates—affected other Hong Kong markets. On October 23, 1997, the Hong Kong interest rate approached 300%.[27] Not surprisingly, this had a negative effect on the Hong Kong stock market. The sharp declines in the Hong Kong market that week and early the week after spilled over to the U.S. stock market on Monday, October 27, 1997.

The speculative attacks on the Hong Kong dollar failed. The currency board worked. Traders who had shorted the Hong Kong dollar in the expectation of an effective devaluation failed and suffered losses. The HKMA had maintained the fixed link to the U.S. dollar but at some cost to other markets. The speculative attacks demonstrated that the interbank interest rate could be pushed sharply higher when massive amounts of Hong Kong dollars are sold as a result of Hong Kong's adherence to the mechanical currency board system. The speculative attacks also demonstrated that a sharp rise in the interbank interest rate would depress stock prices. The sharp rise in the interbank interest rate also imposed a substantial opportunity cost on traders who were short the Hong Kong dollar. If the fixed exchange rate remained impervious to a speculative attack, a trader who was short the stock market could benefit handsomely if a speculative attack drove the interbank interest rate sharply higher and stock prices sharply lower. Shorting stock index futures would be an easy and less risky way to put on a large short stock position.[28] To precipitate an attack on the Hong Kong currency, traders would need Hong Kong dollars to sell. This would expose traders who were short the Hong Kong dollar to substantial costs as short rates rose, unless the trader was able to obtain a sufficient amount of Hong Kong dollars in advance. This problem was solved by swapping into Hong Kong dollars with counterparties who had borrowed money in Hong Kong.

Trading is a game. As such, traders learn from past market behavior. However, so do central banks. As noted earlier, a looming crisis in Russia in August 1998 spilled over to other markets including Hong Kong. In addition, the Long-Term Capital Management crisis was brewing. Against this backdrop, the attempted manipulation of the Hong Kong market occurred. Mr. Joseph Yam, chief executive of the Hong Kong Monetary Authority, described the situation this way in a speech delivered in November 1998.

> …One troubling aspect of the Asian crisis…has been the extreme volatility in markets created by the rapid flows of highly leveraged funds around the world. As markets in the region became more vulnerable, these flows increasingly took on a predatory character and became more and more subtle in their planning and sophistication. This August [1998]…the Hong Kong financial markets became the target of a well planned attack by international hedge funds…

> In August the speculators…introduced a form of double play aimed at playing off the currency board system against the stock and futures markets. First, to avoid being squeezed by high interest rates, they prefunded themselves in Hong Kong dollars in the debt market, swapping US dollars for Hong

Kong dollars with multilateral institutions that have raised Hong Kong dollars through the issue of debt. At the same time, they accumulated large short positions in the stock index futures market. They then sought to engineer extreme conditions in the money market by dumping huge amounts of Hong Kong dollars. This selloff was intended to cause a sharp interest rate hike, which in turn would have sent the stock market plummeting. The collapse of the stock market would have enabled them to reap a handsome profit from the futures contracts they had taken out.

A few figures will help give some idea of the scale of this attack...We estimate that the hedge funds involved had amassed in excess of HK$30 billion in currency borrowings, at an interest cost of around HK$4 million a day. They also held an estimated 80,000 short contracts, which translated into the following calculation: for every fall of 1,000 points in the Hang Seng index they stood to make a profit of HK$4 billion. If they could have engineered that fall within 1,000 days they would have broken even. If they could have achieved it within 100 days they would have netted HK$3.6 billion. All they had to do was to wait for the best moment to dump their Hong Kong dollars, to drive up interest rates and send a shock wave through the stock market. August was an opportune time.[29]

The HKMA recognized the potential market manipulation and sought to discourage similar future attempts by ensuring that the traders who were short 80,000 Hang Seng stock index futures contracts did not profit from their actions. The HKMA bought US$15 billion of stocks and Hang Seng stock index futures contracts. The HKMA also changed some aspects of the currency board system. The actions were successful and the shorts lost money. By November 23, 1998, the value of the HKMA equity portfolio was up US$4 billion from where it was acquired.[30]

The effects of the HKMA intervention did not end immediately. A study by Professors Paul Draper and Joseph Fung [2003] argues that the HKMA's intervention in the stock index futures market had a significant and long-lasting impact on the *basis*, or difference, between the Hang Seng stock index and Hang Seng stock index futures price. The basis was negative rather than positive. Moreover, they argue that arbitrageurs did not exploit the potential arbitrage opportunity that the negative basis implied because of concern that the HKMA might intervene in the stock index futures markets again. Put differently, market participants faced a higher cost of having short stock positions after the intervention than before.[31]

Trading Lessons

The belief that central banks or governments can improve upon the prices generated in a free market is widely held by policymakers and politicians alike. It is the source of many attempts by governments and central banks to induce changes in prices through market interventions. It is also a source of significant profits for the trading community.

Market interventions can exert a dramatic effect on market prices and volatility. Often the effects are powerful but short-lived. Sometimes, they mark a local turning point in the trend of prices. In either case, market interventions by governments and central banks create both risk and opportunity for traders. The risk is that the central bank or government can push prices far enough and long enough to force traders to cut their losses short. The opportunity is that the central bank or government is not price sensitive and may create one-sided bets and allow large traders to bet against it with limited risks.

Central banks are the quintessential example of how one market participant can influence market prices. Market interventions work best (from the policymaker's perspective) when central bank or government actions reinforce an existing trend or exploit a natural tendency of traders to minimize their losses—that is, to cut their losses short. Simply put, well-designed interventions can let the private sector do much of the "heavy lifting" required to achieve the short-term policy objective.

Precisely because the central bank is not required to make a profit on its transactions, it may engage in behavior contrary to what any rational trader would—that is, it frequently fails to cut its losses short. By willingly taking the other side to trades, the central bank enables traders to take a larger position size than might otherwise be available in the open market. For instance, by following a policy of defending an exchange rate that differs from what would prevail in a free market, central banks invite speculative attacks and create one-sided bets.

Trading is a game. As a game, trading strategies do not exist in a vacuum but are dependent upon the expected behavior of other market participants as well as institutional factors that may affect the trading process. Traders learn from their experiences. Although most traders are simply trying to correctly forecast changes in prices or volatility, a few traders try to engineer a desired price change by manipulating the market. These actions can have a substantial impact on even seemingly unrelated markets. Central banks also learn from their experiences and market observations. Sometimes, intervention is necessary to prevent market manipulation as the HKMA argued when it intervened in the stock and stock index futures markets during August 1998.

The trader must assess the probability of a market intervention by the government or its central bank. The trader must also assess the likely magnitude, duration, and direction of impact of the intervention. Many interventions are large but short-lived. Wide stops are not the answer given the potential magnitude of some intervention-induced short-term price moves. Indeed, the prospect of greater risk induced by uncertainty over future market interventions may cause many traders to reduce their overall trading positions when there is a substantial risk of market intervention. It may also cause other traders to substantially increase their positions if they are extremely confident in their beliefs, for instance, that the central bank is no longer able to maintain a nonmarket exchange rate.[32] When governments and their central banks attempt to defend unsustainable exchange rates or prices, they may not only create one-sided betting opportunities but also facilitate larger position sizes for speculators. In a one-sided bet situation, the trader should consider increasing his position size. The trader should also increase the stops on the trade to avoid being prematurely stopped out. Finally, the trader may shorten his trade horizon in an environment where there is substantial risk of market intervention other things being equal.

References

Agence France Presse. "Oil Prices Reach New 10-Year Highs." September 18, 2000.

Agence France Presse. "US Joins Euro Intervention to Limit Potential Damage." September 22, 2000.

American Public Media. *Marketplace*. June 17, 1998.

Bahree, Bhushan and Neil King Jr. "Rising Oil Prices Provide Iraq with New Weapon—Saddam Hussein Could Use Export Power to Seek Gains." *The Wall Street Journal Europe*, September 19, 2000.

Bank for International Settlements. "Triennial Central Bank Survey of Foreign Exchange and Derivatives Market Activity 2004 – Final Results." (http://www.bis.org/publ/rpfx04.htm).

Bank for International Settlements. "Triennial Central Bank Survey of Foreign Exchange and Derivatives Market Activity 2001 – Final Results." (http://www.bis.org/publ/rpfx02t.pdf).

Beveridge, Dirk. "France Bolsters Defense of Franc, And Succeeds, For A Day." The Associated Press, September 23, 1992.

Brancaccio, David. *Marketplace*. June 17, 1998 (http://marketplace. publicradio.org/shows/1998/06/17_mpp.html).

Burdess, Lara. "Analysts—Russian Mkts Fee Fall—Jitters Over Default, Deval." Market News International, August 12, 1998.

Business Week Online. "Don't Let Japan's 'Mr. Dollar' Get Away with It." March 22, 2004.

CNBC. *"After Hours with Maria Bartiromo."* Interview with George Soros, September 16, 2002.

Draper, Paul and Joseph K.W. Fung. "Discretionary Government Intervention and the Mispricing of Index Futures." *Journal of Futures Markets*, Vol. 23, No. 12, 2003, pp. 1159-1189.

Duthie, Stephen. "New Governor at Bank Negara Has Tough Job." *The Asian Wall Street Journal*, April 11, 1994.

Graff, Peter. "Focus-Russian Government Undaunted by Market Slump." Reuters News, August 11, 1998.

Mark Egan. "Gore Urges Sale of Oil from U.S. Strategic Reserves." Reuters News, September 21, 2000.

Market News International. "US TSYS up after Joint Euro Intervention – Global STKS Plunge." September 22, 2000, 8:32 A.M.

Paterson, Lea. "Markets on Standby for Further Euro Intervention." *The Times*, September 23, 2000.

Reuters News. "Dlr Drops More Than 4 Yen in Tokyo on Intervention." April 10, 1998.

Schwager, Jack D. *The New Market Wizards: Conversations with America's Top Traders*. New York: HarperBusiness, 1992.

Spector, Katherine. "Crude Plunges in Anticipation of Strategic Petroleum Reserve Draw." *The Oil Daily*, September 25, 2000.

Studermann, Frederick, and James Blitz. "Revelations on UK Exit from ERM Go from Drama to Farce." *Financial Times*, February 10, 2005, p. 2.

Thompson, Steve. "London Stock Exchange—Euro Intervention Triggers Late Rally in Equities." *Financial Times*, September 23, 2000.

Whitebloom, Sarah. "Sterling Crisis – Forex Frenzy Nets #900m." *The Observer*, September 20, 1992.

Yam, Joseph. Hong Kong Monetary Authority. "Coping with Financial Turmoil." Inside Asia Lecture 1998, Sydney, Australia, November 23, 1998.

Endnotes

[1] Market News International. "US TSYS up after Joint Euro Intervention – Global STKS Plunge." September 22, 2000, 8:32 A.M.

[2] Steve Thompson, "London Stock Exchange—Euro Intervention Triggers Late Rally in Equities." *Financial Times*, September 23, 2000.

[3] Lea Paterson. "Markets on Standby for Further Euro Intervention." *The Times*, September 23, 2000.

[4] The U.S. Treasury is responsible for exchange rate policy in the United States. The Fed, in its role as the U.S. government's banker, executes currency market operations for the Treasury. It should be pointed out, however, that the Treasury's efforts to intervene to support or weaken the dollar impact the money supply by changing the amount of money in circulation. Consequently, the Fed can *sterilize* (or undo) the effects of the intervention by changing the money supply accordingly.

[5] Agence France Presse. "US Joins Euro Intervention to Limit Potential Damage." September 22, 2000.

The article points out that some market participants thought that the upward move in the euro was limited because, "Reports that both the ECB and the US Treasury would be satisfied if the euro stayed above 0.8700, also kept it from gaining further, they added."

[6] Bank for International Settlements. "Triennial Central Bank Survey of Foreign Exchange and Derivatives Market Activity 2004 – Final Results." (http://www.bis.org/publ/rpfx04.htm). To be sure, the average daily amount traded in the foreign

exchange market was lower in September 2000. An April 2001 BIS survey estimated average trading volume of $1.2 trillion. Bank for International Settlements. "Triennial Central Bank Survey of Foreign Exchange and Derivatives Market Activity 2001 – Final Results." (http://www.bis.org/publ/rpfx02t.pdf).

[7] Katherine Spector. "Crude Plunges in Anticipation of Strategic Petroleum Reserve Draw." *The Oil Daily*, September 25, 2000.

[8] Agence France Presse. "Oil Prices Reach New 10-Year Highs." September 18, 2000. The article argues that part of the reason that crude oil prices were as high as they were was the expectation by market participants that the U.S. would not tap into the Strategic Petroleum Reserve.

[9] Bhushan Bahree and Neil King Jr. "Rising Oil Prices Provide Iraq with New Weapon—Saddam Hussein Could Use Export Power to Seek Gains." *The Wall Street Journal Europe*, September 19, 2000.

[10] Mark Egan. "Gore Urges Sale of Oil from U.S. Strategic Reserves." Reuters News, September 21, 2000.

[11] Katherine Spector. "Crude Plunges in Anticipation of Strategic Petroleum Reserve Draw." *The Oil Daily*, September 25, 2000.

[12] David Brancaccio. *Marketplace*. June 17, 1998. (http://marketplace.publicradio.org/shows/1998/06/17_mpp.html).

[13] Reuters reported the following example on April 10, 1998:

> The dollar dropped more than four yen in Tokyo trade on Friday due to aggressive dollar-selling intervention by the Bank of Japan (BOJ), bankers said. The dollar fell toward 127.00 yen from a Tokyo high for the day of 131.55 yen, after…persistent bouts of dollar for yen sales by the central bank from late morning.

Reuters News. "Dlr Drops More Than 4 Yen in Tokyo on Intervention." April 10, 1998.

[14] Business Week Online. "Don't Let Japan's 'Mr. Dollar' Get Away with It." March 22, 2004.

[15] "Defenderé el peso como un perro!" Not surprisingly, President Portillo was contemptuously referred to as "the dog" and barked at by his angry countrymen when he appeared in public.

[16] Peter Graff. "Focus-Russian Government Undaunted by Market Slump." Reuters News, August 11, 1998.

[17] Lara Burdess. "Analysts—Russian Mkts Fee Fall—Jitters Over Defaulat, Deval." Market News International, August 12, 1998.

[18] The Italian lira was allowed to fluctuate within a wider band.

[19] The treaty was narrowly approved by French voters.

[20] CNBC. "*After Hours with Maria Bartiromo*." Interview with George Soros, September 16, 2002.

[21] CNBC. "*After Hours with Maria Bartiromo*." Interview with George Soros, September 16, 2002.

22 Sarah Whitebloom. "Sterling Crisis – Forex Frenzy Nets #900m." The Observer, September 20, 1992.

23 Frederick Studermann and James Blitz. "Revelations on UK Exit from ERM Go from Drama to Farce." Financial Times, Thursday, February 10, 2005, p. 2.

24 Stephen Duthie. "New Governor at Bank Negara Has Tough Job." *The Asian Wall Street Journal*, April 11, 1994.

25 Dirk Beveridge. "France Bolsters Defense of Franc, And Succeeds, For A Day." The Associated Press, September 23, 1992. The article notes: "Foreign-exchange speculators tried to pummel the French franc with waves of selling Wednesday, but a combined defense from the central banks of France and Germany frustrated their effort."

26 Paul Draper and Joseph K.W. Fung. "Discretionary Government Intervention and the Mispricing of Index Futures." *Journal of Futures Markets*, Vol. 23, No. 12, 2003, pp. 1159-1189. Draper and Fung [2003] point out that the HKMA intervened in the stock and stock index futures markets during a two-week period beginning August 14 through 28, 1998. They state:

> …During that period, the government bought in excess of 7.3% of the total market capitalization of all stocks comprising the main market index. The government also indicated that its remaining free reserves would allow it to build up its total holding to more than 30% of the total market capitalization of the index stocks, creating a substantial potential threat to the market and the arbitrage process.

27 Joseph Yam. Hong Kong Monetary Authority. "Coping with Financial Turmoil." Inside Asia Lecture 1998, Sydney Australia, November 23, 1998. Mr. Yam notes in his speech that August 1998 was a particularly good time for speculators to implement their attempt at market manipulation because stock trading volume was about one-third of its usual amount, there was negative news about economic growth, and there were rumors that the currency peg might be abandoned.

28 Shorting individual stocks is sometimes hard to do as the shares shorted have to be borrowed from someone first. It is as easy to go short as to go long with stock index futures. Moreover, traders are able to avoid individual company risk by trading stock index futures.

29 Joseph Yam. Hong Kong Monetary Authority. "Coping with Financial Turmoil." Inside Asia Lecture 1998, Sydney Australia, November 23, 1998.

30 Joseph Yam. Hong Kong Monetary Authority. "Coping with Financial Turmoil." Inside Asia Lecture 1998, Sydney Australia, November 23, 1998.

31 Professors Draper and Fung argue:

> [Central bank] Intervention, however, created a large negative basis between the index and the futures, a reflection of the increased difficulty and cost of short selling due to government intervention. The large negative basis lasted for a month following intervention, suggesting that government action created a risk element impeding arbitrage. A possible explanation arises from the low liquidity observed in the stock market

and the potential for substantial further intervention. These factors increased...the potential cost of covering or rolling over short stock positions...The risk of conducting index arbitrage was aggravated by the absence of term repos in the stock loan market...Despite futures being "cheap", natural holders of stocks did not appear to sell stocks and buy futures, nor did they lend out stocks at (expensive) repo rates despite the apparent profitability of lending.

Paul Draper and Joseph K.W. Fung. "Discretionary Government Intervention and the Mispricing of Index Futures." *Journal of Futures Markets*, Vol. 23, No. 12, 2003, p. 1163.

[32] Stanley Druckenmiller once said that George "Soros has taught me that when you have tremendous conviction in a trade to go for the jugular." Jack D. Schwager *The New Market Wizards: Conversations with America's Top Traders*, New York: HarperBusiness, 1992, p. 208.

7

PERIODIC ECONOMIC REPORTS

"One dog barks at nothing, ten thousand dogs assert its truth."

—Japanese proverb

The Trade Deficit Sparks a Bond Market Rout

On Tuesday morning, April 14, 1987, fixed income, currency, and commodity traders anxiously awaited the release of the latest measure of America's perennial trade deficit with much of the world. The day before, the dollar, Treasury bonds, and U.S. stocks fell sharply, and precious metals rose in response to a late-day rumor that the merchandise trade deficit for February 1987 would be $18 billion—substantially more than the $13.3 billion consensus forecast. Recent price action suggested that bonds and the dollar were in a bear market, whereas stocks remained in a bull market. The question many market participants pondered was whether the bull market in equities would turn bearish anytime soon, and if so, what might trigger it.

At 8:30 A.M. that morning, the Department of Commerce released the merchandise trade balance report for February 1987. The department reported a merchandise trade deficit of $15.06 billion for February, significantly greater (in absolute value terms) than the consensus forecast. In addition, the department revised the previously reported January 1987 trade deficit upward to $12.27 billion.[1] The financial market reaction was swift and negative. The dollar fell, stocks fell, bonds fell, and gold rose. The apparent operative trading thesis among market participants was that a larger-than-expected merchandise trade deficit would cause the dollar to fall and interest rates to rise because of fear of higher inflation (imported goods would cost more) and less demand by foreign (particularly Japanese) investors for dollar-denominated U.S. Treasury securities. The higher interest rates, in turn, would precipitate a decline in stock prices as the required return or discount rate increased. Some of the market's reaction to the report and the economic relationships traders perceived at the time is described in the following excerpt from an article by Tom Herman and Alexandra Peers in *The Wall Street Journal* on April 15, 1987.

> ...Early in the day, actively traded U.S. Treasury bonds plunged in frenzied trading after the Commerce Department reported an unexpected surge in the nation's merchandise trade deficit for February. Also weighing heavily on the bond markets was another sharp increase in the price of gold, which is watched closely as an indicator of inflation.
>
> Nevertheless, Treasury bond prices later rebounded to finish the day with only small declines. After being down nearly two points early yesterday morning, 30-year Treasury issues

wound up with declines of about 1/4 point, or $2.50 for each $1,000 face amount. That brought the total drop since March 26 to about nine points…

The Commerce Department's trade report early yesterday jolted the bond markets even though there had been wide-spread rumors Monday afternoon that the report would show a huge $18 billion deficit…The trade figures helped drive down the dollar in the currency markets.[2]

The article also indicates that the most actively traded 10-year Treasury note actually closed slightly up for day as the yield fell by one basis point to close at 8.19%. The Dow Jones Industrial Average closed down over 34 points or about 1.5% in the second-busiest trading session ever, whereas spot month (April delivery) gold futures closed up $13.80 per troy ounce on the Commodity Exchange.[3] Both moves were attributed to the trade balance report.

Figure 7.1 depicts the reaction of the 30-year, or long, Treasury bond to the report. The bond market reaction to the reported trade deficit for February 1987 underscores both the importance attached to the news in the merchandise trade balance report and the transient nature of the influence of economic reports. Bonds moved two points (or $20 on a thousand-dollar bond) yet recovered most of the early losses by the end of the day. The 10-year Treasury note reversed course and ended the day modestly higher. Moreover, the magnitude of the bond market's reaction—down 2 points initially—was surprising given that the rumor the day before that the February 1987 trade deficit would be $18 billion precipitated a 1 3/4 point slump in bond prices and a fall in the U.S. dollar against the yen.[4] Indeed, the behavior of financial and commodity market prices following the release of the trade balance report raises a number of questions about both the influence of trading catalysts and commonly perceived economic relationships held by many market participants.

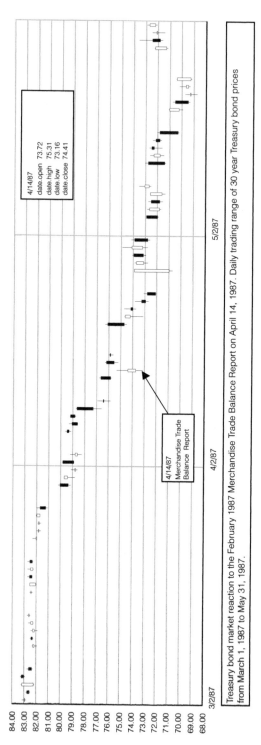

Treasury bond market reaction to the February 1987 Merchandise Trade Balance Report on April 14, 1987. Daily trading range of 30 year Treasury bond prices from March 1, 1987 to May 31, 1987.

FIGURE 7.1   The trade deficit sparks a bond market rout.

Market reactions can be inconsistent across markets. For instance, if the trade deficit report was the proximate cause of the rise in gold spot and futures prices, why did gold futures prices close sharply higher rather than follow the roller-coaster behavior of bond prices? Why did the rally in the price of gold initially adversely affect bond prices but not later? Put differently, if gold is a good barometer of inflation fears, why didn't Treasury bonds end the day substantially lower?

News is contained in the forecast error or the difference between actual and consensus expectations. The consensus forecast is not what economists predict but is the forecast that is in the market—that is, the consensus forecast is what most *traders and other market participants* think. Consensus expectations need not remain constant over time. Indeed, the consensus forecast for the February 1987 trade balance probably increased on Monday, April 13 as the bond market reacted to the rumor of a larger-than-expected trade deficit. Yet, the initial bond market reaction to the trade deficit report news on Tuesday, April 14 was as if the market had not reacted to a higher-than-expected number the previous day. Moreover, the effect did not last because the long bond closed only modestly lower for the day. Was the initial reaction wrong? If so, why was the initial reaction so wrong? After all, the magnitude of the apparent correction was seven times the size of the change in the closing price of the Treasury long bond. If it wasn't a correction, what caused the 1 3/4 point rally in Treasury bond prices from the low of the day to the closing price? The article does not indicate that other news impacted the bond market later in the trading day.

Stock prices also fell on April 13 with much of the decline occurring in the last hour of trading and directly attributable to rumors of the larger-than-expected trade deficit.[5] Spot gold increased $4.25 per troy ounce on Monday with the rumor of a higher trade deficit. Adding to the concerns of traders was the imposition of a new policy of reporting merchandise trade balance data revisions by the Department of Commerce.

Taken alone, the immediate reactions of individual markets to news of a larger-than-expected trade deficit seem plausible and consistent with conventional wisdom about perceived economic relationships. Taken together or viewed over even a marginally longer period of time, both the initial reactions and the duration of the reactions in various markets are more puzzling. For instance, if one argues that all of the relevant bond market reaction occurred on Monday after the rumor circulated about the larger-than-expected size of the trade deficit, why was the increase in the price of gold on Tuesday after the trade balance report announcement three times what it was on Monday? Was there another factor that impacted just the gold market? If so, what was it?

The Trade Deficit Sparks a Bond Market Rally

At 8:30 A.M. on Friday, August 29, 1986, the Department of Commerce released the merchandise trade balance report for July 1986. The department reported a record merchandise trade deficit of $18.02 billion for July 1986, a number that would have been even higher were it not for $930 million of gold mined outside the U.S. but re-exported to Japan for minting commemorative coins.[6] In addition, the merchandise trade balance for June 1986 was revised down from $14.17 billion to $13.25 billion. At the time, the bond market was arguably in a bullish phase. Once again, the market's response to the report was swift and the focus was on the preliminary headline numbers. The dollar fell against its principal counterparts.[7] However, unlike the market reaction to the February 1987 merchandise trade report on April 14, 1987, the prices of U.S. Treasury securities rose sharply as depicted in Figure 7.2. Also, unlike the market reaction to the February 1987 merchandise trade balance report, this time the stock and gold markets were virtually *unaffected*. The Dow Jones Industrial Average closed down less than 2 points for the day to 1898.34. Spot gold was up $1.25 per troy ounce to $387.75.[8] The dollar fell slightly against the yen and Deutsche mark, whereas September 10-year Treasury note futures and 30-year Treasury bond futures rose about 1 point and over 1/2 point, respectively.[9]

The following excerpt of an article by H.J. Maidenhead that was published in *The New York Times* on August 30 illustrates both the perceived relationship between the trade deficit and interest rates and likely future Federal Reserve monetary policy actions.

> Bond investors…aggressively snapped up short- and long-term Treasury debt after the Government reported a record trade deficit for July…The deficit for July…also heightened expectations of another cut in the discount rate by the Federal Reserve…A soaring trade deficit is a bearish economic indicator.[10]

This was likely the operative trading thesis market participants had in August 1986.

As with the April 14, 1987 release of the February 1987 merchandise trade balance report, rumors hit the market the day before that the trade deficit would be a larger-than-expected $16 billion. A spate of earlier rumors on various economic reports—some of which proved prescient—lent credence to the rumor (and prompted a later investigation as to whether there was a leak at the Commerce Department).[11] The rumor precipitated a rally in Treasury bonds and other fixed-income securities on Thursday, August 28.[12] It also prompted a rally in gold with the spot price of gold closing up $5.25 per ounce on Thursday.[13] Although another report, the Index of Leading Economic Indicators, was released the same day, contemporary news accounts attributed the price action solely to the trade balance report.

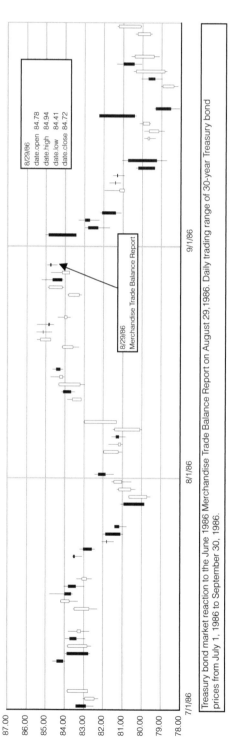

Treasury bond market reaction to the June 1986 Merchandise Trade Balance Report on August 29,1986. Daily trading range of 30-year Treasury bond prices from July 1, 1986 to September 30, 1986.

FIGURE 7.2   The trade deficit sparks a bond market rally.

The apparent operative trading thesis for the bond market during August 1986 was that the larger-than-expected trade deficit signaled the onset of a recession. And recessions are associated with lower interest rates, presumably because of a reduction in the demand for credit holding the supply of credit constant. Therefore, bond prices rose in reaction to the report.

It is interesting to compare the market reactions to the larger-than-expected February 1987 and July 1987 merchandise trade balance reports and the rumors of such that preceded their release. The dollar fell against its principal counterparts in both cases. Although the price of gold rose in both cases, gold increased more on the rumor than on the actual report in August 1986, whereas the reverse was true in April 1987. Stocks fell in reaction to the release of the February 1987 merchandise trade balance report and to the rumor that preceded it. However, stocks largely ignored the news in the July 1986 merchandise trade balance report and the rumor that preceded it.

Perhaps the most bizarre reaction to the two reports was in the bond market. As the preceding excerpts make clear, the reaction of the bond market to the two reports was 180 degrees different. Bonds rallied to both an actual and rumored larger-than-expected trade deficit in August 1986, whereas bonds broke in response to an actual and rumored larger-than-expected trade deficit in April 1987. Moreover, the trade deficit report appeared to impact shorter-term securities more during August 1986 than during April 1987. Why the dramatically different bond market reactions to similar trade reports in the space of less than nine months? Did received economic theory change during the interim?

It would be wrong to focus exclusively on the perceived economic relationship between changes in the trade deficit and interest rates without considering the potential influence of the trade deficit on Federal Reserve monetary policy. An ancillary trading thesis in August 1986, at least, was that the Federal Reserve would lower short-term interest rates. It would do so by reducing the *discount rate*—the rate charged member banks for loans from the Federal Reserve System—in the near future. Put differently, the market reaction to economic announcements is, in part, a reaction to the presumed future actions of an important market participant, the Federal Reserve. Anticipating future monetary policy actions by the Federal Reserve or any central bank is important to traders. Simply put, if the trade balance report is important to Federal Reserve monetary policymakers, it is important to traders.[14] That said, it is not clear that this explanation accounts for the differential reactions of the bond market to similar forecast errors in the merchandise trade balance report between 1986 and 1987. However, it is clear that perceived economic relationships among market participants can change radically over time.

Scheduled Economic Reports

There is a decided preference among many market participants to make trades based on fundamental information and perceived economic information. The large changes in financial and commodity market prices and increased volatility that often follow economic reports and announcements seemingly validate fundamentally based trading strategies. The periodic release of economic reports offers market participants an opportunity to trade off of perceived fundamental economic information. Given that the release of most periodic economic reports is scheduled far in advance, traders have the opportunity to assess the outlook, form expectations, compare their expectations with consensus expectations, determine the appropriate size of their positions, and time their entry and exit so as to bet largely on the outcome of the economic report or announcement.

At first glance, the market's rapid reaction to news contained in the release of economic reports corresponds with what modern financial economic theory would predict[15]—that is, that new information is quickly impounded into financial market prices in an informationally efficient capital market. The academic literature also suggests that much of the volatility in the bond market occurs around economic release days and persists for some time after the release.[16] Upon closer inspection, however, anomalies start to appear that question the presumption of market efficiency and whether the news in economic reports really represents relevant fundamental economic information.

As the two opening examples in this chapter demonstrate, the market's interpretation of the same forecast errors is not constant over time—that is, the "market's" interpretation of the implication of a larger-than-expected forecast error in the merchandise trade balance report changed 180 degrees in the space of less than a year even though received economic theory did not change between August 1986 and April 1987. Interestingly, the present conventional wisdom about the impact of a large forecast error on interest rates remains the view espoused in 1987.

Sometimes, the market appears to overreact to the news contained in economic reports. Other times, markets differ in their interpretation of the news. For instance, gold rose and bonds fell on fears of higher inflation following the release of the trade balance report. Yet, bonds later rallied while gold remained down even though there was no apparent news that sparked the rally. Did the February 1987 merchandise trade balance report contain significant unanticipated negative news about future inflation? If so, which market responded correctly to the news contained in the trade balance report—the bond market or the gold market? It would be misleading to leave the impression that the apparent overreactions of the bond market in the opening examples of this chapter are typical of the market's reaction to most economic reports.

Sometimes, financial markets selectively respond to the news in economic reports, seemingly ignoring the news in some cases or responding opposite to the usual reaction. For instance, as noted earlier, the stock market largely ignored the news in the merchandise trade balance report in 1986 but reacted negatively in 1987. Simply put, the market's reaction to essentially the same piece of information may change over time.

Common sense and financial theory alike would suggest that the larger the forecast error the greater the market's reaction to any news contained in economic reports. Yet, this relationship appears to break down for large forecast errors, even when the forecast errors are adjusted for differences in dispersion across individual forecasts— Simply stated, large forecast errors are less surprising when there are wide differences in opinion among individuals than when there is near-unanimity of opinion among market participants. Often, a multiple standard deviation forecast error—which would be considered extraordinarily unlikely to occur under a normal distribution—does not result in an appreciably larger market response than a much smaller (and more likely to occur) forecast error. The market's response to a given sized forecast error need not be constant.

For example, the *magnitude* of the impact of a three standard deviation forecast error on market prices and volatility may differ over time. The *direction* of the impact does not have to differ over time as it did in the bond market's reaction to the trade balance report between 1986 and 1987. Rather, the direction of the market's reaction may be the same, whereas the magnitude of the market's reaction differs sharply over time. The difference in the magnitude of the market's reaction to economic reports underscores the importance of knowing what the underlying market conditions are.

As discussed earlier, financial markets presumably respond to the forecast error in economic reports—that is, the difference between the actual outcome and the consensus forecast. Because economic reports are scheduled, one measure of consensus forecasts is often available from surveys. Again, the relevant consensus forecast is not what economists think but what is in the market—that is, the collective wisdom of market participants. There is also a common presumption that consensus forecasts—however measured—are rational.

However, that may not be the case because the individual forecasts upon which consensus forecasts are based may not be rational.[17]

Another basic question that arises is which data should the market react to? This seems simple until one understands that most economic reports contain a plethora of data. Notwithstanding the large amount of data to which the market could react, it appears that the market reacts largely to the headline number or numbers—for which consensus expectations have been formed—even though there may be other seemingly relevant news in the report. However, even if one focuses only on the relevant headline numbers in economic reports, the question still arises. What role do revisions to the headline numbers in past economic reports play in impacting market prices? Presumably, fundamentally oriented traders are more interested in accurate data than less accurate data. Yet, the reverse appears to be true. Confronted with a choice of reacting to less precise preliminary data or more precise revised data, participants in financial markets almost always opt for reacting to the less precise preliminary data. This highlights another problem that arises with trading off of fundamental information—namely, the undue weight put on preliminary data. One consequence of this over-emphasis on preliminary data is increased volatility in financial markets. It also means that traders who are able to forecast economic variables more accurately (i.e., closer to the ultimate revised value) may be at a disadvantage to traders who have less accurate forecasting models but produce forecasts closer to the preliminary values of the economic variable in question.

Not all macroeconomic reports are created equal. Certain economic reports such as the Employment Report and the Producers Price Index Report exert more influence on changes in market prices and volatility than other reports do. Interestingly, what market participants consider the most important economic reports changes over time. For instance, during the late 1970s and early 1980s, the weekly money supply report was considered the dominant report for bond market participants. Its significance increased after the Federal Reserve switched to targeting monetary aggregates on Saturday, October 6, 1979. The capability of this report to roil fixed-income markets was substantial. Consider, for instance, the reaction of the Treasury bond market to the release of the money supply report by the Federal Reserve on Friday, April 10, 1981. The bond market's reaction to the news is captured in this excerpt from an April 13, 1981 article in *The Wall Street Journal*.

> The money supply news sent the bond markets into a tailspin late Friday. Prices of some long-term debt securities plunged more than two points or $20 for each $1000 face amount. Short-term interest rates jumped as much as 3/4 percentage point. On the long-term front the Treasury's closely followed 12 3/4 pc bonds due 2010 tumbled to a record low of 95 7/8. The issue closed down at 95 3/4 down from 97 30/32 Thursday.[18]

For a while, the release of the weekly money supply report exerted a tremendous impact on the prices of fixed income securities. Sometimes, long-term bond prices would move as much as three points in reaction to an announcement—a huge move in the bond market. Then suddenly, the weekly money supply report lost its capability to impact financial markets. Journalists are not accustomed to writing stories about nonreactions to apparent fundamental economic news, but sometimes they do.[19]

Weekly money supply reports were once highly important for financial market participants. Today, they are virtually ignored. If money supply reports were once important to bond market participants, why aren't they still important? If money supply reports are not important for bond market participants, why were they once important?

One potential explanation is that the bond market was simply reacting to changes in what it believed the Fed was targeting—that is,

bond market participants were trying to anticipate likely Fed monetary policy actions from the forecast errors of the money supply
report because the Fed was targeting monetary aggregates. Simply
stated, if the Fed targets monetary aggregates, bond market participants should watch monetary aggregates. If the Fed targets something else, bond market participants should watch that. Yet, this
argument fails to persuade for several reasons.

First, why should fixed-income market participants use highly
volatile (and hence likely uninformative) weekly money supply figures to forecast monetary policy actions? Indeed, the Fed considered
changing the frequency of the money supply reports precisely
because the volatile nature of the weekly reported data made such
data a poor indicator of monetary trends.[20] Second, why should highly
erratic *weekly* money supply reports affect *long-term* bond prices?
For long-term bond prices to be affected by the money supply forecast error, the change in the (rate of growth of the) money supply
should be permanent. Again, are short-term fluctuations in the
money supply really indicative of longer-term trends?[21] Third, the
report stopped moving financial markets long before the Federal
Reserve stopped targeting monetary aggregates with the appointment of Alan Greenspan as Fed chairman on August 11, 1987. Put
differently, if market participants watch the weekly money supply
reports simply because the Fed pursues a policy of targeting monetary aggregates, market participants should continue to react to the
report as long as the Fed continues to target monetary aggregates.

What Is Fundamental Economic Information?

Two questions naturally arise. First, do economic reports contain
relevant fundamental economic information of use to traders? Second, does the market process this information correctly and quickly?

But an even more basic question must be answered first—namely, what is fundamental economic information?

At first glance, such a simple question seems irrelevant— everyone knows what fundamental economic information is. Upon further reflection, it is apparent that fundamental economic information is theory dependent—that is, it depends on what financial or economic theory suggests should be the relationship. Do traders and other market participants get these relationships right? Do they understand the nuances of economic theories? Widely believed economic relationships by market participants may be at variance with received economic theory. And, there are often competing explanations or theories of economic relationships. Moreover, the explanatory power of many received economic theories may be limited.[22]

Consider, for example, the relationship between an unexpected change in the rate of growth of the money supply and changes in interest rates.

1. Is there an impact?
2. If so, does it cause interest rates to increase or decrease?
3. Does the immediate impact differ from the longer-term impact?[23]
4. Is the impact on the real rate or on inflation expectations?
5. What is the mechanism of transmission?
6. How long does it last?

What does economic theory suggest is the relationship? The answer depends on which theory one considers correct. Different economic theories posit different relationships. Unfortunately, there are a number of macroeconomic and monetary theories to choose among. Restricting the set of potential choices to those espoused by economists who have won the Nobel Prize in economics gives the following answers.[24]

1. Professor Paul Samuelson, a *Neo-Keynesian* economist who was awarded the Nobel Prize in 1970, would likely argue that an unexpected increase in the rate of growth of the money supply would cause the interest rate to fall initially as the supply of credit increased in the banking system.

2. Professor Milton Friedman, a *monetarist* who was awarded the Nobel Prize in 1976 and believes that individuals form expectations adaptively, would likely argue that the initial decline in interest rates following an unexpected increase in the rate of growth of the money supply would be followed by rising interest rates as individuals slowly became aware of the increased money supply and formed expectations of higher future inflation.

3. Professor Robert Lucas, another *monetarist* who was awarded the Nobel Prize in 1995 and believes individuals form expectations rationally, would likely argue that the initial effect of an unexpected increase in the rate of growth of the money supply on interest rates is a rise in interest rates.

The preceding economic theories have radically different views about the impact of an unexpected increase in the rate of growth of the money supply on interest rates. Which theory, if any, is correct? Do most market participants understand the differences among these theories? Most likely, they do not. The point is that economic relationships are theory dependent and different economic theories offer competing views of economic relationships. To complicate matters even more, other economic theories exist. The preceding three interpretations of the impact of an unexpected change in the money supply are from those economists who believe that the central bank controls the money supply.[25]

Market participants sometimes misunderstand the relevant economic variable in economic theories. For instance, market participants commonly confuse changes in relative prices (the price of one commodity increases relative to another one) with changes in absolute prices (all commodity prices change). Thus, an increase in the price of oil or an increase in grain prices is said to be inflationary when it may simply represent a change in relative prices. Similarly, changes in the level, or *stock,* of an economic variable like the money supply are confused with changes in the *flow,* or rate of growth, of the economic variable. To the extent that changes in the money supply matter, it is the change in the rate of growth of money that matters. This makes the former attention devoted by market participants to the weekly money supply announcements puzzling. Even more puzzling was the substantial response of longer maturity bonds to these periodic announcements, because it implied that market participants assumed the unexpected component of the change in the money supply was permanent.

Market participants sometimes perceive economic relationships that may not be there. An example in this regard is the commonly expressed concern about the relationship between budget deficits and interest rates. Although concern over the potential of large Federal budget deficits on interest rates was at one point shared by all three major candidates in the 1992 U.S. presidential election—and is widely shared by many market participants—there is little evidence to support this notion in the academic literature.

A lot of widely believed relationships are what economists would call *partial equilibrium relationships*—that is, relationships that explain only a part of the effects associated with a price change. To consider but one example, it is widely believed that currency devaluation—for example, in the dollar—improves the trade balance by making foreign currency denominated imports more expensive to U.S. consumers and U.S. dollar-denominated exports less expensive to foreigners. The essential flaw in this argument is that it assumes that prices are set locally rather than globally. For instance, suppose the exchange rate between the euro and the dollar is one to one—that is, $1 sells for €1. Suppose further that gold sells for $400 per troy ounce and €400 in eurozone countries before a sudden 50% devaluation of the U.S. dollar against the euro, so €1 will buy $2. Conventional wisdom would suggest that the U.S. would suddenly export more goods (including gold) because eurozone residents could buy them more cheaply in the States. In the first instant after devaluation, a U.S. gold mining firm faces the choice between selling gold for $400 in the States or the equivalent of $800 (€400) in the eurozone. Would U.S. gold mining firms really sell gold for half of what it would fetch in Europe? No. What would happen to the dollar price of gold? The dollar price of gold would simply double. The point is that rather than stimulating exports and economic output, a devaluation of the dollar against the euro stimulates higher dollar prices on tradable goods. Again, from a trading perspective, it is not important whether other market participants get the theory right but how their actions would likely affect prices.

Noise and Information

There is a presumption that the large price moves that often follow the release of key economic reports is evidence that financial markets must be reacting to the arrival of new fundamental economic information. Furthermore, the rapid reaction of financial markets is often taken as evidence of market efficiency. However, markets need not be efficient, and the news in economic reports need not represent relevant fundamental information for financial market participants.

If financial and commodity markets are not reacting to the arrival of new fundamental economic information when economic reports are released, what are they reacting to? Although financial markets react to news, news need not contain relevant fundamental economic information. It may also contain *noise*—nonfundamental information that impacts market prices. The late Fisher Black, co-developer of the Black-Scholes option pricing model, argued that noise trading is a necessary condition for active, liquid financial markets and that noise traders create the mispricings that value investors exploit.

The quintessential example of noise is the addition of a new stock in an index like the S&P's 500 stock index.[26] The price of the stock that is added to the index typically rises after the announcement as index funds and other portfolio managers rush to include the stock (or increase its weight) in their portfolios. Yet, fundamentally, nothing has changed about the underlying company. It still has the same expected future cash flows. Absent a reduction in the discount rate, the price of the stock should remain unchanged following its inclusion in the portfolio. Another result of noise trading is that it causes excessive volatility in financial market prices in the short-run.

It is possible that much of the puzzling behavior in the preceding examples of the market's reaction to economic reports might be explained by noise. Simply stated, much apparent macroeconomic news is noise rather than fundamental information.

Trade Selection and Trade Horizon

At any point in time, traders face a myriad of choices as to where to place their trades and how large to make their bets. Simply stated, some markets may not be as sensitive to the news contained in an economic report as other markets. For those traders with a view on the likely forecast error and market reaction, the size of the trading position should vary directly with their confidence in their forecasts.

For instance, at 8:30 A.M. on Friday, September 5, 2003, the Department of Labor released the Employment Report for August 2003. The attention of traders and other market participants was initially focused on two headline numbers: the unemployment rate and the change in nonfarm payrolls, a measure of new jobs created during the month. Attention focused on the Employment Report because of the widespread belief among many market participants that the strength of the economy (as reflected in the employment situation) and interest rates are inversely related and that the Employment

Report may be a harbinger of Federal Reserve monetary policy actions. Some market participants squared or hedged trading positions going into the employment report; others took out new or adjusted existing positions in advance of the report's release. Fixed income traders were especially interested in the report but the report influenced the currency, equity, and commodity markets as well.

The Department of Labor reported that the unemployment rate in August 2003 fell to 6.1% and the number of new jobs created during August (i.e., nonfarm payrolls) fell by 93,000. The department also reported that the number of new jobs created in July 2003 was revised to down 49,000. The average work week remained unchanged, whereas average hourly earnings were up 2 cents. Jobs were lost in the manufacturing sector for the 37th consecutive month. The consensus forecasts for the unemployment rate and the change in nonfarm payrolls was 6.2% and +12,000, respectively.[27] If the consensus forecasts were the actual forecasts in the market, the forecast errors were -.1% for the unemployment rate and 105,000 for nonfarm payrolls.

The operative trading thesis going into the report was that a weakening economy as evidenced by a higher unemployment rate or fewer jobs created would boost bond prices as people anticipated reduction in the demand for credit and lower interest rates. In this instance, traders are faced with conflicting information—the unemployment rate is down indicating a strengthening economy, whereas the number of new jobs created is down indicating a weakening economy. Traders must decide how the market will react if there is conflicting information about the state of the economy in the report. And if so, which data should the trader focus on? At one time, more attention was paid to the unemployment rate; at present, more attention is paid to the nonfarm payrolls number.

As should be readily apparent by now, it is not important to understand what economic theory suggests about how the market should react to the forecast errors in the Employment Report.

Rather, it is important to understand how the market, as a whole, is likely to respond to it and which market will be most sensitive to the report. In addition, the trader who wants to bet primarily on the report's outcome must determine when the trade should be put on and taken off.

Consider the reaction of the December 2003 10-year Treasury note futures contract traded on the Chicago Board of Trade. At the time of the report, the December 2003 T-note futures contract was the most actively traded contract month. The futures price was at 109-20 at 8:20 A.M. on Friday, September 5, 10 minutes before the report was released. The market stood at 109-20+ a moment before the news came out at 8:30 A.M. By the end of the first minute of trading after the announcement, the market was at 110-08+. The minimum price move, or tick, is 1/64 and has a dollar value of $15.625. Thus, the 40-tick move by 8:31:00 A.M. translates into a $625 profit or loss per futures contract. One minute later, the market stood two ticks higher at 110-09+. Five minutes after the announcement, the market traded at 110-08+. The market remained around the 110 level for almost the next half hour and then moved slightly higher. The market started to climb higher around 12:36 P.M. The high of the day (110-31+) was reached toward the end of the regular trading session. The market closed at 110-30+ or 48.5/32 (97 ticks) above the previous close of 109-14.

A long position in the 10-year Treasury note futures contract entered at Thursday's closing price of 109-14 and exited at Friday's close of 110-30+ would have made $1515.62 per contract, ignoring transaction costs—that is, $15.625 x 97 or 48.5 x $31.25. This position would have entailed the risk of holding the position overnight and long after the report came out. In contrast, a long position placed at the opening of pit trading (i.e., at 8:20 A.M.) on Friday at 109.20 and exited after the first two minutes of trading at 110.09+ would have made $671.87 per contract (i.e., $31.25 x 21.5) and exposed the trader to risk for 12 minutes.

This ignores transaction costs and assumes that the trader would have entered or exited at the indicated prices. In reality, a trader would face the prospect of *slippage*, *execution delay*, and brokerage commissions, all of which would reduce the potential profit from such a trading position.

The question naturally arises as to whether there were better trades in the fixed income or currency markets that might have been made. The answer depends on the desired *trade horizon*—how long a trading position is kept open. Table 7.1 compares the potential trading profits and losses from buying a single futures contract in the 2-year Treasury note futures, 10-year Treasury note futures, 30-year Treasury bond futures contract, EuroFX futures, or Japanese yen futures contract in advance of the employment report and holding it for as short as 12 minutes or as long as one day. The 2-year Treasury note and 30-year Treasury bond futures contracts are traded on the Chicago Board of Trade, whereas the EuroFX (i.e., the euro currency futures contract) and Japanese yen futures contracts are traded on the Chicago Mercantile Exchange. The sensitivity of interest rate futures contracts to changes in interest rates depends upon the implied duration—a measure of interest rate risk. The 2-year Treasury note futures contract has the smallest duration, whereas the 30-year Treasury bond futures contract has the greatest duration. The 2-year Treasury note is considered more sensitive to Fed monetary policy actions. It trades in quarter points on $200,000 of notional principal.[28] The tick value is $15.625.

The potential profits from the long 10-year Treasury note futures position and 30-year Treasury bond futures position are similar. Not surprisingly, given its lower sensitivity to changes in interest rates (or implied duration), the 2-year Treasury note futures contract produced smaller trading profits than either the 10-year Treasury note or 30-year Treasury bond futures contracts. A quick examination of Table 7.1 reveals that the largest profits occurred with trades held for an entire day. Although it worked out in this instance for traders with long positions, it is a fundamentally flawed strategy, however, because it entails assuming unnecessary risks. It is not clear whether the large end-of-day price moves can be attributed to the employment report. It is also possible that, the subsequent price changes were due to other news.

TABLE 7.1   Market Reaction of Selected Futures Contracts to the August 2003 Employment Report on September 5, 2003

	2-Year T-Note Dec. 2003 Futures	10-Year T-Note Dec. 2003 Futures	30-Year T-Bond Dec. 2003 Futures	Euro Sept. 2003 Futures	Yen Sept. 2003 Futures
Thursday Close	106-21	109-14	104-27	109.22	.8569
Friday 8:20	106-22+	109-20	105-04	109.23	.8563
Friday 8:29:59	106-22+	109-20+	105-05	109.23	.8565
Friday 8:31:00	106-26	110-08+	105-21	109.55	.8568
Friday 8:32:00	106-27+	110-09+	105-24	109.70	.8573
Friday 8:35:00	—	110-08+	—	109.80	.8574
Friday Close	107-032	110-30+	106-22	111.03	.8562
Max. Potential Profit 12-minute Trade Horizon 8:20:00-8:32:00	$312.50	$671.87	$625	$587.50	$125
Max. Potential Profit 1-Day Trade Horizon Close to Close	$890.62	$1515.62	$1,843.75	$2,262.50	–$87.50

The 2-year Treasury note futures contract has a notional principal of $200,000, whereas the 10-year and 30-year Treasury bond futures contracts have a notional principal of $100,000. The Japanese yen futures contract has a notional principal of ¥12,500,000 and the EuroFX futures contract has a notional principal of €125,000. All of the contracts are traded on a quarterly expiration cycle with futures contracts expiring in March, June, September, and December.

The trading lesson is simple. If the bet is on the outcome of an economic report, the trade horizon should be relatively short to avoid exposing the trading position to unnecessary risks. Another lesson that emerges is that the highest trading profit came from holding a currency futures position rather than an interest rate futures position.

It is not apparent that the differential reaction between the currency and interest rate futures markets could have been ascertained in advance. Moreover, an individual who bet on yen futures rather than the EuroFX futures would have lost money. Therefore, it is also important to pick the currency that will react as anticipated. Table 7.1 indicates the importance of placing the bet on the right security but also illustrates the difficulty in doing so.

Trading Lessons

The release of economic reports often acts as a trading catalyst in financial markets by precipitating substantial changes in market prices and volatility. Although scheduled economic reports offer market participants a seeming opportunity to trade off of fundamental economic information, the opportunity may be more apparent than real. Much of the news in the reports may represent *noise* rather than *fundamental economic information*.

Fundamental economic information is theory dependent—that is, theory determines what fundamental economic information is. Sometimes, economic theory is silent on the impact of forecast errors from economic reports on financial market prices. In other cases, the existence of plausible competing economic theories means that even the *direction* of the impact of forecast errors from some economic reports may be controversial.

Many commonly held beliefs about economic relationships by market participants may differ substantially from received economic theory. For instance, market participants often confuse changes in relative prices (e.g., an increase in the price of oil) with changes in absolute prices (i.e., inflation). Moreover, consensus beliefs about the meaning of forecast errors from economic reports can change suddenly. Witness the 180-degree difference in interpretation of a larger-than-expected trade deficit report on bond prices between

August 1986 and April 1987. In other cases, formerly closely watched economic reports can suddenly lose their capability to move markets—as happened with money supply announcements during the 1980s.

Sometimes, forecast errors from an economic report will occasionally act as a trading catalyst that pushes the market in the direction opposite of what was expected. Sometimes, the market won't react at all to the forecast error in an economic report that usually moves markets. More frequently, the duration of the impact of a forecast error on financial markets may be short-lived. This need not be indicative of an efficient market. Indeed, it often suggests the reverse, especially on days when the initial impact of the economic report is reversed soon after the report is released.

Even when the market interprets the news in forecast errors in the same way over time, the magnitude of the response to the forecast error may not always vary directly with the size of the forecast error. Simply put, an extremely large (i.e., rare) forecast error may not have as much impact as a far smaller (and more frequent) forecast error. Another anomaly is the market's differential reaction to preliminary and revised data. Presumably, more accurate data is preferred to less accurate data, yet the market appears to react more to preliminary data than to more accurate revised data. There is a presumption that the consensus forecast is rational. Yet, the consensus forecast of the news in economic reports may not be rational if market participants fail to take into account seasonal influences, which they frequently fail to do. All of the preceding reasons suggest that the news in many economic reports is noise rather than fundamental economic information. It also suggests that a good economic forecaster may not have an edge when trading with other market participants.

From a trading perspective, whether market participants understand the nuances of economic theory or mistake noise for fundamental economic information is not important. *The objective of trading is to make money.* It is not to educate other market participants on their mistaken beliefs or to correctly predict the outcome of economic reports. Correctly anticipating the forecast error is only part of it. Often, what is more important is correctly anticipating how other market participants and the market as a whole are likely to react to the forecast error or perceived information in an economic report. One important market participant is the Federal Reserve. In many cases, traders use the forecast errors from economic reports as an indicator of likely future Federal Reserve monetary policy actions. How the Federal Reserve responds to the news in the reports may drive perceived economic relationships among market participants as well as the responses of the market to economic reports.

This means that it is important for traders to not only have a view on the likely sign and size of the forecast error from an economic report but also on the market's reaction to the forecast error. Traders must also be able to anticipate how the market will interpret the forecast error. Traders must anticipate the sign, magnitude, and duration of the market's response to a forecast error. As a result, there is another risk that must be considered when trading off of economic reports—the risk of how the market will react to the forecast error. Financial markets not only respond to the news in key economic reports; they frequently but not always overreact to it. This creates an opportunity for traders to bet on economic reports after they have been released.

There is a more general trading lesson that arises from trading off of perceived fundamentals: that the correlation between economic variables may be transitory. That is, the relationship among assets need not be the same over time. Indeed, correlation among financial and commodity markets is often transitory due to misguided notions of economic relationships such as the BOB (beans over bonds) spread discussed in Chapter 5, "Weather and Natural Disasters." As will be seen in a later chapter, correlation can be unstable, especially during market crises, and can cause diversified bets to become undiversified.

Trading off of the apparent news in economic reports is tantamount to gambling if the trader doesn't have a view on the likely forecast error and the market's likely reaction to it. However, even if one chooses not to trade on the outcomes of economic reports, the market's reaction to the reports may provide valuable information in placing other trades. How a market responds or reacts to news may be informative in itself. For instance, a muted reaction to seemingly bearish news may signal a future rally, whereas a muted reaction to seemingly bullish news may signal a future break.

It is worth repeating that the principal objective of trading is to make money. Whether economic reports contain fundamental economic information or noise is largely irrelevant. Economic reports and announcements are likely to continue to serve as significant trading catalysts in financial and commodity markets. The large price changes and increased volatility that they induce create attractive trading opportunities as well as substantial risks for traders.

References

Balduzzi, P., E.J. Elton, and T.C. Green. "Economic News and the Yield Curve: Evidence from the U.S. Treasury Market." *Journal of Financial and Quantitative Analysis*, Volume 36, 2001, pp. 523-543.

Berry, John M. "Trade Deficit Data Revised Downward." *The Washington Post,* April 17, 1987.

Black, F. "Noise." *Journal of Finance*, Volume 41 (3), July 1986, pp. 528-550.

Chicago Sun-Times. "Stocks, Dollar Take Tumble as Gold Leaps." April 15, 1987.

Clark, T.D., D.H. Joines, and G.M. Philips. "Social Security Payments, Money Supply Announcements, and Interest Rates." *Journal of Monetary Economics*, Volume 22, pp. 257-78, 1988.

Cornell, Bradford. "Money Supply Announcements and Interest Rates: Another View." *Journal of Business*, Volume 56, (1), 1983, pp. 1-23.

Dow Jones News Service. "US Trade Deficit Stood at Record $18.04 Billion in July." August 29, 1986.

Dow Jones News Service. "Fed Reconsidering System of Weekly Money Supply Reports." April 2, 1981.

Ederington, L.H., and J.H. Lee. "How Markets Process Information News Releases and Volatility." *Journal of Finance*, Volume 48, 1993, pp. 1161-1191.

Ederington, L.H., and J.H. Lee. "The Short-Run Dynamics of the Price Adjustment to New Information." *Journal of Financial and Quantitative Analysis*, Volume 30, pp. 117-134.

Fleming, M.J., and E.M. Remolona. "What Moves the Bond Market?" *Economic Policy Review*, Federal Reserve Bank of New York, 1997, Volume 3, Issue 4, pp. 31-50.

Herman, Tom, and Edward P. Foldessy. "Bond Prices Rise Slightly Amid Rumors About Forthcoming Reports on Economy." *The Wall Street Journal*, August 29, 1986.

Herman, Tom. "Interest Rates Surge, Stock Prices Fall 51.71 Points; Rumor About Trade-Deficit Report Batters Market—Some Treasury Bond Quotes Plunge Over 1 3/4 Points; Fed Funds Rate Rises." *The Wall Street Journal*, April 13, 1987.

Herman, Tom, and Alexandra Peers. "Bond Prices End Lower in Erratic Day; Fears About the Dollar, Inflation Persist." *The Wall Street Journal*, April 15, 1987.

The Journal Record. "Dollar Mixed, Gold Jumps by More Than $5 an Ounce." August 29, 1986.

Kadlec, Daniel. "Dollar, Trade Deficit Fears Clobber." *USA Today*, April 14, 1987.

Lyons, Richard K., and Martin D. Evans. "Order Flow and Exchange Rate Dynamics." University of California, Berkeley, January 19, 2001.

Mackenzie, Michael. "Treasurys Close Higher Amid Continued Deflation Talk." *Dow Jones Business News*, September 4, 2003.

Maidenhead, H.J., Credit Markets. "Treasury Bill Rates Plunge." *The New York Times*, August 30, 1986.

Morris, Bailey. "Dollar Suffers as US Deficit Soars to Record 18 Billion Dollars." *The Times*, August 30, 1986.

The New York Times. "Did Wall Street Receive a Tip?" August 31, 1986.

Newton, Maxwell. "US Notebook: Reality Behind Wealth: Market Effects of the US Trade Deficit." *The Times*, September 1, 1986.

Quint, Michael, Credit Markets. "Rate-Cut Hopes Are Growing." *The New York Times*, September 2, 1986.

The San Francisco Chronicle. "Trade Report Sends Dollar into Skid." August 30, 1986.

The Wall Street Journal. "Bond Marts: Surge in Money Supply Growth." April 13, 1981.

The Washington Post. "Rumors of Leak Discounted." August 30, 1986.

Webb, Robert. *Macroeconomic Information and Financial Trading*. Oxford: Blackwell Publishers, 1994.

Endnotes

[1] The reported number includes the cost of transporting and insuring the goods acquired. At the time, the Department of Commerce was required by law to separately report the merchandise trade balance including transportation and insurance and 48 hours later release the trade deficit without taking into account transportation and insurance costs. On April 16, 1987, the Department of Commerce reported that the merchandise trade deficit for February 1987 was $13.65 billion or $1.4 billion less when the cost of insuring and transporting foreign

goods to the United States was excluded. For more information on the monthly revision, see "Trade Deficit Data Revised Downward," by John M. Berry, in the April 17, 1987 issue of *The Washington Post*.

[2] Tom Herman and Alexandra Peers. "Bond Prices End Lower in Erratic Day; Fears About the Dollar, Inflation Persist." *The Wall Street Journal*, April 15, 1987.

[3] *Chicago Sun-Times*. "Stocks, Dollar Take Tumble as Gold Leaps." April 15, 1987.

[4] Tom Herman. *The Wall Street Journal*. "Interest Rates Surge, Stock Prices Fall 51.71 Points; Rumor About Trade-Deficit Report Batters Market—Some Treasury Bond Quotes Plunge Over 1 3/4 Points; Fed Funds Rate Rises." April 13, 1987. The article notes that the 1 3/4 point decline in the long bond brought the cumulative decline in the preceding two weeks to 8 3/4 points for an increase in yield of 87 basis points for the long bond.

[5] Daniel Kadlec. "Dollar, Trade Deficit Fears Clobber." *USA Today*, April 14, 1987.

[6] Dow Jones News Service. "US Trade Deficit Stood at Record $18.04 Billion in July." August 29, 1986.

[7] Bailey Morris. "Dollar Suffers as US Deficit Soars to Record 18 Billion Dollars." *The Times*, August 30, 1986.

[8] *The San Francisco Chronicle*. "Trade Report Sends Dollar into Skid." August 30, 1986.

[9] Maxwell Newton. "US Notebook: Reality Behind Wealth: Market Effects of the US Trade Deficit." *The Times*, September 1, 1986.

[10] H.J. Maidenhead, Credit Markets. "Treasury Bill Rates Plunge." *The New York Times*, August 30, 1986. The article gives a sense of the magnitude of the impact by noting that the yield on three-month Treasury bills fell by 12 basis points by the close of trading, whereas the prices of the on-the-run 10-year Treasury note and 30-year Treasury bond rose by 25/32 and 19/32, respectively.

[11] The Department of Commerce did not find evidence of a leak and argued that the rumor hit the street on Tuesday morning before the trade deficit number was even compiled. *The Washington Post*. "Rumors of Leak Discounted." August 30, 1986.

[12] Tom Herman and Edward P. Foldessy. "Bond Prices Rise Slightly Amid Rumors About Forthcoming Reports on Economy." *The Wall Street Journal*, August 29, 1986. The article reports:

> Bond prices wound up with small gains yesterday, after wide swings earlier in the day amid a flurry of rumors about economic reports to be issued today and next week. Some actively traded Treasury bonds rose about 1/4 point, or $2.50 for each $1,000 face amount. At one point... these issues were up about 3/4 point.

[13] *The Journal Record*. "Dollar Mixed, Gold Jumps by More Than $5 an Ounce." August 29, 1986.

[14] Michael Quint, Credit Markets. "Rate-Cut Hopes Are Growing." *The New York Times*, September 2, 1986. The article states:

> ...for the time being many traders are focusing on the trade deficit as a litmus test for the economy and Federal Reserve policy.
>
> "If you are trying to anticipate the Fed's next move, you want to look at the economy like they do," said one Treasury note trader who asked not to be identified, "and the July F.O.M.C. meeting showed they are focusing intently on the trade sector."
>
> "If they eased in July, the fact that the trade deficit is even larger now suggests they will ease again," the trader said.

[15] For example, see L.H. Ederington and J.H. Lee. "How Markets Process Information News Releases and Volatility." *Journal of Finance*, Volume 48, 1993, pp. 1161-1191; and L.H. Ederington and J.H. Lee, "The Short-Run Dynamics of the Price Adjustment to New Information," *Journal of Financial and Quantitative Analysis*, Volume 30, pp. 117-134. Also see Robert I. Webb, *Macroeconomic Information and Financial Trading*, Oxford: Blackwell Publishers, 1994.

[16] For example, see M.J. Fleming and E.M. Remolona. "What Moves the Bond Market?" *Economic Policy Review*, Federal Reserve Bank of New York, 1997, Volume 3, Issue 4, pp. 31-50; or P. Balduzzi, E.J. Elton, and T.C. Green, "Economic News and the Yield Curve: Evidence from the U.S. Treasury Market." *Journal of Financial and Quantitative Analysis*, Volume 36, 2001, pp. 523-543.

[17] T.D. Clark, D.H. Joines, and G.M. Philips. "Social Security Payments, Money Supply Announcements, and Interest Rates." *Journal of Monetary Economics*, Volume 22, pp. 257-78, 1988.

[18] *The Wall Street Journal*. "Bond Marts: Surge in Money Supply Growth." April 13, 1981. The article goes on to note that some observers thought that the bond market "overreacted" to the news because of large transfers from savings accounts into checking accounts.

[19] Tom Herman and Edward P. Foldessy. "Bond Prices Rise Slightly Amid Rumors about Forthcoming Reports on Economy." *The Wall Street Journal*, August 29, 1986. The article notes:

> The credit markets showed little reaction late yesterday to a Fed report showing another unexpectedly large increase in the nation's money supply.

[20] Dow Jones News Service. "Fed Reconsidering System of Weekly Money Supply Reports." April 2, 1981. The article quotes then Fed Chairman Paul Volcker as saying:

> There is nearly unanimous agreement by all observers that weekly money statistics are extremely erratic and therefore poor indicators of underlying trends.

The article also quoted Fed Chairman Volcker as saying:

> In general, there is considerable merit to the view that weekly data as such convey little information and that weekly seasonal adjustments are subject to substantial uncertainty.

[21] Bradford Cornell. "Money Supply Announcements and Interest Rates: Another View." *Journal of Business*, Volume 56, (1), 1983, pp. 1-23. In it, Cornell argues:

> [We are left] with no explanation of why the market participants react so violently to short-term announcements. It hardly seems rational for an investor to adjust his long-run inflation expectations significantly on the basis of 1 week's announcement.

[22] There is extensive evidence in the empirical economic literature that suggests that most conventional macroeconomic models of exchange rates are poor predictors of changes in exchange rates. Richard Lyons and Martin Evans argue that a model that includes order flow as an explanatory variable predicts changes in exchange rates better.

[23] The nominal interest rate can be decomposed into a real rate component—the rate of interest in a world without inflation—and an expected inflation component.

[24] There is no Nobel Prize in economics. Instead, there is the Bank of Sweden Prize in Economic Sciences in Memory of Alfred Nobel.

[25] Some economists contend that the central bank does not control the money supply, so its actions should have no immediate impact on interest rates. Fisher Black, co-developer of the Black-Scholes option pricing model and likely co-recipient of the Nobel Prize in 1997 had he lived, would likely have argued that the central bank does not control the money supply and consequently an unexpected increase in the rate of growth of the money supply would have no effect on a change in interest rates. The late James Tobin, who was awarded the Nobel Prize in 1981 and was a proponent of the *Keynesian New View*, would likely have argued that there is no effect as the money supply is too broad (given the existence of near-monies like savings accounts) to be controlled by the central bank. Professor Robert Mundell, an international economist who was awarded the Nobel Prize in 1999, would likely argue that the answer depends on the size and openness of the economy—with an absence of relationship in small open economies.

[26] F. Black. "Noise." *Journal of Finance*, Volume 41 (3), July 1986, pp. 528-550.

[27] Michael Mackenzie. "Treasurys Close Higher Amid Continued Deflation Talk." *Dow Jones Business News*, September 4, 2003.

[28] The sensitivity of the 2-year Treasury note futures contract to changes in interest rates would be even smaller were its sensitivity not increased by its larger notional principal.

8

SIZE MATTERS

"In telling this tale I attempt no compliment to my own sagacity. I claim not to have controlled events, but confess plainly that events have controlled me."

—Abraham Lincoln[1]

Blood in the Water 1: Sumitomo Is Long and Wrong

On Friday, May 17, 1996, London Metals Exchange (LME) copper futures prices fell almost 5% in volatile trading before recovering slightly.[2] The proximate cause of the decline was unknown and many market observers were puzzled by it. However, some media accounts at the time attributed the price decline to rumors that Sumitomo and other large copper market players were unwinding long positions and to rumors that Mr. Yasuo Hamanaka, Sumitomo's long-time head copper trader, was being reassigned to a nontrading position at Sumitomo.[3]

Supposedly, the rumors indicated that Sumitomo had decided to stop trading copper futures and would trade only physical copper in the future.[4] If true, it meant that Sumitomo's massive long copper futures positions would have to be liquidated. The rumor that Mr. Hamanaka was being reassigned only reinforced the notion that Sumitomo would be selling copper. The reason is that Mr. Hamanaka was widely known for his bullish views on copper; consequently, his reassignment to a nontrading position at Sumitomo could mean only one thing: Sumitomo had substantial losses from copper trading. This interpretation of the rumors swirling around the copper market that day proved prescient as later developments would show.

On Monday, May 20, 1996, a Sumitomo spokesperson confirmed the rumor that Mr. Yasuo Hamanaka had been reassigned, but noted that Mr. Hamanaka had been given more responsibility. Market participants did not buy this interpretation. As has been stressed repeatedly throughout this book, trading is a game. Participants have an incentive to disguise their true intentions from other market participants to avoid adversely affecting the value of their trading positions. Traders recognize the potential for conflicting incentives and may discount the public statements of other market participants accordingly. Sumitomo had an incentive not to make announcements that would adversely affect its widely known massive long copper futures position. On Monday, May 20, 1996, LME copper futures prices for July delivery fell another 5%.

Notice that the factors driving the price decline were largely internal to the market—in this case, fear of massive selling by traders attempting to exit long positions in copper. Sometimes, large price changes become trading catalysts in themselves. One reason for this is that, at some point, traders who are losing money try to cut their losses short by exiting their losing trading positions. The timing of their exit depends upon the losing traders' willingness and ability to tolerate losses. If other traders think they can push prices enough to trigger an exit by one or more key players, the implicit or explicit stop-loss orders that follow may push prices even further in the same direction.

Uncertainty over the exact cause or causes for the sharp declines in copper futures prices increased market volatility. Although copper futures prices bounced around, sometimes wildly, copper futures prices largely continued their downward descent during May and June of 1996. One factor driving the price declines were rumors of massive trading losses at Sumitomo. This meant that at some point Sumitomo might be forced to liquidate its massive long positions in copper, which would push prices down even further.

On Monday, June 6, 1996, copper futures prices crashed. The wild price action is captured in the following excerpt from an article by Kenneth Gooding that appeared in the June 7, 1996 issue of the *Financial Times*.

> Pandemonium broke out in the copper market yesterday as the price…plummeted by 15% in two hours on the London Metal Exchange.
>
> Traders…said the combined scale and the speed of the drop was unprecedented. Dealers increased the "spread" or difference between the prices at which they were willing to buy or sell to $50 a tonne—a level previously unheard of…At one point early yesterday, copper for delivery in three months on the LME dropped to $1,910 a tonne, down $337 from Wednesday's closing price. The price recovered to close…at $2,105 a tonne, $142 below Wednesday's close…Traders suggested the rout was started on Wednesday by two US hedge funds…The funds' objective was to drive copper down to below $2,424 a tonne at which point…[traders] that had granted 'put' options…—or promised to buy copper…at a certain price—would have to start selling.[5]

The huge increase in the bid/ask spread (to $50 per tonne) shows how liquidity dries up in markets under stress. The preceding excerpt also illustrates some of the game-like characteristics of trading— namely, it illustrates how other large market participants were perceived to be selling copper futures in an attempt to force longs to liquidate their positions and those who sold put options to protect themselves by selling copper futures. Of course, it is impossible to determine whether the rumored involvement of the hedge funds named in the preceding excerpt was real or imagined. Many instances where the actions of certain hedge funds are rumored to be moving the market are simply wrong. However, that misses the point. Traders *perceived* the market moves as the result of the actions of large traders and acted accordingly. The sharp changes in copper futures prices are depicted in Figure 8.1.

Another reason large price changes by themselves act as trading catalysts is the widespread knowledge that most sellers or writers of options *delta-hedge* their option price risk exposure. Delta-hedging is the financial market equivalent of just-in-time hedging. The delta of an option represents how the price of an option changes when the price of the underlying security changes. As noted earlier, the value of delta ranges from 0 to 1 for calls and between 0 and -1 for puts. Delta is also known as the hedge ratio. The absolute value of the delta of an option can be thought of as akin to the probability of exercise.

Large price changes will change the delta of the options written. In turn, this requires the option writer to sell futures to protect his exposure to price risk for put options when the price of the underlying falls or buy futures to protect his exposure to the price risk for call options when the price of the underlying rises. Either way, the additional selling or buying pressure may reinforce the prevailing price move.

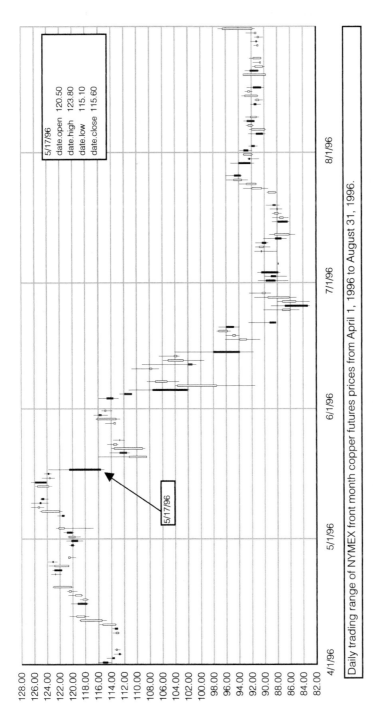

Daily trading range of NYMEX front month copper futures prices from April 1, 1996 to August 31, 1996.

FIGURE 8.1 "Not worth a copper": The market suspects problems at Sumitomo.

The sharp price declines in copper futures prices in May and June of 1996 forced copper put option writers to sell more copper futures contracts in order to remain delta-hedged.[6] This increased the decline in copper futures prices. Later short-covering by funds and the unwinding of previously acquired cover by option sellers had the opposite effect and caused futures prices to rise. All in all, these actions created a very volatile market.[7]

Again, price declines were exacerbated by factors internal to the market; in this case, delta-hedging activity by organizations that had sold put options on copper and short-covering as traders attempted to take profits from previously executed short sales of copper futures.

On June 13, 1996, a Sumitomo official admitted that the firm had about $1.8 billion in copper trading losses.[8] These losses were incurred over a 10-year period through allegedly rogue trading by Mr. Hamanaka. Interestingly, Sumitomo claimed that it first found evidence of rogue trading on June 5, 1996, the day when copper futures prices fell 15% in two hours.

One common thread in many trading debacles is that the initial reported trading loss is too low. For instance, Orange County, California initially reported a loss of $1.5 billion in its investment pool on December 1, 1994. The loss was later revised up to $1.7 billion. Sumitomo's initially reported copper trading losses were understated as well. The final loss was raised to $2.6 billion. Some market rumors had Sumitomo suffering a loss of $4 billion. Although that amount proved to be too high, market participants anticipated correctly continued downward pressure on copper futures prices and larger trading losses for Sumitomo.[9]

The losses were blamed on rogue trading by Mr. Hamanaka who was dismissed from Sumitomo and later arrested, charged with violating the law by Japanese authorities, tried, convicted, and imprisoned. It should be pointed out that Sumitomo's trading activities were supposed to be limited to hedging. Classification as a hedger allowed

Sumitomo to circumvent restrictions on position size imposed on speculators by the LME and other regulatory bodies.

The delayed admission by Sumitomo that Mr. Hamanaka had incurred massive trading losses for the firm became a trading catalyst in itself. Copper futures prices fell in "panic selling" as traders feared that Sumitomo would sell more of its massive copper position.[10] The admission of rogue trading by Sumitomo not only precipitated a sharp decline in copper futures prices; it also led to an increase in volatility that persisted for some time after the admission. This is yet another example of how trading catalysts can be long-lived in their influence on the level and volatility of commodity and financial market prices.

Finally, it should be noted that Sumitomo, under Mr. Hamanaka's direction, was thought to be behind many attempted squeezes and other manipulations of the copper market in the past.[11] On May 11, 1998, the U.S. Commodity Futures Trading Commission (the federal government agency that regulates futures markets in the United States) announced a settlement with Sumitomo over alleged price manipulation during 1995 and 1996. Sumitomo agreed to pay a $125 million fine and $25 million in partial restitution to those injured by the artificially high prices Sumitomo's copper trading actions created. Sumitomo also agreed to pay the United Kingdom's Financial Services Authority $8 million. As with most such settlements, Sumitomo neither admitted nor denied that it had engaged in price manipulation.[12]

Blood in the Water 2: The Yen Suddenly Rises

On Wednesday, October 7, 1998, the dollar fell sharply against the yen. It was a day of exceptional volatility in the dollar yen exchange rate. Much of the volatility occurred during Tokyo trading hours when the foreign exchange market against the yen is most active and liquid. At one point, the dollar was down almost 12 yen or over 9.15% intraday.[13] This is an incredible intraday move in a major currency under floating exchange rates. Wednesday's rout came after the dollar fell earlier in the week and was followed by another decline in the dollar against the yen on Thursday. The dollar rebounded somewhat in a volatile trading session on Friday. Figure 8.2 depicts the sharp rise in the yen on that day.

What was the catalyst that precipitated the massive slide in the dollar and sharp increase in volatility? It was not a comment by a politician or policymaker or intervention in the currency market by the Bank of Japan. It was not a larger-than-expected forecast error from an economic report. It was not a natural disaster or a geopolitical event. In fact, it was not fundamental news of any kind. Rather, it was the unwinding of massive short yen and yen-carry positions by hedge funds and other market participants. Simply put, the attempt by key market participants to exit a formerly popular trade acted as a catalyst that stimulated a reaction by other market participants and resulted in a sharp decline in the dollar against the yen.

Currency carry trades attempt to profit from interest rate differentials across countries with different currencies. Carry traders borrow the foreign currency in the low interest rate country (e.g. Japan) and invest the sums borrowed (exchanged, of course, into the domestic currency) in the higher interest rate country (e.g. the United States). When the investments mature, the domestic funds are exchanged into the foreign currency and used to repay the initial loan. If the exchange rate remains unchanged, the currency carry trader picks up the yield differential between the two currencies.

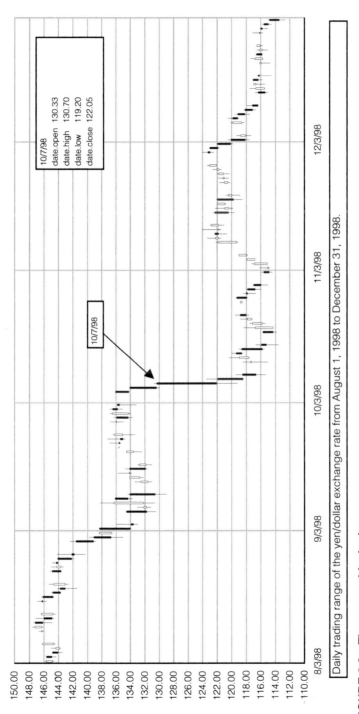

Daily trading range of the yen/dollar exchange rate from August 1, 1998 to December 31, 1998.

FIGURE 8.2   The yen suddenly rises.

For instance, suppose 100 yen equals US$1 and that the short-term interest rate in Japan is 1%. Suppose further that the short-term interest rate in the United States is 4%, while the long rate in the U.S. is 5%. Borrowing yen at 1% in Japan and exchanging the proceeds of the yen loan into dollars and investing at 4% in the Unites States provides the yen-carry trader with the opportunity to make an additional 300 basis points if the exchange rate does not change. Many traders attempt to maximize the interest rate differential by mismatching the maturities of the yen loans and dollar investments. Typically, funds are borrowed on a shorter-term basis than they are invested at. This allows traders to *ride the yield curve* as well (when the yield curve slopes upward)—that is, exploit the fact that if longer-term rates are higher than shorter-term rates, a trader can profit from borrowing at lower short-term rates and investing at higher long-term rates.

In the preceding example, the carry trader would borrow short term at 1% in Japan and invest for a longer term at 5% in the United States. This trade works well as long as the dollar does not fall against the yen or the yield differential reverses. The trade works even better if the dollar rises against the yen or long rates fall after the carry trader has put his position on. Keep in mind that the carry trader would make an extra 300 (or 400) basis points if the two positions were held for a year (if interest and exchange rates remained unchanged). However, a significant fall in the value of the dollar against the yen could easily wipe out the profits associated with the carry trade in a short period of time.

The power of internal market catalysts to move markets is captured in the following excerpt from an October 9, 1998 news report by Dow Jones Business News that discusses the large appreciation in the yen during October 1998 and its likely cause.

> …The dollar began the week trading at 135 yen in Tokyo and fell as low as 111.73 yen Thursday…Friday the currency bounced around in a four-yen range in Asia, finishing the session at 116.90 yen, down from 119.45 yen in New York late Thursday…

It is widely believed that U.S. hedge funds sparked the dollar rout by rushing to unwind "yen-carry" positions, through which they had borrowed yen at low interest rates to invest in high-yielding assets denominated in other currencies. The massive shift in capital was aimed at taking profits.[14]

Some background is in order to better appreciate the market conditions that prevailed during September and October 1998. Financial markets had just come off of a crisis precipitated by the near collapse of the hedge fund Long-Term Capital Management (LTCM) during August and September of 1998. The financial market crisis was accompanied by dramatic changes in the prices of some of the trading positions that LTCM had on. Many market participants suspected that major hedge funds including Tiger Management, at the time the largest hedge fund in the world with assets in excess of $20 billion, and LTCM had massive yen carry positions on. A sudden rally in the yen could set off a stampede by hedge funds for the exits.

Often, a significant price break is preceded by smaller declines in prices. Such was the case here. The sharp slide in the foreign exchange value of the dollar in early October was preceded by a significant selloff in early September that was also attributed to unwinding activities by hedge funds. This is illustrated in the following story reported by Reuters on Monday, September 7, 1998 (which was also the Labor Day holiday in the United States).

> Asian regional currencies extended early gains in thin trade as the dollar lost over two yen on sales by U.S. hedge funds and a late surge in Tokyo stocks. The dollar lost over three yen as hedge funds aggressively unwound short yen positions...
>
> Senior Japanese Finance Ministry official Eisuke Sakakibara said on Monday that Japan and the U.S. were both concerned about "excessive" yen weakness. Sakakibara said the yen's correction had just begun, and...that investors don't realize the risk of a yen rise.[15]

Mr. Sakakibara's comment about investors not realizing the risk of rise in the value of the yen proved more prophetic than perhaps even he realized.

According to *The Wall Street Journal*, Tiger Management lost over 10% of its assets during the first two weeks of September 1998 in the wake of the LTCM hedge fund debacle.[16] The principal implication of these losses is that it may have made Tiger and other hedge funds that were short yen more likely to get out of their losing positions if the dollar fell further. Tiger still had an enormous short yen position on. Put differently, in the eyes of some other market participants, Tiger became a weak hand with a large short yen position. A sudden rise in the yen could induce a short-covering rally as hedge funds that were short would cover their positions. According to a news report on CNNfn, Tiger Management lost more than $2 billion dollars on one day in October 1998 (presumably October 7, 1998) from a short bet on the yen.[17]

Was the sharp slide in the value of the dollar against the yen simply a distant echo of the LTCM crisis? To be sure, rumors that LTCM had a yen-carry position on added to the belief that a sudden and adverse move in its position could force it out at extremely disadvantageous prices. On the floor of open outcry futures markets, the phrase "gunning for stops" is used to indicate the tendency of the market to gravitate toward levels where stop-loss orders are thought to be clustered in the hopes of triggering stops and the momentary imbalances in supply and demand that result. Something analogous may have happened with respect to Tiger's position. Although Tiger Management did not use explicit stops, market participants knew that implicit ones had to exist.

Another point that deserves attention is that a significant number of market participants use technical analysis to guide their trading decisions. The failure of key technical support levels (such as 133.50 yen to the dollar) to hold earlier during the week of October 5, 1998 may have changed the trading preferences of technically oriented traders. Simply put, the repeated breaching of dollar support levels would have encouraged technical traders to reverse their long dollar (short yen) position and short the dollar (and go long the yen). This would add to the selling pressure on the dollar against the yen.

Internal Market Catalysts

Although much of this book has focused on the impact of external trading catalysts on market prices, some of the largest price changes are often the result of trading catalysts internal to the market, as the preceding examples demonstrate. The impact of internal market catalysts may arise from the influence of large orders or the triggering of trades as various price levels are breached.

Internal trading catalysts may arise suddenly and seemingly unexpectedly. In large part, this is due to the fact that internal trading catalysts need not be tied to news. This may make the market's response to internal trading catalysts puzzling to many market observers and policymakers alike. Internal trading catalysts may be triggered accidentally or intentionally as part of a trading strategy.

The impact of an internal trading catalyst induced price change need not be limited to the market in which it arises. Sometimes, internal trading catalysts in one market influence price changes and volatility in other markets.

The game-like nature of trading becomes even more apparent when the impact of internal trading catalysts on financial markets is examined. It is imperative to know how other market participants will behave in certain circumstances and react to potential trading catalysts. Many of the large price changes witnessed in financial markets involve cascading waves of buy or sell orders. Although these waves of buy or sell orders could be prompted by the arrival of news, many of these episodes arise when trading appears to feed upon itself—that is, *positive feedback trading*.[18] As the preceding examples also demonstrate, many trading strategies may be based on the expectation of igniting positive feedback trading by other market participants.

The manner by which news is incorporated into speculative prices has long fascinated financial economists. Nobel Laureate and Cornell University Professor Robert Engle together with Professors Takatoshi Ito and Wen-Ling Lin published an article in *Econometrica* in 1990 that suggests that patterns in the volatility of changes in speculative prices are the result of either the arrival of new information or market dynamics in response to the arrival of new information. In an interesting article, Professors Bradford J. DeLong, Andrei Shleifer, Lawrence H. Summers, and Robert J. Waldman advance a model in which *positive feedback trading* (i.e., trading that feeds on itself) makes rational speculation potentially price *destabilizing*; causes speculative prices to *overreact* to news; increases price volatility; and induces serial correlation and mean reversion in price changes. They attribute much positive feedback trading to *extrapolative expectations* among market participants and argue that it persists due to impediments to learning.[19]

The sequential series of crises in Asian financial markets following the devaluation of the Thai baht on July 2, 1997 brings into sharp relief the impact of volatility spillover, contagion risk, transitory correlation, illiquidity, and positive feedback trading on the behavior of speculative prices.[20] This chapter focuses on the impact of positive feedback trading on the behavior of speculative prices during periods of market stress.

There are a number of sources of positive feedback trading. These include technical analysis, stop-loss orders, margin calls, portfolio insurance, and dynamic hedging or delta-hedging. In each case, traders exacerbate a price move by buying when prices are rising or selling when prices are falling. A trend-following trader would buy when prices are rising and sell when prices are falling. A stop-loss order requires selling out of a losing long position when prices are falling or covering a losing short position when prices are rising. Similarly, a margin call forces an individual to either post more funds when a position moves against the individual or exit the position. Exiting a losing long position entails selling when prices are falling. Examples of positive feedback trading occur very frequently.

Portfolio insurance was a popular trading strategy before the stock market crash of October 19, 1987. Basically, it entailed buying a put option to protect the value of a stock portfolio against a substantial decline in prices. However, because options are expensive, most portfolio insurance programs created synthetic options on an as-needed basis instead of buying actual ones for the entire period—that is, portfolio insurers replicated the payoffs on a synthetic put option only *when* they feared they needed a put. The creation of synthetic put options was accomplished by selling stock index futures whenever stock prices fell below a certain trigger amount. In practice, this meant that stock index futures would be sold in a falling market. Moreover, these trigger amounts were widely known by other market participants.

The Sumitomo copper debacle example discussed how delta-hedging by option writers exacerbated the price decline of copper. The essence of hedging is to take an opposite position to the initial position such that a decrease in the value of the initial position is offset by an increase in the value of the hedge position, and vice versa. If the changes in the initial and hedge positions exactly offset each other, one has a perfect hedge. As noted earlier, the delta of an option shows how the value of the option changes with the value of the underlying security or commodity. Again, the absolute value of delta is akin to the probability that the option will be exercised. It is also akin to the fraction of the underlying security or commodity. Thus, an option with a delta of $-.1$ is equivalent to a tenth of the underlying security in the sense that it will move by 10 cents if the underlying security moves by a dollar. Put differently, a bank that sold 10 put options would hedge itself by selling one copper futures contract. If the delta changed to −.2, the bank would sell another copper futures contract to maintain its hedge. If the delta changed to −.3, the bank would sell yet another copper futures contract to remain delta neutral. Delta-hedging essentially requires that firms only hedge what they need to hedge.

It was noted that two banks lost roughly $25 million each from writing put options on copper and delta-hedging their exposure to falling copper futures prices. The question naturally arises as to how the two banks lost money when they were delta-hedged. The answer is that delta-hedging works well when prices change in small increments. Large price moves down in the case of puts (or up in the case of calls) means that the firms are not able to hedge completely. In this instance, hedging meant selling more copper futures contracts, thus exacerbating the downward price move. One component of the cascade of selling in the copper futures market in May and June of 1996 was due to banks delta-hedging their short put option positions.

Order Size as a Trading Catalyst

Perhaps the most fundamental internal trading catalyst is order size. Although financial economic theory suggests that order size alone should not influence market prices in an informationally efficient capital market, in practice, large orders do. The mechanism by which large orders influence financial market prices is called *price pressure*. The influence of large orders is especially pronounced when they are executed in a short period of time and in less liquid markets—that is, the price impact of large orders is greater the smaller market *depth*.

To be sure, another component of the influence of large orders is the suspicion that the party for whom the large order is executed has information that other market participants do not have. Large traders can capitalize on that fear by taking into account the likely reaction of other traders to large orders when they develop their trading strategies. An interesting example in this regard occurred in a series of bond market trades executed by Citigroup during August 2004.

Electronic Trading Games: Citigroup Hits All Bids— August 2004

In the space of 18 seconds between 10:28 and 10:29 A.M., on Monday, August 2, 2004, Citigroup sold €11.3 billion of eurozone government bonds on the MTS cash bond trading platform by hitting most of the bids that rival dealers were obligated to make.[21] The amount sold by Citigroup equaled the average daily trading volume on the MTS trading platform. Around the same time, Citigroup sold approximately €1.5 billion of eurozone bonds elsewhere to bring its total bond sales to about €12.9 billion. Not surprisingly, Citigroup's trade set off a eurozone bond market slide as competing dealers raced to dump the inventory they acquired or hedge it in the futures market. These actions helped to drive cash and futures market bond prices sharply lower. The markets' reaction to the Citigroup trades was entirely predictable and, most likely, anticipated by the Citigroup traders.[22]

A subsequent investigation by the United Kingdom's Financial Services Authority (FSA) showed that after putting on these positions, Citigroup was net short €3.8 billion. This position was covered at 11:25 A.M. on August 2, 2004 at substantially lower prices. Again, the effects on the market were entirely predictable—namely, wider bid ask spreads, lower market depth, and lower trading volume on the MTS. Some dealers reacted by suspending their participation in the MTS trading platform. It should be pointed out that Citigroup is a part owner of the MTS trading platform along with other commercial and investment banks.

Citigroup made an estimated $18.2 million from the various trades. Citigroup's action was neither illegal nor against the rules of the MTS trading platform. However, it did exert considerable pressure on the MTS and anger many traders and the governments whose bonds fell as a result of Citigroup's actions.

The question naturally arises as to whether Citigroup's trades constituted an attempt to manipulate the market in their favor. The facts are as follows. Citgroup acquired a significant long position in German government note and bond (i.e., bund) futures contracts traded on Eurex prior to the rapid fire sale. Indeed, Citigroup bought 66,214 interest rate futures contracts on Eurex between 9:17 and 10:29 A.M. on Monday, August 2, 2004, according to a subsequent investigation by the FSA. The interest rate futures contracts acquired were of various maturities. The FSA estimated the preceding futures position was equivalent to 55,000 bund futures contracts. The FSA notes that bund futures prices rose from €114.25 to €114.61 while the 5-year note futures (known as the bobl) rose in price from 111.06 to 111.21. This caused a rise in the cash market prices of the corresponding bonds and notes.[23]

Apparently, the intended trade by Citigroup was a *basis trade*— that is, a trade that attempts to profit from differences between cash and futures market prices. The FSA concluded that Citigroup did not engage in price manipulation but

> executed a trading strategy…which…caused a temporary disruption to the volumes of bonds quoted and traded on the MTS platform, a sharp drop in bond prices and a temporary withdrawal by some participants from quoting on that platform.[24]

On June 28, 2005, the United Kingdom's Financial Services Authority announced that Citigroup agreed to pay about £14 million in fines (£4 million) and forfeited profits (£9.96 million). The FSA determined that while Citigroup

> did not intend to disrupt or distort the market, [it violated] FSA Principles 2 and 3 by failing to conduct its business with

due skill, care and diligence and failing to control its business effectively.[25]

Although the FSA determined that Citigroup had not attempted to manipulate the market, the German financial regulator, Bafin (i.e., the Federal Financial Supervisory Authority or *Bundesanstalt für Finanzdienstleistungsaufsicht*), disagreed at least with respect to Citigroup's actions in German futures markets. Bafin argued that there was sufficient evidence that Citigroup attempted to manipulate the Eurex futures market. The prosecutor's office disagreed and no charges were brought by the German authorities for the Eurex bond futures trades.

The Citigroup bond trading episode illustrates how large trades alone can act as a trading catalyst. But more important than size was the fact that the large trades occurred within a short period of time—18 seconds—and Citigroup knew, or should have anticipated, the likely reaction of other market participants (i.e., the firms that suddenly acquired a large inventory of bonds that they did not want to hold). This example exemplifies the effect that large buy or sell orders can have on market prices even in the absence of the arrival of new fundamental economic information.

As already noted, Citigroup's trades were neither illegal nor against the rules of the MTS trading platform. However, collectively, it was a bad trade despite making over $18 million for the firm. Much trading is a *repeated play* game. The bond traders at Citigroup would likely have to trade again with the counterparties to the trades it made on the morning of August 2, 2004. These counterparties would likely remember being disadvantaged by Citigroup for a long, long time. In addition, the episode made the MTS a less desirable trading platform. Bid ask spreads widened, depth narrowed, and subsequent trading volume declined. However, the most important trading error that Citigroup made was to offend the governments that regulate it.

The Citigroup bond trades illustrate once again that it is important to anticipate the reaction of other market participants to a potential trade. It is also important to remember that trading is a game that
is often played repeatedly rather than for a single time. This affects
how a market participant will "play the game." Finally, the Citigroup
bond trades also illustrate an obvious but sometimes overlooked fact:
that the real trade a party may be making may be a spread or basis
trade rather than an outright trade.

Size Matters: March 1996 CBOT Wheat Futures

The preceding example illustrates the impact that large trades can
have on market prices. Size matters. Of course, what constitutes a
large order depends upon the circumstances and the market. In some
markets, a relatively small order can exert a substantial impact on
market prices under certain conditions. One such market condition is
proximity to expiration for futures contracts. An example of how a
comparatively small order exerted an out-sized impact on market
prices occurred on the Chicago Board of Trade (CBOT) wheat
futures market on March 20, 1996 when a single order of 80 contracts
pushed up March 1996 wheat futures by 49% in a matter of minutes.
At the time, the cash market price for wheat was less than $5 per
bushel. The price rose to $7.50 per bushel before closing at $6.40 per
bushel, or up $1.33 for the day. The increase in price was not due to
the arrival of news (fundamental information or otherwise) but rather
the resistance by locals to taking the other side of a transaction minutes before contract expiration.[26] This was a bizarre event that did not
really affect the prices of deferred wheat futures contracts.[27]

The CBOT wheat futures market is a relatively liquid market in
normal circumstances. This example illustrates how sensitive futures
prices are to relatively small trading volumes near expiration due to
market illiquidity. It also illustrates how market conditions (in this
case, proximity to expiration and the concomitant reluctance of locals

to enter a position that might result in taking or making delivery) can exert a large influence on the behavior of speculative prices.

Trade Execution Matters

Perhaps the penultimate example of the impact of order size on market prices occurred on Thursday, October 22, 1987 when an order (attributed to George Soros) to sell 5,000 December 1987 S&P 500 stock index futures contracts at the opening on the Chicago Mercantile Exchange resulted in a massive decline in S&P 500 stock index futures prices.[28] The December 1987 S&P 500 stock index futures contract had closed at 258.25 the day before, but sentiment turned negative again by Thursday's opening.[29] Thursday's opening range (202.00 to 195.00) was an exceptionally wide 7 points, or $3,500. Moments after the large sell order had been filled, the market bounced back rising as high as 250.50 before closing for the day at 244.50. (The closing range was 244.00 to 245.00.) An individual who was fortunate enough to buy a single December 1987 stock index futures contract at 195.00 and who held it to the end of the day would have made $24,750. The spectacular price action in the S&P 500 stock index futures pit on Thursday, October 22, 1987 is described in the following excerpt from the November 2, 1987 issue of *Barron's*.

> ...[A]fter a two-day rebound in U.S. stock prices, the psychology had turned bearish again. Reports circulated of large margin calls. U.S. stocks had opened sharply down on foreign exchanges. Using Shearson as a broker, Soros apparently decided to pitch out his entire [5,000 futures contracts] position on the opening. On the bell, the Shearson floor broker began offering thousand lots. The other pit traders, picking up the sound of a whale in trouble, hung back, but circled the prey. The offer went from 230 down to 220 to 215 to 205 to 200. Then, the pit traders attacked. The Soros block sold from 195 to 210. The spiral was ghastly. It was Soros's block

and not program trading that drove the futures to a cash discount some 50 points, or 20%, below the cash value of the S&P contract. The discount on the 5,000 contracts represented some $250 million. The futures fund manager covered there, as did a number of local traders who made millions off the immediate snapback in price. The contract that day closed at 244.50, or some $222 million higher, based on Soros's position. Soros's loss from the previous day was estimated at more than $200 million.[30]

This episode illustrates several points. First, the magnitude of the decline in the value of the S&P 500 stock index futures contract from Wednesday's close to Thursday's opening was 21.8% to 23.8%, roughly the same size as the decline in the cash S&P 500 stock index on Monday, October 19, 1987.[31] Unlike Monday, October 19, prices in the stock market did not fall very much—at one point, the December 1987 S&P 500 stock index futures contract was trading at a 50-point discount to the cash index.[32] Also, unlike October 19, prices quickly bounced back after the large sell order had been filled. Simply stated, the large sell had about the same impact on market prices as the Monday, October 19, 1987 market crash did except that it was localized to the S&P 500 stock index futures market and was short-lived. Second, the episode illustrates the importance of market conditions and sentiment. The large sell order probably would not have exerted much impact on prices in a normal trading environment. As a result, the execution of the trade was flawed. Third, the episode illustrates once again the game-like nature of trading. Recall that the excerpt notes that the locals in the pit assumed that the large sell order meant that there was a large trader in trouble and refused to buy at the initially higher offers. It is important to point out that the original long futures position was acquired the day before, perhaps in a single order, and that order did not drive prices substantially higher. Fourth, the episode illustrates that although the initially reported trading catalyst—a missile attack on Kuwait and negative comments by market guru Robert Prechter—may have stimulated the large sell order, it was a factor internal to the market—the belief that there was a large trader in trouble—that precipitated the massive price decline and immediate bounce back.

Precursor to the 1987 Crash

The crash of 1987 (which is discussed in detail in the next chapter) took many investors by surprise. However, market participants got a taste of what it would be like earlier in the year during an especially volatile session on Friday, January 23, 1987. In the space of an hour, the U.S. stock market as measured by the Dow Jones Industrial Average plunged 115 points, or over 5%, only to bounce back and then close down 44 points, or 2% lower for the day. Big Board trading volume set a record as over 302 million shares changed hands. The reasons for the sharp decline and volatility were not known. Many analysts attributed the volatility to computerized *program trading*.[33] The wide trading range on January 23, 1987 is depicted in Figure 8.3.

The speed of the decline was apparent in the stock index futures markets on the Chicago Mercantile Exchange and the Chicago Board of Trade. The lower cost of trading on futures markets means that futures markets often lead the corresponding cash or spot market. In this case, the stock index futures market leads the stock market.

The S&P 500 stock index futures contract, which is traded on the CME, was the most actively traded stock index futures market. It had a "nickel" tick, or minimum price move, at the time.[34] Most of the time, the S&P 500 stock index futures market moved a "nickel" up or down. However, on Friday, January 23, 1987, the S&P 500 stock index futures contract suddenly started to move in "dollar" or full-point increments rather than nickels—that is, $500 at a time.

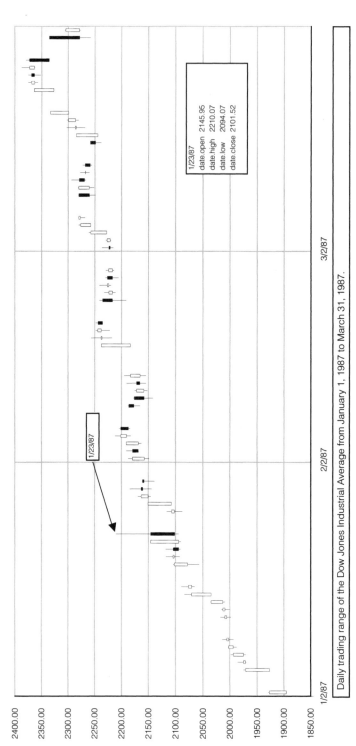

1/23/87
date open   2145.95
date high   2210.07
date low   2094.07
date close 2101.52

Daily trading range of the Dow Jones Industrial Average from January 1, 1987 to March 31, 1987.

FIGURE 8.3   Harbinger of the crash? January 23, 1987.

Many observers attributed the various intraday ups and downs in market prices to waves of program trading.[35] Not surprisingly, major program traders denied that program trading was the culprit.[36] Program trading can itself be decomposed into various types ranging from any computerized program that generates buy and sell orders to programs that specialize in *index arbitrage* (i.e., arbitrage between stock index futures contracts and a subset of the stocks that comprise the stock index on which the futures contract is based). By far, the dominant form of program trading at the time was index arbitrage. Academic financial economists would generally argue that index arbitrage is stabilizing rather than destabilizing and would reduce rather than exacerbate volatility. Whether the proximate cause of the volatility was due to program trading is less important than the fact that the cause was internal to the market.

The exceptional volatility on Friday, January 23, 1987 returned on Monday, October 19, 1987 when a more severe decline occurred. The events of January 23, 1987 may have had a possible precedent on September 11, 1986 when the Dow Jones Industrial Average suddenly fell and closed down over 86 points, or 4.6%. Analysts attributed that decline to an external trading catalyst (i.e., adverse interest rate news) whose impact was exacerbated by an internal trading catalyst (i.e., program trading activities).[37]

Trading Lessons

Internal trading catalysts often exert a larger impact on market prices than external catalysts. A seemingly innocuous shock can precipitate a large change in market prices in an environment where the trading positions of key market participants are both similar and concentrated by triggering positive feedback trading. In such an environment, it is imperative for traders to anticipate how key market participants would likely react to a sudden internal or external shock.

The most basic type of internal trading catalyst is order size. Large orders may exert pressure on market prices and influence trader behavior as traders attempt to determine whether the party placing the large order has information other market participants do not. This was demonstrated in the Citigroup eurozone bond trading example. What constitutes "large" depends upon the particular market and other factors such as when the order is placed. A comparatively small futures trade executed near expiration can exert a powerful impact on market prices, as was shown in the CBOT March 1996 wheat futures example.

Equally important are the real and perceived positions of key market participants. If the market suspects a key trader is in trouble, prices often move in a direction adverse to that trader's perceived position. This occurred during the Sumitomo copper debacle in 1996 and in the yen/dollar market during September and October 1998 when major hedge funds were rumored to be under pressure to exit huge short yen positions.

The examples discussed in this chapter also demonstrate that internal trading catalysts can seemingly come out of nowhere to impact market prices. Sudden changes in market prices for no apparent reason may be explained in many cases by internal catalysts. Another lesson that emerges is that although the impact of most internal catalysts on market prices is relatively short-lived, the impact of some internal catalysts on market prices can last a significant time, as the sharp appreciation of the Japanese yen against the U.S. dollar during early October 1998 demonstrates. Finally, the impact of internal market catalysts on market prices can last even longer if the resultant price action changes market sentiment. Such effects are readily observable in the aftermath of bubbles, corners, squeezes, and crashes, which are considered in the next chapter.

References

Barron's. "A Bad Two Weeks—A Wall Street Star Loses $840 Million." November 2, 1987.

Collett-White, Mike. "Traders Count Cost of LME Copper Swings." Reuters, June 7, 1996.

CNNfn. "Tiger Wounded as Losses Bite." November 2, 1998, 6:41 A.M. ET.

DeLong, B.J., A. Shleifer, L. Summers, and R.J. Waldman. "Positive Feedback Investment Strategies and Destabilizing Rational Speculation." *Journal of Finance*, Vol. 45, No. 2 , (June 1990a) pp. 379-396.

DeLong, B.J., A. Shleifer, L. Summers, and R.J. Waldman. "Noise Trader Risk in Financial Markets." *Journal of Political Economy*, 98, (4), (August 1990b), pp. 703-738.

Donovan, Patrick, Tony May, and Owen Bowcott. "Copper Crash Baffles Experts." *The Guardian*, May 18, 1996.

Dow Jones Business News. "Dollar's Slump Leaves Japanese Officials Puzzled, Guarded." October 9, 1998.

Engle, R.F., T. Ito, and W. Lin. "Meteor Showers or Heat Waves? Heteroskedastic Intra-Daily Volatility in the Foreign Exchange Market." *Econometrica*, Vol. 58, No. 3, (May 1990), pp. 525-542.

Financial Times. August 10, 2004.

Gooding, Kenneth. "Hedge Funds Blamed as Copper Falls 15% in Two Hours' Trading." *Financial Times*, June 7, 1996.

Gooding, Kenneth. "Commodities and Agriculture—Hamanaka Rumours Helped to Trigger Sales." *Financial Times*, May 21, 1996.

Hayes, Martin. "Sumitomo Copper Squeezes Date Back to Late 1980s." Reuters News, June 26, 1996.

Holter, James T. "Case Closed? CFTC Nails Sumitomo with a $150 Million Fine." *Futures Magazine*. May 11, 1998.

Houston Chronicle. "Wheat Futures Jump Nearly 50% to Set Record." March 21, 1996.

Lenzner, Robert. "Don't Blame Program Trading, Firms Say." *The Boston Globe*, January 27, 1987.

Lincoln, Abraham. Letter to Albert G. Hodges, April 4, 1864.

McMurray, Scott. "Chicago Merc Sets Daily Limit On Price Swings—Aim Is to Reduce Volatility in Stock-Index Futures and Options Trading." *The Wall Street Journal*, October 23, 1987.

McMurray, Scott. "Free Fall: Interest Rate Worries and Program Trading Send Stocks Plunging—Automated Selling Generates Biggest One-Day Decline as Volume Sets a Record—A Fluke or a Positive Omen?" *The Wall Street Journal*, September 12, 1986.

Munter, Paivi, and Ivar Simensen. "Citigroup Eurozone Bonds Ploy Leads to Panic and Clampdown on Trading." *Financial Times*, August 10, 2004.

Pender, Kathleen. "'Craziest I've Ever Seen'/Wild Trading Day for Stock Market/Dow Goes Way Up, Way Down." *San Francisco Chronicle,* January 24, 1987.

Reuters. "Sakakibara Says 'No Comment' on Forex-Jiji." October 8, 1998.

Reuters. "Asia FOREX-Withering Dollar Boosts Regionals." September 7, 1998.

Reuters. "Dollar Battered by Aggressive BOJ Action in Tokyo." April 10, 1998.

Reuters. "Sumitomo Copper Losses Could Hit $2.5 Bln—Trade." June 14, 1996.

Reuters News. "Full Text of Sumitomo Corp. Statement." June 14, 1996.

Rowley, Anthony and Neil Behrmann. "US$1.8B Loss at Sumitomo Rocks World Copper Market." *Business Times Singapore*, June 15, 1996.

Siconolfi, Michael, Anita Raghavan, Mitchell Pacelle, and Michael R. Sesit. "Why a World-Wide Chain Reaction Set Financial Markets into a Spin." *The Wall Street Journal,* September 22, 1998.

Sterngold, James. "Wall Street Day: Torrid Start, Sudden Chill." *The New York Times*, January 24, 1987.

The Wall Street Journal. Thursday, March 21, 1996.

United Kingdom Financial Services Authority. "FSA Fines Citigroup £13.9 Million (€20.9mn) for Eurobond Trades." June 28, 2005 (http:/www.fsa.gov.uk/pages/Library/Communication/PR/2005/072.shtml).

Endnotes

[1] Abraham Lincoln. Letter to Albert G. Hodges, April 4, 1864.

[2] Patrick Donovan, Tony May, and Owen Bowcott. "Copper Crash Baffles Experts." *The Guardian*, May 18, 1996.

[3] Patrick Donovan, Tony May, and Owen Bowcott. "Copper Crash Baffles Experts." *The Guardian*, May 18, 1996.

[4] Kenneth Gooding. "Commodities and Agriculture—Hamanaka Rumours Helped to Trigger Sales." *Financial Times*, May 21, 1996.

[5] Kenneth Gooding. "Hedge Funds Blamed as Copper Falls 15% in Two Hours' Trading." *Financial Times*, June 7, 1996.

[6] Large price changes make it difficult to delta-hedge option positions. Two prominent banks incurred substantial losses from delta-hedging the copper put options they had written according press reports.

[7] Mike Collett-White. "Traders Count Cost of LME Copper Swings." Reuters, June 7, 1996. The article notes: "… 'The delta on these options may have only been 10 percent before the market crashed, but it got to fifty or even sixty percent,' one trader said."

[8] The text of the company's announcement indicated that "[t]he Company first discovered evidence of the unauthorized trading activities on June 5, 1996." The announcement also noted that "[p]reliminary estimates indicate the possible loss that the Company may have to absorb is approximately $1.8 billion, based on current copper market prices." Reuters News. "Full Text of Sumitomo Corp. Statement," June 14, 1996.

[9] Reuters. "Sumitomo Copper Losses Could Hit $2.5 bln—Trade." June 14, 1996.

[10] Anthony Rowley and Neil Behrmann. "US$1.8B Loss at Sumitomo Rocks World Copper Market." *Business Times Singapore*, June 15, 1996. The article provides more evidence for the game-like nature of trading when it notes: "Sumitomo holds long positions in copper and is widely believed to have been involved in a price tug-of-war with major [hedge] funds ... which decided to short the market."

[11] Martin Hayes. "Sumitomo Copper Squeezes Date Back to Late 1980s." Reuters News, June 26, 1996.

[12] James T. Holter. "Case Closed? CFTC Nails Sumitomo with a $150 Million Fine." *Futures Magazine*, May 11, 1998.

[13] Reuters News. "Sakakibara Says 'No Comment' on Forex-Jiji." Thursday, October 8, 1998.

[14] Dow Jones Business News. "Dollar's Slump Leaves Japanese Officials Puzzled, Guarded." October 9, 1998.

[15] Reuters. "Asia FOREX-Withering Dollar Boosts Regionals." September 7, 1998.

[16] Michael Siconolfi, Anita Raghavan, Mitchell Pacelle, and Michael R. Sesit. "Why a World-Wide Chain Reaction Set Financial Markets Into a Spin." *The Wall Street Journal*, September 22, 1998.

[17] CNNfn. "Tiger Wounded as Losses Bite." November 2, 1998, 6:41 A.M. ET.

[18] Academic thought on positive feedback trading has been strongly influenced by two articles by Professors Bradford DeLong, Andrei Schleifer, Lawrence Summers, and Robert Waldman that were published in the *Journal of Finance* and the *Journal of Political Economy* in 1990.

[19] Extrapolative expectations refer to forming expectations about the future assuming that the pattern of recent price changes continues. Positive feedback trading persists because various impediments to learning slow the speed at which market participants learn.

[20] *Volatility spillover* is the tendency for turbulence in one market to spill over to another market. It is related to contagion risk. *Correlation* is a measure of how closely two variables move together. Sometimes, two (usually unrelated) variables (e.g., silver and sugar) move closely together for a short period of time. This is known as *transitory correlation*. *Illiquidity* refers to markets where it is difficult to buy or sell a large quantity without adversely affecting the price.

[21] MTS SpA runs a trading platform for the electronic trading of eurozone bonds.

[22] Paivi Munter and Ivar Simensen. "Citigroup Eurozone Bonds Ploy Leads To Panic and Clampdown on Trading." *Financial Times* August 10, 2004, p. 1. The article notes: "…Traders said the Bund futures contract on Eurex, the main hedging instrument for eurozone government bonds, fell about 20 ticks in 30 seconds compared with a typical daily move of only a few ticks. [Each tick has a value of €10.]"

[23] Financial Services Authority. "Final Notice to Citigroup Global Markets Limited." June 28, 2005 (http://www.fsa.gov.uk/pubs/final/cgml_28jun05.pdf)

[24] United Kingdom Financial Services Authority. "FSA Fines Citigroup £13.9 million (€20.9mn) for Eurobond Trades." June 28, 2005 (http:/www.fsa.gov.uk/pages/Library/Communication/PR/2005/072.shtml).

[25] Ibid.

[26] *The Wall Street Journal*. Thursday, March 21, 1996.

[27] *Houston Chronicle*. "Wheat Futures Jump Nearly 50% to Set Record." March 21, 1996, p. 3. The article notes that wheat futures for delivery during May 1996 closed up 6 cents per bushel for the day.

[28] *Barron's*. "A Bad Two Weeks—A Wall Street Star Loses $840 Million." November 2, 1987.

[29] The article notes: "…[T]he pit was deluged with sell orders when trading resumed [Thursday], forcing the contract down more than 60 points within seconds. The sell-off was tied to a missile attack on a Kuwaiti oil facility, and negative comments from the widely followed market technician Robert Prechter, traders said…"

Scott McMurray. "Chicago Merc Sets Daily Limit On Price Swings—Aim Is to Reduce Volatility In Stock-Index Futures And Options Trading." *The Wall Street Journal*, October 23, 1987.

[30] *Barron's*. "A Bad Two Weeks—A Wall Street Star Loses $840 Million." November 2, 1987.

[31] The magnitude of the decline the large order sparked was tremendous even if one measures the price impact from the initial 230 offer to 195.

[32] *Barron's*. "A Bad Two Weeks—A Wall Street Star Loses $840 Million." November 2, 1987.

[33] Kathleen Pender. "'Craziest I've Ever Seen'/Wild Trading Day for Stock Market/Dow Goes Way Up, Way Down." *San Francisco Chronicle*, 24 January 1987. The article notes:

> …Analysts said there was no economic news from the government or from abroad that would have set off the pandemonium. They blamed the volatility on computerized trading programs operated by big brokerage houses.

[34] The contract specifications called for the value of the futures contract to be $500 times the stock index futures price. This gave the minimum tick a dollar value of $25. This was later changed to $250 times the index on November 1, 1997. The tick size was increased to a "dime," or .1, to maintain the dollar value of $25.

[35] James Sterngold. "Wall Street Day: Torrid Start, Sudden Chill." *The New York Times*. January 24, 1987.

[36] Robert Lenzner. "Don't Blame Program Trading, Firms Say." *The Boston Globe*, January 27, 1987.

[37] Scott McMurray. "Free Fall: Interest Rate Worries and Program Trading Send Stocks Plunging—Automated Selling Generates Biggest One-Day Decline as Volume Sets a Record—A Fluke or a Positive Omen?" *The Wall Street Journal*, September 12, 1986.

9

BUBBLES, CRASHES, CORNERS, AND MARKET CRISES

"A conventional valuation which is established as the outcome of the mass psychology of a large number of ignorant individuals is liable to change violently as the result of a sudden fluctuation of opinion due to factors which do not really make much difference to the prospective yield; since there will be no strong roots of conviction to hold it steady. In abnormal times in particular, when the hypothesis of an indefinite continuance of the existing state of affairs is less plausible than usual even though there are no express grounds to anticipate definite change, the market will be subject to waves of optimistic and pessimistic sentiment, which are unreasoning and yet in a sense legitimate where no solid basis exists for a reasonable calculation."

—John Maynard Keynes[1]

The Silver Corner

During the fall and winter of 1979, the prices of silver and gold rose sharply in volatile markets. At one point in late August and early September, silver rose for 13 consecutive trading sessions.[2] Concern that the sharp increase in the price of silver was the result of manipulation prompted an investigation by the Commodities Exchange (COMEX) where most silver futures were traded at the time.[3] Market participants were concerned about a potential *squeeze* or a *corner* in the silver market where individuals who were short silver would be forced to cover their positions at artificially high prices. These fears intensified as the price of silver continued to jump and deliverable supplies of silver shrunk during the fall of 1979. This can be seen in the following excerpt from the November 29, 1979 issue of *The Wall Street Journal*.

> ...Traders agree that a key factor in the market's behavior is the potential shortage of silver available for immediate delivery. Silver in warehouses approved by the London Metals Exchange has declined by more than half in the past month, to 9.5 million ounces.
>
> On the COMEX, the number of contracts outstanding for delivery in December represents about 45 million ounces, or two-thirds of all the Exchange's deliverable supplies.[4]

In reaction to these concerns, the two principal U.S. exchanges that traded silver futures, the COMEX and the Chicago Board of Trade (CBOT), imposed new position limits on silver futures and raised margin requirements.[5] Fears of an immediate squeeze fell but returned in December 1979. Contemporary news accounts attributed much of the silver purchases to Nelson Bunker Hunt and his brother William Jefferson Hunt (members of an immensely wealthy Texas family) and their largely foreign business associates. To be sure, there were other factors besides the rumored efforts by the Hunt brothers and their allies to drive the price of silver up. Fear of inflation buoyed the demand for precious metals. Two geopolitical factors also helped spur the price rises in silver, gold, and platinum: the Iranian hostage crisis that began on November 4, 1979 and the Soviet invasion of Afghanistan that began on December 25, 1979. Nevertheless, the repeated use of the silver futures markets by the Hunt brothers and their allies to purchase and take delivery of large quantities of silver induced a shortage in the deliverable supply of silver that reinforced the price increases. Simply put, silver futures shorts were being squeezed as the Hunt brothers and their allies amassed large quantities of silver. The extensive rally in silver futures prices is depicted in Figure 9.1. Figure 9.2 depicts the largely coincident rally and subsequent break in gold futures prices during 1979 and 1980.

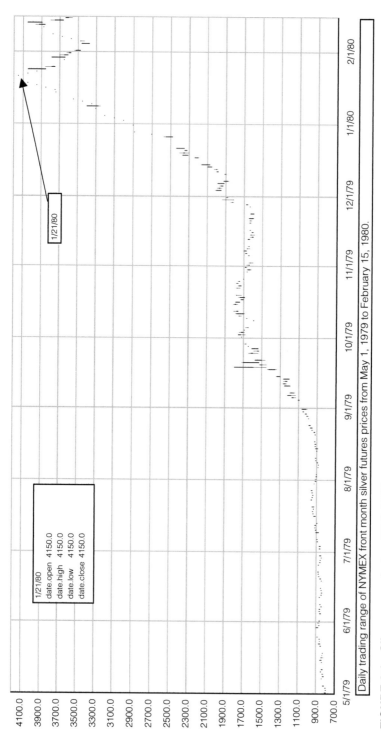

FIGURE 9.1   Silver soars during 1979-1980.

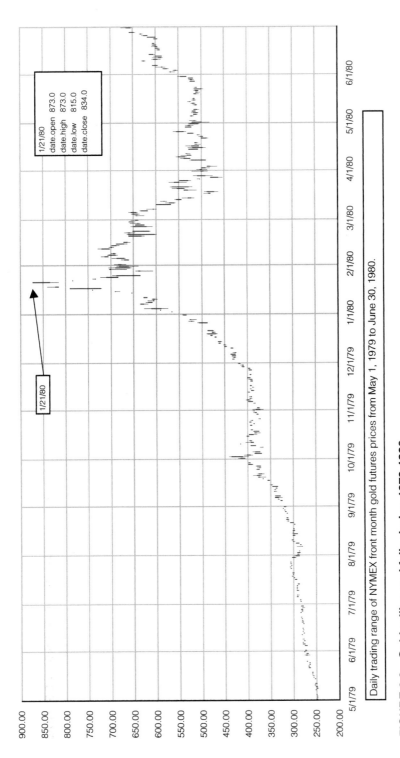

FIGURE 9.2 Gold rallies and falls during 1979-1980.

On January 21, 1980, the price of spot silver reached a high of $52.50 per troy ounce, and COMEX silver futures prices also set a new high. The spot price of gold reached a high of $850 per troy ounce that same day. The COMEX and the CBOT reacted by restricting the silver futures market to liquidation-only trades and sharply increasing margin requirements on existing positions. These actions prevented the perceived shortage in the deliverable supply of silver from being exacerbated by parties who used new purchases of silver futures contracts to acquire physical silver. Not surprisingly, silver futures prices fell sharply in response to the new restrictions imposed by the exchanges, as the following excerpt from *The Wall Street Journal* reveals.

> Silver plummeted $10 to $34 an ounce a record single-day drop in prices. The slump followed restrictions placed by New York's Commodity Exchange [COMEX] on silver trading Monday. The Chicago Board of Trade yesterday... [forbid] traders to add on new positions in January, February, and March contracts.

> ...Silver's decline was accelerated by the record $143.50 drop in gold in New York...During the day Nelson Bunker Hunt, one of the big speculators whose buying helped push silver to record prices, said he offered to buy up to five million ounces at $40 an ounce, deliverable in Zurich, New York or London from anybody who has silver that's deliverable.[6]

Notice that Nelson Bunker Hunt's proposed offer to buy up to 5 million ounces of deliverable silver at $40 per ounce did not prevent the futures price of silver from falling significantly below $40. Notice also how the sharp price decline in gold adversely impacted the silver market. A period of sharp price volatility followed for both gold and silver, but the record high prices for both gold and silver would not be topped. For instance, the spot price of gold fell nearly $200 per troy ounce in two days, or about 24%. The spot price of silver fell $22.25 per troy ounce, or nearly 43%, during the same two day period. The prices of both precious metals then climbed substantially higher.[7]

The U.S. Commodity Futures Trading Commission subsequently investigated whether the Hunt brothers and their allies were actively trying to corner the market for silver. The price action during 1979 and early 1980 suggests that, if they were attempting to do so, they succeeded for a while.

There are two problems with attempted corners. The first problem is that supply may dramatically increase as price increases because alternatives are found (thus reducing demand) and previously unavailable private holdings enter the marketplace (thus increasing supply). This lessens the effectiveness of an attempted corner. There is anecdotal evidence that some heavy industrial users of silver (like firms in the photography industry) were able to obtain needed silver by reprocessing it from old film after the price of silver rose dramatically. There is also anecdotal evidence that India (where many women store their wealth in the form of silver jewelry) went from being a net importer of silver before the attempted silver corner to a net exporter of silver. Similarly, there were numerous anecdotal reports of individuals selling their family silverware to take advantage of the high price of silver. Keeping the price of silver high requires continued purchases of silver if new supplies enter the market.

The large holdings of silver that the Hunt brothers and their associates controlled needed to be financed. The Hunt brothers could control more silver if they borrowed to finance it. The Hunt brothers used the high value of their existing silver holdings as collateral to finance the purchase of additional silver—that is, they were pyramiding on an existing trading position. This set the stage for a possible positive feedback trading episode in silver futures prices if a price decline—that required longs to post additional margin—induced selling by other longs (cutting their losses short) and further price declines. This is exactly what happened during early March 1980 when the price of silver fell repeatedly and the Hunt brothers received a series of margin calls. The question that other market participants had to answer was whether the Hunts could continue to meet the margin calls if the price of silver continued to fall. News that the Hunts faced margin calls pushed prices down but the price of silver still remained relatively high.

The second problem with attempted corners is also fundamental—namely, the only way to take a profit is to sell the commodity that was cornered. However, selling the commodity that was cornered may cause prices to fall, reducing the value of the remaining holdings. Moreover, the price decline associated with a sale might be magnified if other market participants believed that the corner could not be maintained.

The Hunt brothers devised a seemingly clever way around this problem. On Wednesday, March 26, 1980, Nelson Bunker Hunt announced in Paris the planned issuance of interest-bearing commodity bonds backed by 200 million ounces of silver—that is, bonds whose principal is redeemable in silver or in currency at the option of the issuer. According to press accounts at the time, the Hunt consortium planned to issue between $3 billion to $3.5 billion of bonds. The announcement was made after the silver market in New York was closed. Silver closed at $15.80 or down $4.40 from March 25. The next day, silver fell $5 to close at $10.80 per troy ounce.

The announcement may have acted as a trading catalyst. Bonds are forward contracts on money and commodity bonds are forward contracts on the commodity in question. The bond issuer is selling forward contracts, whereas the bond buyer is buying forward contracts. The proposed issuance of commodity bonds was an ingenious way of selling silver forward and locking in profits.[8] However, it didn't work because market participants saw the proposed commodity bonds for what they were—an end run around selling in the forward market directly and depressing the price of silver. Figure 9.3 depicts the sharp decline in silver futures prices during the first few months of 1980.

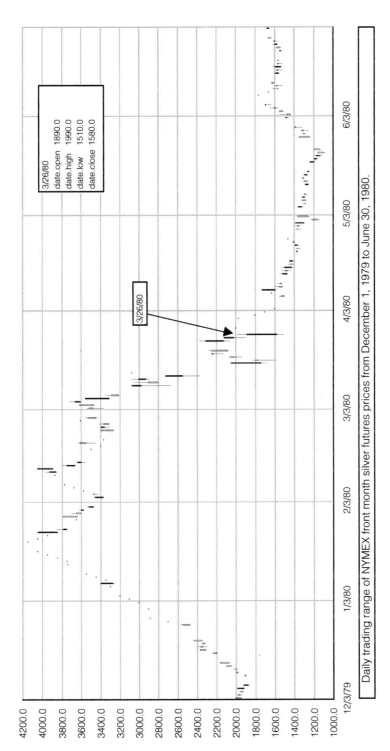

FIGURE 9.3 Silver plummets during 1980.

A simpler explanation is that word of the Hunts's inability to meet margin calls at Bache Halsey Stuart—a large brokerage firm at the time—leaked out and market participants smelled blood in the water. The Hunts had approximately $90 million in equity at Bache to cover the over 4,000 silver futures contracts they had outstanding on Wednesday, March 26. The Hunts held both spot and deferred month silver futures contracts. Price limits in futures markets meant that the Hunts's sizable positions in deferred futures contracts months were not fully marked to market. Bache estimated that if the deferred futures prices were marked to the spot price of silver, the Hunts's equity would be approximately $50 million.[9]

In May 1980 report to the Committee on Agriculture, Nutrition, and Forestry of the United States Senate, the U.S. Commodity Futures Trading Commission described the situation as follows.

> The Commission's Division of Trading and Markets was informed at approximately 1:15 P.M. [on Wednesday, March 26, 1980] that the Hunts had failed, for the first time, to meet their margin calls at [their broker] Bache. On the evening of Tuesday, March 25, 1980, Bache advised Mr. W.H. Hunt that additional margin of $135,000,000 was required. Mr. Hunt reportedly advised Bache by telephone that he was unable to meet the margin call and acquiesced in the Bache position that it would begin immediately to liquidate collateral held for the Hunt accounts. Bache informed the Division that the Hunt's activity and positions in silver were so substantial that daily margin calls in excess of $10,000,000 had been commonplace. Upon learning of Bache's situation, members of the Division of Trading and Markets' staff contacted the CBOT and COMEX at approximately 1:30 P.M....As of the close of business on Tuesday, March 25, 1980, the Hunt account at Bache held a net long silver position of 4,070 contracts. On Wednesday morning, Bache liquidated for the Hunt's accounts silver bullion in the approximate amount of

$100,000,000 which had been previously deposited by the Hunts as collateral. On Thursday, March 27, Bache liquidated 636 futures contracts so that the Hunt's net long position as of the close of the business on Thursday, March 27 was 3,434 contracts. On Friday, March 28, 1980, Bache advised the CFTC that they had sold 3,316 additional futures contracts. Thus, as of the close of business on Friday, March 28, 1980, the Hunts' position at Bache was represented by 38 net long futures contracts and 80 warehouse receipts.[10]

In any event, the market soon rebounded after the forced liquidation. The spot month silver futures contract price closed at $12.00 per troy ounce on Friday, March 28, 1980.

News of the Hunts's plight acted as a trading catalyst in silver and in other markets. It sparked a flight to safety rally in Treasury bills and bonds and a selloff in stocks. It precipitated a rise in the U.S. dollar and declines in commodity prices (with some seemingly unrelated commodities experiencing limit down moves). Put differently, the internal market catalyst in the silver market became an external market catalyst for price changes in other commodity and financial markets. The spillover effects of this event for other markets are described in the following excerpt from an article by George McNair that appeared in *The Globe and Mail* on March 28, 1980.

A collapse of silver futures prices…is having wide ranging effects on other commodity and financial markets…Led by silver, commodity prices fell sharply. Gold was down $41 to $463 (U.S.) an ounce and copper fell 3.7 cents to 84.2 cents a pound. Sugar, cotton, cattle and hogs all fell by as much as permitted in a single day. Grains fell moderately.

The stock markets' decline was attributed in large part to the collapse of silver and other commodity prices and the resulting forced selling. Bond prices, however, were firm.[11]

At one point, the stock market as measured by the Dow Jones Industrial Average was down almost 3% on news of stock market liquidations by Bache Halsey Stuart to meet some of the Hunt brothers's margin calls on silver. The market later rebounded and closed at 759.58, or down only 2.14 points, for the day.[12] Not surprisingly, the financial crisis that the silver market meltdown precipitated induced a flight to safety. Treasury bill prices rose sharply as 13 week T-bill yields fell almost one percentage point to 14.85% and the overnight Federal funds rate tumbled from 25% to 19%.[13]

It is interesting to speculate on why the sharp decline in silver futures prices affected a broad array of commodities. Although the sympathetic reaction of gold and copper futures prices makes some intuitive sense, the limit down moves of sugar, cotton, hogs, and cattle futures prices and the moderate reaction of grain futures prices to the decline in silver futures prices do not. The connection is weak at best. Perhaps, the commodities were all inflation hedges. Otherwise, there is no apparent reason individuals or firms who were *long* silver to be *long* hogs, cotton, cattle, sugar, or grain futures. The common argument that individuals or firms who are long both silver and any of the aforementioned commodities need to sell these commodities to raise money is dubious.

It would be misleading to leave the impression that the massive rise in silver prices was solely due to the actions of the Hunt brothers. Clearly, it was not. Geopolitical factors and fear of inflation contributed significantly to the run-up in precious metal prices. The price of gold rose sharply during this time period and its price changes sometimes led changes in silver prices. The actions of exchanges also impacted silver futures prices. This is shown in the reaction of the silver futures market to the imposition of trading restrictions and increased margin requirements on silver on January 22, 1980 when silver dropped $10 per troy ounce. That said, the actions of the Hunt brothers in acquiring their silver spot and futures market positions and repeatedly taking delivery of expiring silver futures positions had a substantial positive impact on silver (and other commodity) prices. Likewise, the unwinding of the Hunts's silver positions exerted a substantial negative impact on silver (and other commodity) prices. This is shown in the reaction of silver futures prices to news of the Hunt brothers's inability to meet margin calls and plan to issue silver-backed bonds in late March 1980. These incidents demonstrate how factors internal to the market (e.g., an attempted corner, trading restrictions, and margin calls) can push prices either sharply higher or sharply lower.

Finally, the inability of the Hunts to meet margin calls illustrates another problem that traders with large positions sometimes encounter—that is, *cash flow risk*. Simply put, a trader needs to have the cash flow necessary to meet margin calls arising from short-term movements in prices. Otherwise, the trader may be stopped out or forced out of a trading position due to a sudden sharp adverse move in prices.

Internal Market Catalysts

No discussion of trading catalysts would be complete without an examination of market corners, squeezes, bubbles, crashes, and crises and the factors that precipitate them. These market events are the quintessential examples of the effects of internal trading catalysts on market prices and volatility. These events also demonstrate the importance of the trading decisions of key market participants and the game-like nature of trading. These events are related in that each is associated with significant changes in financial market prices and volatility. They are oftentimes unrelated to fundamental economic factors. These market events also exert a powerful impact on the popular imagination about the behavior of financial markets. However, these market events also differ in important ways.

Corners and squeezes are attempts by some market participants who have significant long positions to drive prices higher by forcing market participants who are short to cover their short positions. For this reason, corners are also known as *short squeezes* as the principal objective is to force shorts to cover their positions at higher prices. Corners and squeezes are simply attempts to manipulate market prices upward through strategic control of deliverable supply. The subsequent price increases largely result from reasons unrelated to fundamental economic factors.

As the attempted corner of the silver market by the Hunt brothers and others demonstrates, successful corners are difficult to conduct, maintain, and profit from. Although a number of external factors (such as perceived inflation and the taking of American hostages in Iran) reinforced the rally in silver prices, few observers would argue that silver prices weren't distorted for a considerable time period as a result of the machinations of certain silver market participants.

A more ingenious strategy for squeezing shorts occurred during the Salomon Brothers Treasury bid-rigging scandal of 1991. At the time Salomon Brothers was a large investment bank and arguably the premier fixed-income trading firm on the Street. Salomon submitted phony customer orders from large trading firms (which it later reversed) at Treasury auctions with the objective of acquiring a larger supply of new 2-year Treasury note issues than the 35% it was allowed to purchase under existing Treasury guidelines. In one instance, Salomon was able to acquire 44% of 2-year Treasury notes sold at auction.[14] Salomon used its control over a large fraction of the supply of newly issued 2-year Treasury notes to squeeze dealers who were short the security in the when-issued market.[15]

Many of the Treasury securities that dealers hold are financed in the "repo" or collateralized lending market. Market participants can pledge (or lend) securities and borrow money or borrow securities and lend money in the repo market—that is, repo market participants must do both. The rate at which money can be borrowed or lent is the *general collateral rate* if no securities are specified or the lower *special rate* if a dealer wants to borrow specific Treasury securities. When a security is in high demand or short supply, the price of the security will rise and the *special repo rate* can approach zero if a trader needs to borrow the security in the repo market. Much of the profit from the squeeze was earned in the repo market where dealers who were short the 2-year Treasury note in the when-issued market were forced to lend money to Salomon at the below market special repo rate in order to borrow the 2-year Treasury notes that they were short.

Neither the SEC nor the Treasury took kindly to Salomon's bid-rigging actions. Salomon was fined and almost closed as a result of its attempted manipulation of the Treasury market. It also lost a large number of institutional clients who ended or suspended their dealings with the firm as a result of the scandal. Key executives resigned and Warren Buffet was brought in to temporarily run the firm.[16]

Market *crashes* represent a sharp downward revaluation of an individual asset, a market sector, or the overall market. Like bubbles, a market crash can occur over a protracted period of time (such as occurred in the U.S. stock market during the 1973-1974 stock market) or very quickly. The popular imagination and most attention focus on crashes that occur quickly.

A *bubble* is a situation in which the price of an asset feeds off of past price increases of the asset without regard to economic fundamentals—that is, past price increases of an asset class increase current demand for, and the price of, the asset class. A bubble may occur in an individual asset, a market sector, or in the overall market. The rate of price increase tends to accelerate as time passes until the bubble peaks. The inflation of asset prices may occur over a protracted period of time or very quickly. Similarly, a bubble may deflate slowly or very quickly.

Bubbles may be driven by fads, fashions, herd behavior, or manias.[17] Commonly cited examples of bubbles are the tulip bulb mania in The Netherlands during 1634-1635, the Mississippi Company bubble in France during 1719-1720, the South Sea Company bubble in Britain during 1720, the Japanese stock market in the late 1980s, and the dot.com and technology stock bubble in the U.S. during the late 1990s and early 2000.

Although there is little debate about whether sudden market crashes exist, the existence (and even definition) of market bubbles is controversial.[18] The observation of a market crash does not mean that the crash was preceded by a bubble. Nor does the existence of a perceived market bubble mean that it will be followed by a sudden market crash. Thus, there need not be a single catalyst that precipitates the deflation of a market bubble.

For instance, some market observers contend that there was a bubble in the Japanese stock market during the late 1980s. However, the deflation of the Japanese stock market (which peaked at 38,915.87 on December 29, 1989 as measured by the Nikkei 225 stock index) started during early 1990 and occurred over an extended period of time. Numerous factors such as rising interest rates, a falling yen, and a shift in focus by Soviet President Mikhail Gorbachev from foreign to domestic issues were catalysts for periodic selloffs in the Nikkei during January and early February 1990. Meanwhile, there was substantial demand outside Japan for newly issued put warrants on the Japanese stock market (which were presumably hedged by selling Japanese stock index futures).

On Monday, February 26, 1990, the Nikkei 225 fell 1,569 points, or 4.5%, to close at 33,321. It had been down over 2,413 points during the trading day. As a result of this and earlier market declines (the Nikkei was down 6.9% the previous week), the Tokyo Stock Exchange imposed some temporary restrictions on index arbitrage selling.[19] Prices continued to bounce around but drift lower in the days that followed. On Monday, April 2, 1990, the Nikkei fell almost 1,938 points, or 6.59%, to close at 28,002. The decline came on top of a 3.4% loss the previous Friday. The apparent trigger for the second-largest daily decline in stock prices was concern that major institutional investors would start selling stocks. [20] The low for the Nikkei 225 for 1990 was 20,221.90, and it closed the year at 23,848.70. How much of the decline should be attributed to the deflation of the bubble in Japanese stock prices is difficult to ascertain. In any case, the Japanese economy entered an extended downturn, and the Nikkei 225 stock index reached a low of 7607.88 at one point during 2003. The decline of the Japanese stock market during 1990 is depicted in Figure 9.4.

It is widely believed that there was a bubble in U.S. technology and dot.com stocks (many of which were traded on Nasdaq) during the late 1990s and early 2000. The Nasdaq Composite Index closed at 751.96 on December 30, 1994 and closed at 1,005.89 on July 17, 1995. The Nasdaq Composite Index closed at 1291.03 on December 31, 1996, 1570.35 on December 31, 1997, and at 2,192.69 on December 31, 1998. The index continued to increase during 1999 and closed at 3,028.51 on November 3 and at 4,041.16 on December 29. The dot.com bubble peaked on March 10, 2000 when the Nasdaq Composite Index hit an intraday high of 5132.52 and closed at 5048.62. Like the deflation of the Japanese bubble, an extended period of volatility and decline in Nasdaq stock prices followed. The rise and subsequent decline of the Nasdaq Composite Index is depicted in Figure 9.5.

There was no universal euphoria over technology stocks prior to March 10, 2000. Many market participants were wary that a bubble in technology stock prices existed. Indeed, concern by policymakers and others that there was a potential bubble in U.S. stock prices was expressed far earlier at substantially lower levels of stock prices. As was noted in Chapter 3, "Talk Isn't Cheap," Fed Chairman Alan Greenspan made his famous "irrational exuberance" speech in December 1996 when the Nasdaq Composite Index stood at almost 1300 even and the Dow Jones Industrial Average at 6437.10.[21]

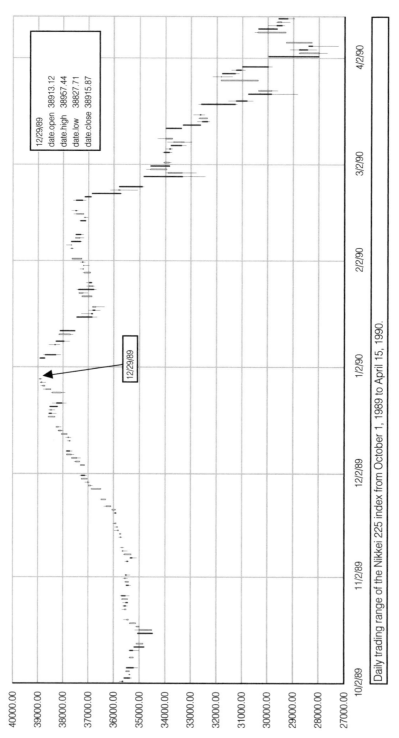

12/29/89

date.open 38913.12
date.high 38957.44
date.low 38827.71
date.close 38915.87

12/29/89

Daily trading range of the Nikkei 225 index from October 1, 1989 to April 15, 1990.

FIGURE 9.4   The Japanese stock market peaks.

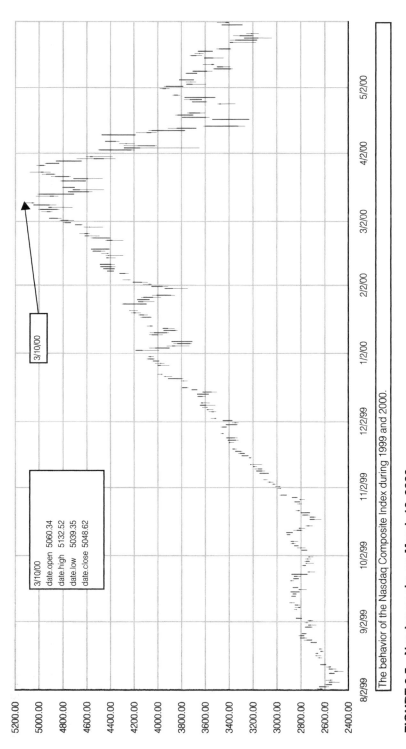

3/10/00

3/10/00
date.open 5060.34
date.high 5132.52
date.low   5039.35
date.close 5048.62

The behavior of the Nasdaq Composite Index during 1999 and 2000.

FIGURE 9.5 Nasdaq peaks on March 10, 2000.

The perceived bubble in dot.com stocks traded on the Nasdaq in the U.S. pales in comparison with the performance of technology stocks traded on the Neuer Markt in Germany. The Neuer Markt was introduced in 1997 as part of the Deutsche Börse. The Neuer Markt's Nemax all-share index closed at 506.48 on the first day of trading in 1997. It soared to a peak of over 8,000 in early 2000 and fell almost 95% by September 2002. This is a far greater percentage rise and decline than occurred on Nasdaq over the same 5 1/2-year time period. The Neuer Markt was subsequently closed by its parent Deutsche Börse.[22]

Financial panics and market crises may encompass many of the preceding events such as market crashes, corners, or squeezes. However, market crises merit their own examination. *Market crises* are periods where markets fail to function normally due to a lack of confidence or liquidity. Market crises may be driven by fundamental economic factors or factors internal to the market. They may be localized or general. Market crises may be relatively short-lived as occurred on Thursday, March 27, 1980—in response to the sharp decline in silver prices when the corner was effectively broken—or last for a protracted period of time as occurred with the Asian Financial Crisis of 1997 and 1998. Extreme examples of market crises are financial *panics*. The Federal Reserve System was established, in part, to eliminate financial panics.[23]

Many financial market crises are often attributed to an external event. For instance, the devaluation of the Mexican peso in December 1994 by the newly elected government of President Ernesto Zedillo triggered a crisis in Mexican financial markets that quickly spread to the financial markets of other emerging market countries. Similarly, the apparent trigger for the Asian Financial Crisis of 1997 and 1998 was the decision by the Thai government to devalue the Thai baht on July 2, 1997. Given that market crises often have a plausible external factor that precipitates them, the question naturally arises as to whether market crises should be considered internal or external trading catalysts. One argument for classifying market crises as internal trading catalysts is that much of the initial impact of market crises on financial and commodity prices stems from market dynamics. Indeed, in some cases, the external factor that is perceived to have triggered the market crisis is often the result of an internal factor, such as a speculative attack on a currency. This does not mean that devaluations are always the result of speculative attacks by currency traders. Devaluations are often the result of the pursuit of flawed economic policies by governments. However, speculative attacks on an overvalued currency may accelerate the inevitable change in exchange rates.

Volatile financial prices are an important characteristic of market crises. Another characteristic is a flight to safety. Market crises are also characterized by a lack of liquidity and a sharp increase in the *liquidity risk* premium. The sharp increase in *liquidity risk* can have devastating effects on traders pursuing certain arbitrage trading strategies, as Long-Term Capital Management (LTCM) found out during 1998.

LTCM was a large hedge fund that specialized in *convergence, conditional convergence*, and *relative value arbitrage* trading strategies to exploit price differences among similar securities. (The fund was also engaged in various directional bets that accounted for approximately one-fifth of its trades.) Because most price differences among similar securities are small, LTCM was highly levered to increase potential profits. Although the fund diversified its bets across markets, many of LTCM's trading strategies were *liquidity provision* strategies and subject to the risk of a sudden change in the liquidity premium.[24] Simply stated, LTCM held illiquid securities and hedged its exposure to interest rate risk by shorting liquid default-free securities. In such an environment, hedges can backfire as traders lose money on both the illiquid securities held long and the liquid securities that were shorted. Leverage magnifies the losses.

Like the Hunt brothers, LTCM faced cash flow risk as a result of the flight to safety during the liquidity crisis. LTCM lost almost

$4 billion. Even though its convergence trades were right in the long-run (i.e., the expected convergence occurred), the firm had trouble surviving in the short-term. The firm was effectively bailed out by a consortium of investment banking firms.

The August 17, 1998 devaluation of the rouble and default by Russia on its rouble and foreign currency denominated sovereign debt is blamed for exacerbating a sharp selloff in emerging market debt and prompting a flight to safety. Some attribute the near collapse of LTCM to this event. The near collapse of the hedge fund Long Term Capital Management in late August and September of 1998 highlights several trading risks. One risk is the danger of unwinding a position when too many other participants have the same trading position on. It also highlights the importance of liquidity risk. In a liquidity crisis, there are only two relevant assets: cash or its equivalents and everything else. The highly levered nature of arbitrage funds means that such firms are susceptible to massive losses if their hedges go awry during a liquidity crisis.

Although individual stocks may experience sudden large price moves up or down that greatly exceed changes in the overall market much public attention is focused on the sharp declines in the overall market associated with market crashes. This makes analysis of the catalysts that precipitate a market crash especially interesting. The stock market crash of 1929 occurred over two days with the Dow Jones Industrial Average falling 12.8% on Black Monday and another 11.7% on Black Tuesday. The stock market crash of 1987 occurred within a single day, Monday, October 19, 1987.

The Crash of 1987

On Friday, October 16, 1987, the Dow Jones Industrial Average fell 108.36 points, or 4.6%, on record volume of 343 million shares. The sharp decline precipitated a minor *flight to quality and safety* at the end of the trading day. Treasury bills were bid up. Treasury bonds were not. The market decline on Friday came on top of a 95.46-point decline in the DJIA on Wednesday and (coupled with other daily changes) resulted in a 9.5% decline in the DJIA for the week. Interestingly, some news accounts attributed the Friday, October 16, 1987 decline to concern among market participants that the stock market rally was over.[25] Although it is impossible to ascertain if that was indeed the catalyst for the sharp selloff, it is interesting that some market observers believed that the prospect of an end to the stock market's rally was enough to trigger a decline in stock prices on Friday, October 16, 1987.

Whatever the cause of the decline on Friday and earlier in the week, many market participants were anxious about the course and direction of the market. Some market observers and policymakers advocate trading halts as a means to settle anxious market participants and thereby calm volatile markets. Indeed, the Presidential Task Force on Market Mechanisms—which was formed in the wake of the October 1987 crash—recommended the imposition of *circuit breakers* (i.e., mandatory trading halts when prices move by a set amount up or down) on stock and stock index futures markets to reduce the likelihood of future stock market crashes. It is not apparent that if circuit breakers had been operative before the market crash that it would have made any difference. In this instance, market participants had a natural two-day trading halt—the weekend—to reflect on the market. Rather than calming market jitters, the weekend trading halt exacerbated them because they could not get out of their positions.

On Monday, October 19, 1987, the stock market reopened. By the end of the trading day, the stock market had plunged 508 points on the DJIA, or 22.6%, on record volume of 604.33 million shares.[26] This was the second largest one-day decline in the history of the U.S. stock market, exceeded only by a 24% decline on December 14, 1914 when the NYSE reopened after being closed for several months after

World War I started in July 1914. Figure 9.6 depicts the October 19, 1987 stock market crash. A sense of the breadth and depth of the decline in stock prices is captured in the following excerpt of an October 19, 1987 article by Peter Coy of the Associated Press.

> ...The market [decline] fed on itself in wave after wave of selling...Earlier Monday panic selling gripped [foreign] stock exchanges...And...continued with ferocity Tuesday morning as share prices plunged when the Tokyo and Australian stock markets opened...
>
> The Wall Street rout was all the more stunning because there did not seem to be any major news event that caused it. A selling trend that picked up speed in the middle of last week simply gained unstoppable momentum and turned into a frenzy...
>
> ...Money continued to pour out of stocks and bonds into gold and short-term Treasury securities, which are considered safe havens in times of crisis...The price of a benchmark 30-year Treasury bond with a face value of $1,000 fell about $5 as its yield rose to 10.2 percent by 3:30 P.M. EDT.
>
> The dollar was also relatively stable...The price of gold... gained another $12 an ounce to $483 an ounce by 3:30 P.M. EDT.[27]

The report argues that there were underlying concerns among many market participants about "rising interest rates and a weakening dollar" and that money continued to "pour out of stocks and bonds into gold and short-term Treasury securities." The excerpt points out that the Treasury long bond had declined one-half point by 3:30 P.M. This initial *negative* reaction of the Treasury long bond to the stock market crash stands in sharp contrast to the frenzied *positive* reaction that occurred later that night when the market experienced the largest one-day rally ever in Treasury bonds. To be sure, the bond market closed before the equity market closed, but it was apparent even before the bond market closed that equity markets would likely experience a record point loss and a percentage loss far in excess of the Black Monday component of the October 1929 crash.

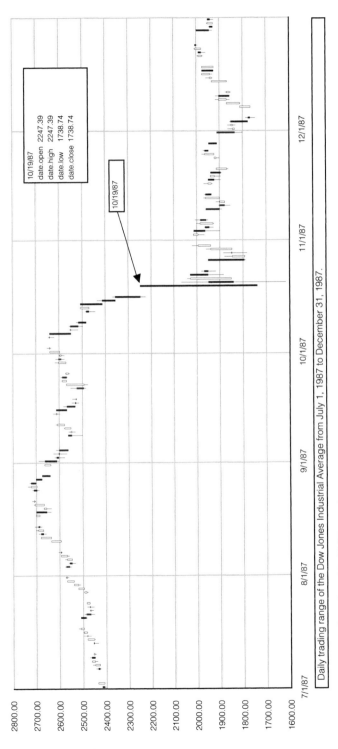

FIGURE 9.6   The October 19, 1987 crash.

Notice that the preceding excerpt suggests that there was no obvious external trigger for the sharp decline in stock prices. If anything, the account seems to suggest that the decline resulted from wave after wave of selling that fed upon each other. Floyd Norris described the action in the October 26, 1987 issue of *Barron's* as follows.

> ...Just what set off the selling at the opening Monday is not completely clear. Portfolio insurance played the largest role, but that alone could not be the whole story...[M]ostly what happened was panic. After the first wave of selling sent prices down more than 200 DJIA points, there was a rally that gained back more than 100 of them...The portfolio insurers kept selling [stocks or futures]...The DJIA dipped below 1960 to show a drop of 12.8% for the day, and soon there was talk of Oct. 28, 1929, or Black Monday...when a record 12.8% decline set off a crash...[P]rices soon rallied, with the Dow climbing back to the 2000 level. But that level couldn't hold, and when prices fell below 1950, the remaining decline was precipitous.[28]

To be sure, other explanations were offered at the time as potential catalysts for the crash such as comments by U.S. Treasury Secretary James Baker that the U.S. would pursue a weak dollar strategy against the Japanese yen and German mark or a proposed bill by Congressional Democrats to increase taxes and discourage hostile takeovers. However, even when other catalysts were blamed for precipitating the crash, program trading (in the form of *index arbitrage* between individual stocks and stock index futures contracts) and *portfolio insurance* were blamed for the exacerbating the severity of the crash.

Portfolio insurance was a very popular risk-management technique during the mid 1980s. The essential idea behind it is to replicate a synthetic put option on a portfolio in order to limit the downside risk of equity portfolios.[29] However, put options are expensive and short-lived. To minimize the cost of acquiring portfolio insurance, fund managers were persuaded that they could sell an appropriate number of stock index futures contracts after the cash stock market fell by a certain percentage or trigger amount. The dollar amount of stock index futures sold would only be a fraction of the total value of the portfolio. A commonly used rule was to sell stock index futures equivalent in value to twice the percentage amount of the portfolio as the trigger percentage market decline. If stock prices fell further, the losses on the long stock portfolio would be partially offset by gains on the short futures stock index futures position. Additional declines beyond a certain percentage would trigger additional selling of stock index futures. The trigger points for many large insured portfolios were well-known to market participants. Indeed, one investment bank, Kidder Peabody, pursued a policy where it would announce to other market participants whenever it wanted to enter or exit a position due to a portfolio insurance transaction. The idea was to get better prices for its transactions by assuring counterparties that the firm was not executing a large order because its customer had information that the counterparties did not have. How well this strategy worked on October 19, 1987 is not clear.

Portfolio insurance was partially the victim of its own success. The technique worked well for portfolios that sold stock index futures on Friday, October 16, 1987. The technique did not work as well for those portfolios that sold or attempted to sell stock index futures on Monday, October 19, 1987. The technique relied on a flawed underlying assumption that there would always be someone willing to buy stock index futures at small deviations from the current price. This meant that market participants who were short on the day of the crash had every reason to believe that the selloff would worsen as the day progressed and more sell orders flowed in from portfolio insurers. It also meant that locals or scalpers in the stock index futures pits had no incentive to take the other side of the sell orders except at sharply lower prices. Portfolio insurance is a form of positive feedback trading. Arguably, the sell orders from portfolio insurers and the expectations of other market participants of those orders exacerbated the price decline.

On November 5, 1987, U.S. President Ronald W. Reagan ordered the creation of the *Presidential Task Force on Market Mechanisms* (commonly called the Brady Commission because it was chaired by Dillon Read investment banker Nicholas Brady) to investigate the causes of the stock market crash. The Task Force viewed the crash from the perspective of several days starting on Wednesday, October 14, 1987 and ending on Tuesday, October 20, 1987. The Task Force had the following comments on the causes and nature of the decline.

On Wednesday morning, October 14, 1987, the U.S. equity market began the most severe one-week decline in its history. The Dow stood at over 2,500 on Wednesday morning. By noon on Tuesday of the next week, it was just above 1,700, a decline of almost one third. Worse still, at the same time on Tuesday, the S&P 500 futures contract would imply a Dow level near 1,400…

During October 14 to 16, the Dow fell by over 250 points. The selling was triggered primarily by two proximate causes: disappointingly poor merchandise trade figures, which put downward pressure on the dollar in currency markets and upward pressure on long term interest rates; and the filing of anti-takeover tax legislation, which caused risk arbitrageurs to sell stocks of takeover candidates resulting in their precipitate decline and a general ripple effect throughout the market. The market's decline created a huge overhang of selling pressure—enough to crush the equity markets in the following week. This overhang was concentrated within two categories of reactive sellers, portfolio insurers and a few mutual fund groups, and exacerbated by the actions of aggressive trading-oriented institutions selling in anticipation of further declines...[T]he typical portfolio insurance model calls for stock sales in excess of 20 percent of a portfolio in response to a 10 percent decline in the market.

Various sources indicate that $60 to $90 billion of equity assets were under portfolio insurance administration at the time of the market break. Two consequences were evident. First, portfolio insurers were very active sellers during the Wednesday to Friday period. In the futures market, where they concentrated their activity during the week, they sold the equivalent in stocks of approximately $530 million on Wednesday, $965 million on Thursday and $2.1 billion on Friday. Second, they approached Monday with a huge amount of selling already dictated by their models. With the market already down 10 percent, their models dictated that, at a minimum, $12 billion (20 percent of $60 billion) of equities should already have been sold. Less than $4 billion had in fact been sold.

A small number of mutual fund groups were also confronted with an overhang...On Friday alone, customer redemptions at these funds exceeded fund sales of stock by $750 million...These funds also received substantial redemption requests over the weekend.

The activities of a small number of aggressive trading-oriented institutions both contributed to the decline during this week and posed the prospect of further selling pressure on Monday. These traders could well understand the strategies of the portfolio insurers and mutual funds. They could anticipate the selling those institutions would have to do in reaction to the market's decline. They could also see those institutions falling behind in their selling programs. The situation presented an opportunity for these traders to sell in anticipation of the forced selling by portfolio insurers and mutual funds, with the prospect of repurchasing at lower prices...

Index arbitrage was active throughout the three day period to transmit selling pressure from the futures market to the stock market. But…it was the timing of arbitrage activities, rather than the aggregate daily level, which had specific impact on the stock market.[30]

The preceding excerpt views the crash as part of a larger one-week period of market turbulence. Although it suggests that there were two trading catalysts for the selloff, it is clear that the existence of "reactive" and "price-insensitive" sellers sharply exacerbated the severity of the decline. The excerpt also illustrates the game-like nature of trading when it discusses the role that "a small number of aggressive trading-oriented institutions" that understood the reactive and price-insensitive "strategies of the portfolio insurers and mutual funds" and could anticipate the future selling these market participants "would have to do in reaction to the market decline"—that is, there was an opportunity to short the market that was not related to fundamental economic factors but to the likely trading behavior of some market participants.

A closer examination of the price action on Monday, October 19, 1987 illustrates the important role that portfolio insurers and reactive mutual funds played in exacerbating the price declines during the day of the crash. It also highlights the impact that the cessation of index arbitrage after 2:00 P.M. had on the market. Again, the Brady Commission's report describes it as follows.

[Foreign markets fell before New York opened on Monday, October 19, 1987. By midday London] was down 10 percent. Selling of U.S. stocks on the London market was stoked by some U.S. mutual fund managers who tried to beat the expected selling on the NYSE by lightening up in London…

[T]he S&P 500 futures also opened down under heavy selling pressure by portfolio insurers. During the first half hour of trading, a few portfolio insurers sold futures equivalent to just under $400 million of stocks, 28 percent of public volume.

By the scheduled 9:30 A.M. opening on the NYSE, specialists faced large order imbalances…[and as a result] did not open trading in their stocks during the first hour…[Some portfolio insurers started to sell stock directly rather than stock index futures.]…

The selling pressure in futures led to discounts of historic size. In response to these huge discounts, three mechanisms came into play to transmit selling pressure from futures to stocks. First, index arbitrage executed $1.7 billion of program sales through DOT [the NYSE's designated order turnaround system], matched by equivalent futures purchases. Second, there were additional straight program sales of stock equal to $2.3 billion. Most of this was portfolio insurance selling diverted from the futures market to the stock market by the large discount. Taken together, arbitrage and straight sell programs totaled $4 billion, almost 20 percent of the sales on the first 600 million share day in the NYSE's history…

Starting around 11:40 A.M., portfolio insurance sales overwhelmed the rally. Between then and 2:00 P.M., the Dow fell from 2140 to 1950, a decline of just under 9 percent. The last 100 points of this decline occurred after reports began circulating that the NYSE might close…Over these two hours, the futures index fell 14.5 percent. Portfolio insurance activity intensified. Between 11:40 A.M. and 2:00 P.M., in the futures market portfolio insurers sold approximately 10,000 contracts, equivalent to about $1.3 billion and representing about 41 percent of futures volume exclusive of market makers (i.e., locals). In addition, portfolio insurers authorized to sell stock directly sold approximately $900 million in stocks on the NYSE during this period. In the stock and futures markets combined, portfolio insurers contributed over $3.7 billion in selling pressure by early afternoon…After about 2:00 P.M., index arbitrage slowed because of concerns about delays in DOT and the consequent ineffective execution of basket sales…Relieved of these selling pressures…the Dow rallied back to the psychological important 2,000 level by 2:24 P.M.

The result of the withdrawal of some index arbitrage and diverted portfolio insurer sales from the DOT system was that neither mechanism was sufficient to keep the stock and futures markets from disconnecting...

The rest of Monday afternoon was disastrous. Heavy futures selling continued by a few portfolio insurers. In the last hour and one half of futures trading, these institutions sold 6,000 contracts, the equivalent of $600 million of stock...[The virtual absence of index arbitrage activity resulted in futures contracts trading at] a discount of 20 index points...

All told, Monday, October 19 was perhaps the worst day in the history of U.S. equity markets. By the close of trading, the Dow index had fallen 508 points, almost 23 percent, on volume of 604 million shares worth just under $21 billion. Even worse, the S&P 500 futures had fallen 29 percent on total volume of 162,000 contracts valued at almost $20 billion.

This record volume was concentrated among relatively few institutions...The contribution of a small number of portfolio insurers and mutual funds to the Monday selling pressure is even more striking. Out of total NYSE sales of just under $21 billion, sell programs by three portfolio insurers made up just under $2 billion. Block sales of individual stocks by a few mutual funds accounted for another $900 million. About 90 percent of these sales were executed by one mutual fund group. In the futures market, portfolio insurer sales amounted to the equivalent of $4 billion of stocks or 34,500 contracts, equal to over 40 percent of futures volume, exclusive of locals' transactions; $2.8 billion was done by only three insurers... Huge as this selling pressure from portfolio insurers was, it was a small fraction of the sales dictated by the formulas of their models.[31]

The report indicates that portfolio insurers executed only a small fraction of the amount of selling they should have executed if they followed their models faithfully—that is, $20 to $30 billion. Simply stated, as bad as the crash was, it could have been much worse. The excerpt also suggests that the crash was even worse (29% versus 22.6%) if one measured it by the decline of stock index futures. The report describes Monday, October 19, 1987 as "perhaps the worst day in the history of U.S. equity markets." Yet, the report makes clear that the behavior of only a few large portfolio insurers and mutual funds exerted most of the adverse effect on prices on "the worst day in U.S. equity markets."

On Tuesday, October 20, 1987, the U.S. financial system almost seized up and ceased to function. After rising almost 200 points as measured by the Dow Jones Industrial Average shortly after the open, stocks fell by an even larger amount by midday and threatened to fall further. Although the New York Stock Exchange technically remained open during the day of the crash and on Tuesday, October 20, effectively it was closed as many of the largest stocks were not open for trading due to delayed openings and temporary closings.[32] At one point, both the Chicago Mercantile Exchange and the Chicago Board Options Exchange temporarily halted trading in stock index futures and equity options, respectively, under the assumption that the New York Stock Exchange would soon close. The Chicago Board of Trade remained open as did its thinly traded Major Market Index futures market. (The Major Market Index resembled the Dow Jones Industrial Average.) Suddenly, stock prices rose. The catalyst for the turnaround was a sharp inexplicable rally in the thinly traded Major Market Index stock index futures contract traded on the Chicago Board of Trade. (To be sure, a number of announcements of stock buybacks by corporations may also have played a role.) Some observers contend that the Major Market Index futures contract price may have been manipulated to induce substantial buy orders of major stocks.[33] The Dow Jones Industrial Average closed up 102.27 points or 5.9% on record trading volume. The S&P 500 stock index closed up over 5%. The rally was not broad-based in that NYSE losers far outnumbered NYSE gainers and the Nasdaq Composite Index closed down 9.9%.[34]

The October 1987 crash has been much studied. Not surprisingly, the causes of the October 19, 1987 stock market crash remain controversial. Many academic studies suggest that the event was consistent with informationally efficient capital markets.[35]

Other market observers dispute that point. For example, legendary trader George Soros argues that *reflexive* (i.e., positive feedback type) behavior among market participants makes "financial markets inherently unstable."[36] Mr. Soros goes on to argue that "trend-following speculation (such as indexing, performance measurement, and technical analysis) and trend-following devices (such as portfolio insurance and option writing) disrupt the balance" between buyers and sellers on financial markets.

There are several lessons from the crash of October 19, 1987.

1. There may not be any apparent fundamental economic reason for a crash.

2. Institutional considerations such as trading strategies and positions of key market participants can play an important role.

3. Selling may be concentrated among a few market participants, rather than widespread, and still have a significant adverse impact on market prices if the orders are insensitive to transaction prices.

4. Other financial markets may not react immediately to news of a crash in equity prices. For instance, Treasury bonds were down for most of the day and did not start to rally until *after* stocks closed 508 points lower on the day. The magnitude of the subsequent rally was enormous. Treasury bonds had their biggest one-day rally ever. The move was not approached until October 31 and November 1, 2001 when Treasury bonds rallied sharply on the news that the 30-year Treasury bond would be discontinued.

5. Trading theses may change suddenly. After the 1987 stock market crash, Treasury bond prices became linked to stock market prices. If stock prices rose, bond prices would fall, and vice versa. Once again, traders did not want to miss out on a bond market rally as large as occurred after the October 1987 stock market crash.

6. Another sobering lesson from the crash and the days immediately following it is the fragility of the financial system. The U.S. Treasury bond market dwarfs the stock market in trading volume. Yet, none of the major commercial and investment banks would make a market on Tuesday, October 20, 1987 because the CBOT Treasury bond futures market was *lock-limit up*.[37] Although some might cite counterparty risk, the unwillingness of dealers to make a market in Treasury securities was true for any of their customers including the World Bank whose obligations are guaranteed by the member countries who own it. The unwillingness of dealers to make a market in U.S. Treasury securities to even the World Bank illustrates the hesitancy of many financial institutions to take on directional risks outright. Put differently, the amount of risk taking was dependent on the relatively thinly capitalized locals on the floor of the Chicago futures markets.

On Friday, October 13, 1989, the U.S. stock market fell sharply in what came to be called the mini-crash. The DJIA closed down 6.9% with most of the 190-point price decline occurring in the last hour of trading. Although there was an external trading catalyst for the event—the collapse of the proposed buyout of United Airlines (UAL)—many market observers attributed the sharp decline to waves of selling from computerized program trades. Given the sharp rise in Treasury bond prices that followed the 1987 stock market crash, Treasury bond prices were bid up in an apparent flight to safety while junk bond prices fell.[38]

As is readily apparent, the preceding paragraph discusses how market participants reacted to the sharp declines in equity prices on Friday, October 13, 1989 by bidding up Treasury bond prices. This is what happened on a delayed basis after the crash of 1987. Notice that both the dollar and junk bond prices fell.

Asian Financial Crisis and Market Contagion

Financial crises may be localized to a single market or affect several markets. As was noted in an earlier chapter, the effects of the Asian Financial Crisis extended beyond Asian financial markets. Price declines on Asian markets affected emerging markets in Central and Eastern Europe and Latin America. To be sure, the U.S. dollar rose against several Asian currencies and the stock prices of individual companies were affected. However, the overall U.S. stock market was largely unaffected by the Asian Financial Crisis. Arguably, the most significant single impact of the Asian Financial Crisis on the U.S. stock market occurred on Monday, October 27, 1997 in the wake of sharp declines in the Hong Kong stock market. U.S. stocks fell 554 points, or over 7%, as measured by the DJIA. However, the duration of the impact was essentially limited to a single day. On Tuesday, October 28, 1997, the U.S. stock market rose sharply.

Not only was the impact of falling Asian stock prices on the U.S. stock market short-lived, the magnitude of the decline in the DJIA was significantly lower than other markets. Brazilian markets were especially hard hit. For instance, Brazilian stocks fell 6% on Wednesday, October 29, 1997 and 9.8% on Thursday, October 30, 1997.[39] Again, the trading catalyst was sharp (but smaller) declines in Asian stocks. In this case, the contagion of the Asian Financial Crisis was largely limited to emerging markets. The trading lesson that emerges is that foreign financial market crises are less likely to affect U.S. financial markets than U.S. financial market crises are to affect other financial markets.

Trading Lessons

Large price changes can occur in financial markets without any apparent fundamental economic reason. This was illustrated by the crash of October 19, 1987 ("the worst day in history for the U.S. equity market") and the subsequent rally on Tuesday, October 20, 1987. It was also apparent in the attempted silver corner during 1979 and 1980 and in the prospective unwinding of the corner during March 26 and 27, 1980. In the preceding incidents, the trading actions of key market participants exerted substantial impact on the behavior of market prices. These episodes were also characterized by substantial volatility in prices. Although the trading catalysts were often localized to one market, the impact of the resulting price changes spread to other markets. This does not mean that fundamental economic information does not matter; rather, in the short run, other considerations—namely, market dynamics or the trading positions and strategies of key market participants—may play a large role in determining price changes.

Moreover, such incidents are not a phenomenon of the seemingly "distant" past but remain a recurring feature of financial markets. A more recent example in this regard is the nearly 14% decline in NYMEX April 2006 silver futures prices on Thursday, April 20, 2006, which is depicted in Figure 9.7. Despite a 15-minute trading halt, the decline in silver futures prices continued after trading was allowed to resume. Contemporary news accounts attributed the decline to "profit-taking."[40] The steep price decline in New York silver futures prices precipitated an even larger, almost 16% decline in the front month April 2006 silver futures contracts traded on the Tokyo Commodities Exchange (TOCOM) on April 21, 2006.[41]

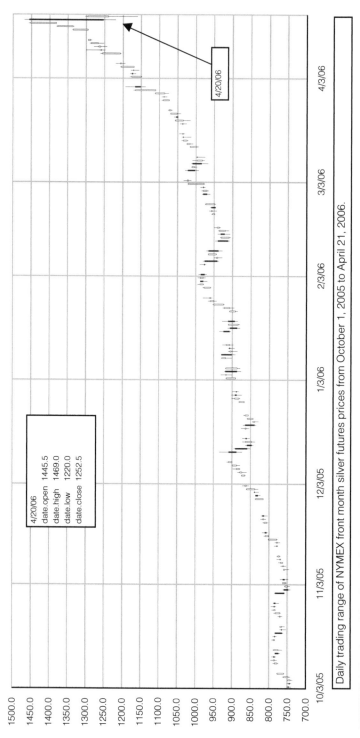

4/20/06

4/20/06
date.open 1445.5
date.high 1469.0
date.low   1220.0
date.close 1252.5

Daily trading range of NYMEX front month silver futures prices from October 1, 2005 to April 21, 2006.

FIGURE 9.7   A sudden break in silver futures prices.

The most important lesson is that trading is a game. Many trading strategies have an objective of inducing positive feedback trading. This means that market participants may try to force weaker hands out of the game by pushing prices enough in one direction to set off stops. Similarly, knowing how other market participants are likely to react to large changes in market prices may assist other traders in anticipating future short-run price changes. The widespread knowledge that some market participants during the October 1987 crash used portfolio insurance strategies encouraged other traders to short the market in advance of likely mechanical sales from portfolio insurers.

Special risks may arise in trading during these time periods. For instance, liquidity may dry up, making it difficult to trade. Rapidly changing prices may entail considerable trade execution or slippage risk. Exchanges may impose restrictions that effectively change the rules of the game mid-stream and benefit one side of a trade resulting in sharp price changes. In addition, a crisis in one market may degenerate into a general liquidity crisis in which losses may arise on both legs of "hedged" positions.

The examples considered in this chapter demonstrate that internal market catalysts often exert a more powerful effect on market prices and volatility than external market catalysts. Moreover, the influence of internal market catalysts on market prices often lasts longer than external market catalysts. However, the game-like nature of trading is more apparent with internal market catalysts.

References

Brancaccio, David. *Marketplace*. October 30, 1997 (http://marketplace.publicradio.org/shows/1997/10/30_mpp.html).

Chancellor, Edward. *Devil Take the Hindmost: A History of Financial Speculation*. New York: Farrar, Straus and Giroux, 1999.

Coll, Steve. "Stock Market Takes Biggest Nose Dive Yet; Dow Falls 108 Points in Frenzied Trading." *The Washington Post*, October 16, 1987.

Coy, Peter. "Panic Sweeps Stock Market; Plunge Rivals 1929 Crash." The Associated Press, October 19, 1987.

The Financial Times. September 27, 2002.

Garber, Peter M. *Famous First Bubbles: The Fundamentals of Early Manias*. Cambridge, MA: MIT Press, 2000.

Harvard Business School. "Long-Term Capital Management, L.P. (D)." 1999.

Hiatt, Fred. "Japanese Stocks, Yen Sink; Nikkei's 28,002 Close Lowest in 17 Months." *The Washington Post*, April 3, 1990.

Keynes, John Maynard. *The General Theory of Employment, Interest and Money*. New York: Harcourt, Brace & World, 1936, p. 154.

Kindleberger, Charles P. *Manias, Panics and Crashes, A History of Financial Crises*. John Wiley, 2001.

Maidenhead, H.J. "Silver Prices Decline on New York Commodity Exchange on Sept 12 After..." *New York Times* Abstracts, September 13, 1979.

McNair, George. *The Globe and Mail*. January 26, 1980.

McNair, George. "Silver Price Drop Is Felt in Markets." *The Globe and Mail*, March 28, 1980.

Mittelstaedt, Martin. "Stock Prices Plunge in Panic Selling UAL Buy-out Problems Trigger Drop." *The Globe and Mail*, October 14, 1989.

Norris, Floyd. "Shadow on a Market." *The New York Times*, August 18, 1991.

Norris, Floyd. "The Crash of 1987—Men and Machines Wreak Havoc on Wall Street." *Barron's*, October 26, 1987.

Partridge, John. "Silver Dive Halts Trading, Rattles Markets, Analysts Blame Speculators, Profit Taking for 14 Per Cent Drop Biggest since 1983." *The Globe and Mail*, April 21, 2006.

[10] U.S Commodity Futures Trading Commission. "Report of the Commodity Futures Trading Commission on Recent Developments in the Silver Futures Markets." Committee on Agriculture, Nutrition, and Forestry of the United States Senate, U.S. Government Printing Office, May 1980, pp. 83-86.

[11] George McNair. "Silver Price Drop Is Felt in Markets." *The Globe and Mail*, March 28, 1980.

[12] Vartanig G. Vartan. "Dow Jones Industrial Average Declines 2.14 Points to Close at 759.58 on March 27." March 28, 1980.

[13] *The Wall Street Journal*. "Bill Rates Drop; Dealers Say Mart Went 'Nuts' on Hunt Woes." March 28, 1980.

[14] Floyd Norris. "Shadow on a Market." *The New York Times*, August 18, 1991.

[15] To understand how Salomon Brothers profited from the short squeeze, it is important to know some institutional details of the Treasury market. The Treasury market is enormous and the dollar value of trading easily dwarfs the stock market. Treasury securities are even traded before they are issued in the when-issued market—a kind of informal forward market that exists between the announcement of a Treasury auction and the actual issuance of the securities.

[16] As a side note, at the time, legendary trader John Meriwether ran the bond arbitrage group at Salomon, which accounted for virtually all of the firm's profits. He was also vice chairman and head of Salomon's fixed income department at the time but unaware of, and uninvolved in, the Treasury bid-rigging scandal. Meriwether left Salomon and later formed his own hedge fund, Long-Term Capital Management, taking a number of talented Salomon coworkers with him.

[17] Andrei Schleifer. *Inefficient Markets*. New York: Oxford University Press, 2000.

[18] Peter Garber contends that most commonly considered bubbles were actually consistent with rational expectations and a generally efficient market.

Peter M. Garber. *Famous First Bubbles: The Fundamentals of Early Manias*. Cambridge, MA: MIT Press, 2000.

In contrast, Charles Kindleberger and Edward Chancellor make the case for the existence of manias and bubbles in their separate books. Edward Chancellor. *Devil Take the Hindmost: A History of Financial Speculation*. New York: Farrar, Straus and Giroux, 1999. Charles P. Kindleberger. *Manias, Panics and Crashes, A History of Financial Crises*. John Wiley, 2001.

[19] *The Toronto Star*. "Tokyo Stock Plunge Drags Down Asian Markets." February 26, 1990.

[20] Fred Hiatt. "Japanese Stocks, Yen Sink; Nikkei's 28,002 Close Lowest in 17 Months." *The Washington Post*, April 3, 1990.

[21] As noted earlier, the Federal Reserve Board chose not to increase margin requirements during this time period, which would have reduced the ability of individual investors to lever their stock holdings.

[22] *The Financial Times*. September 27, 2002.

[23] Market participants may disagree over whether the Federal Reserve has been successful in this regard.

[24] Andre F. Perold. "Long-Term Capital Management, L.P. (D)." Harvard Business School Publishing, 1999. This case consists of a letter from John Meriwether to LTCM investors during the crisis. Liquidity provision strategies are strategies designed to profit from investing in less liquid securities.

[25] Steve Coll. "Stock Market Takes Biggest Nose Dive Yet; Dow Falls 108 Points in Frenzied Trading." *The Washington Post*, October 16, 1987. The article notes: "…Investors and analysts attributed today's heavy retreat to snowballing fears that the stock market's huge five-year rally may be ending. They also worried that the sharp selloff may roll into other financial markets around the world or undermine the growth of the U.S. economy."

[26] The short-term peak of the Dow Jones Industrial Average occurred on August 25, 1987 when the Dow closed at 2722.42.

[27] Peter Coy. "Panic Sweeps Stock Market; Plunge Rivals 1929 Crash." Associated Press, October 19, 1987.

[28] Floyd Norris. "The Crash of 1987—Men and Machines Wreak Havoc on Wall Street." *Barron's*, October 26, 1987. The article notes that at one point on Tuesday, October 20, 1987, Japanese stock index futures traded in Singapore at a discount to cash that was so large that it implied a 75% decline in Japanese stock prices.

[29] That is, create a security whose payoffs match those of a put option.

[30] Report of the Presidential Task Force on Market Mechanisms, January 1988, U.S. Government Printing Office, pp. 29-42.

[31] Report of the Presidential Task Force on Market Mechanisms, January 1988, U.S. Government Printing Office, pp. 29-42.

[32] *The Washington Post* reported that 95 NYSE stocks had delayed openings and 183 stocks had trading due to order imbalances. David A. Vise, "Dow Regains 102 Points in Another Wild Day; Other Indexes Slide, Blue Chips Rally on Record Volume," *The Washington Post*, October 21, 1987.

[33] James B. Stewart and Daniel Hartzberg. "Terrible Tuesday: How the Stock Market Almost Disintegrated a Day After the Crash—Credit Dried Up for Brokers AND Especially Specialists Until Fed Came to Rescue—Most Perilous Day in 50 Years." *The Wall Street Journal*, November 20, 1987.

[34] David A. Vise. "Dow Regains 102 Points in Another Wild Day; Other Indexes Slide, Blue Chips Rally on Record Volume." *The Washington Post*, October 21, 1987.

[35] For example, G.J. Santoni. "The October Crash: Some Evidence on the Cascade Theory." Federal Reserve Bank of St. Louis.

[36] George Soros. "Brady Commission Should've Stressed Market Stability." *The Wall Street Journal*, January 14, 1988. Soros argues:

> …The concept of rational expectations doesn't apply when those expectations relate to events that are themselves contingent on the participants' decisions. The events cease to be uniquely determined and participants are confronted with genuine uncertainty. They are forced to take a view and the bias they bring to bear plays a role in the outcome.

[37] Some futures contracts are restricted in terms of the maximum price move up or down they can make during a trading day. A limit move essentially closes trading for the day as market participants are unwilling to sell at a below market price in the case of a lock-limit up move or buy at an above market price in the case of a lock-limit down move.

[38] Martin Mittelstaedt. "Stock Prices Plunge in Panic Selling UAL Buyout Problems Trigger Drop." *The Globe and Mail*, October 14, 1989. The article notes:

> …long-term U.S. Treasury bond[s]…rallied nearly $17 for each $1,000 face amount and the yield declined to 7.88 per cent from 8.03 per cent. Meanwhile, junk bonds…dropped precipitously. The prices of some issues fell more than $20.

[39] David Brancaccio. *Marketplace*. October 30, 1997 (http://marketplace.publicradio.org/shows/1997/10/30_mpp.html).

[40] John Partridge. "Silver Dive Halts Trading, Rattles Markets, Analysts Blame Speculators, Profit Taking for 14 Per Cent Drop Biggest since 1983." *The Globe and Mail*, April 21, 2006.

[41] Platts Commodity News. "TOCOM Front-Month Silver Plunges by 16% Friday on Panic Sell-Off." April 21, 2006.

10

THE ACCIDENTAL
CATALYST

"We learn little from victory, much from defeat."

—Japanese proverb

The Large Cost of Small Errors

At 9:27 A.M., on December 8, 2005, a trader at Mizuho Securities Company—a prominent Japanese brokerage firm—inadvertently offered to sell 610,000 shares of J-Com, a newly issued stock, at one yen each rather than offering one share of J-Com at 610,000 yen. Given that the exchange rate was approximately 120.27 yen to the dollar, this was the equivalent of offering to sell a $5,072 stock at less than a penny a share. Although the trader quickly recognized his error and attempted to cancel the order several times, it was too late.

A malfunction in the Tokyo Stock Exchange trading system, coupled with inadequate exchange oversight over unusual orders, prevented the trader from canceling the erroneous order.[1]

At the time the order was placed, another broker was bidding ¥672,000 for J-Com stock. That bid was hit as were all other bids above ¥572,000. Within three minutes, the large sell order caused the price of J-Com stock to plunge by ¥100,000—the maximum daily decline allowed under exchange rules—as the unfilled balance of the order automatically became an order to sell at the lower limit of ¥572,000 per share. Note that no one was able to buy J-Com at ¥1 per share. However, the balance of the large sell order was still in the system. Rumors quickly spread that the trade was an error and by 9:40 A.M., the price of J-Com rose to ¥772,000—the maximum amount the stock was allowed to rise—as traders jockeyed to buy shares.[2] The price impact of the error was exacerbated by the fact that the stock was newly listed on the Tokyo Stock Exchange and there were only 3,000 shares available for trading.[3] Trading in J-Com stock was suspended until December 14, 2005.

Over 700,000 shares of J-Com stock were traded on December 8, 2005 and a special settlement price of ¥912,000 was established for J-Com stock traded on December 8, 2005 with settlement occurring on December 13, 2005.[4] Individuals or organizations that bought J-Com stock on that day were paid the difference between their purchase price and the special settlement price.[5]

The price of J-Com continued its upward spiral after trading resumed on December 14, 2005 and the stock peaked in late December 2005. The (subsequent split-adjusted) price action in J-Com stock on December 8, 2005 and subsequent days is depicted in Figure 10.1.[6]

The eventual cost of the error for the Mizuho Financial Group— parent of Mizuho Securities Company—was 40.5 billion yen, or about $350 million at an exchange rate of 115.89 yen to the dollar.[7]

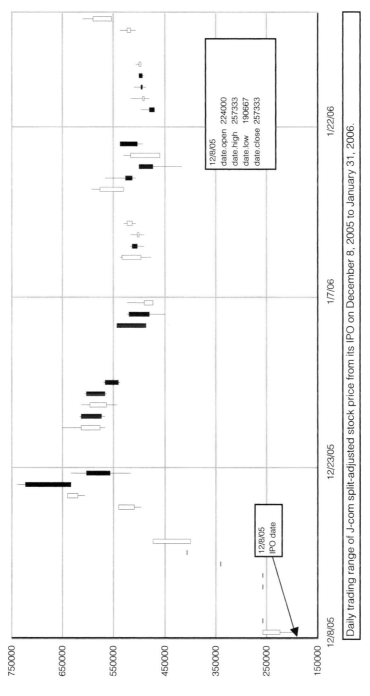

Daily trading range of J-com split-adjusted stock price from its IPO on December 8, 2005 to January 31, 2006.

FIGURE 10.1 The accidental catalyst: J-Com December 2005.

However, the influence of the erroneous order did not end simply with a volatile market for J-Com stock on December 8, 2005. The identity of the firm that made the erroneous trade was not known immediately. Many market participants assumed that it was a Japanese brokerage firm or investment bank. Mizuho did not own up to it until after the market closed. Not surprisingly, traders sold shares in major Japanese brokerage firms and investment banks. Nomura closed down 3.7%. Daiwa closed down 3.3%. Nikko closed down 3.3%. Mizuho closed down 3.4%. Indeed, some observers blamed the 2% decline in the Nikkei 225 stock index on December 8 to Mizuho's erroneous J-Com trade, although other reasons could explain the overall market decline.[8] Figure 10.2 depicts that trading range for the Nikkei 225 in the days immediately before and after December 8, 2005.

Although the Tokyo Stock Exchange (TSE) initially denied any responsibility for the error, this episode is an illustration of how a flawed trading system allowed an error to occur. Managers of the TSE trading system failed to intervene in a timely fashion to cancel the unusually large trade at an unusually low price. To be sure, Tokyo Stock Exchange rules limited the price that the stock could be sold at. This helped limit the ultimate loss to the Mizuho Financial Group. Following the admission of TSE responsibility for not allowing the erroneous order to be cancelled, three senior TSE officials resigned, including the president and the senior managing director. Six other managing directors and executive directors voluntarily agreed to a 10% pay cut for three months as a result of this incident. The incident provided the impetus for the TSE to change its trading system to prevent similar problems in the future.[9]

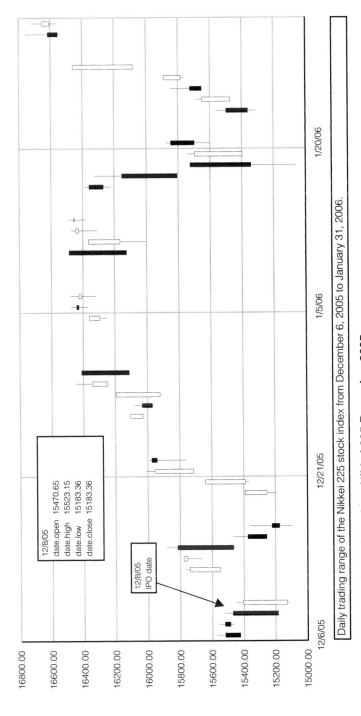

12/8/05
date.open   15470.65
date.high   15523.15
date.low   15183.36
date.close   15183.36

12/8/05
IPO date

Daily trading range of the Nikkei 225 stock index from December 6, 2005 to January 31, 2006.

FIGURE 10.2   The accidental catalyst: Nikkei 225 December 2005.

The principal trading lesson is that erroneous orders can impact not only the security or commodity in question but may extend to other markets as well. An ancillary lesson that this episode teaches is that an electronic trading system may not protect traders from erroneous orders. Not surprisingly, there were calls for the firms that had profited from the trade to return their trading profits. Another trading lesson is that the ability to keep trading profits arising from erroneous orders of counterparties may be limited by political concerns.

Lost in Translation

The opening example in this chapter illustrates how a mistake in order size can impact both the market for an individual stock and the overall market. An earlier chapter showed that the trading theses of market participants may, at times, differ sharply from received economic theory, yet the market reacts according to the trading thesis—that is, traders are trading off of *noise* rather than *fundamental economic* information. Put differently, the information is correct but the *interpretation* of the information by traders is not correct.

Sometimes, the supposedly important information that the market is reacting to is mistaken—that is, the market reaction is appropriate if the information is correct but the information is wrong. This happens with rumors. The trader is in a difficult position as the rumored information may, in fact, be correct. In such cases, the mistaken information acts as a trading catalyst, at least until the facts come out and the markets have readjusted. Once again, existing trader positions may exacerbate the market reaction to the mistake.

To be sure, the market usually reacts sharply to the occurrence of *extreme events* (i.e., perceived low probability events). The market is also likely to react sharply to an erroneous report if the report confirms a commonly held belief and trading position. For instance, during much of 2004 and the first half of 2005, many traders anticipated a sudden revaluation of the Chinese yuan against the dollar.

News reports at the time suggested that the Chinese currency could be as much as 40% undervalued. At the same time, political pressure from the U.S. and, to a lesser extent from other countries, added to a chorus of voices encouraging the Chinese government to revalue its currency, the renminbi (RMB), upward against the dollar. Not surprisingly, traders paid close attention to any news that the Chinese government might revalue its currency.

Many traders attempted to bet on the anticipated revaluation. Those who were able to acquire Chinese assets or RMB-denominated securities directly (despite official impediments) did so. Other traders took positions in the non-deliverable forward (NDF) market that would benefit if the Chinese authorities revalued the yuan before the NDF contract matured.[10] Those who could not bet on the revaluation of the RMB directly bet on it indirectly by taking positions that would likely benefit after the news came out. A common trading thesis at the time was that a revaluation of the Chinese yuan would cause the U.S. dollar to fall against certain Asian currencies such as the Japanese yen and South Korean won. The conditions were ideal for the market to respond to erroneous news that the Chinese government was about to revalue its currency.

One instance occurred on Wednesday, May 11, 2005 when Bloomberg News ran a story that quoted the online English language version of a *Peoples Daily* story that suggested a revaluation of the Chinese yuan was imminent. Other news outlets picked up the report (which was later modified by Bloomberg News). The market reacted in a predictable fashion. The U.S. dollar fell against the Japanese yen, Singaporean dollar, and South Korean won soon after the news report came out. The discounts in the yuan NDF market rose sharply to reflect the greater probability of a revaluation of the RMB. The market reaction was also short-lived as the report was denied by the People's Bank of China—China's central bank—later in the afternoon and exchange and NDF rates reversed course.[11] Interestingly, although the impact of the report on spot exchange rates largely washed out after the erroneous report was denied, the impact persisted on the one-month NDF rate with the discount ending sharply down from the high of the day, but two-thirds higher than the low for the day before the erroneous news report came out.[12]

The news report underlying the *People's Daily* report was written in Chinese and poorly translated by *People's Daily* staff into English. Basically, the market responded to a poorly translated report. There is an old Wall Street adage: "Buy on the rumor and sell on the news." The essential idea is that the time to act is before all the facts are known because after all the facts are known, the new information is fully priced into the market. This makes market participants very sensitive to rumors and raises a very important point—namely, a trader needs to be ready to respond to both rumors and facts.

A trader must limit her exposure to any one position and be ready to exit trades early enough such that she has enough capital to trade again. A rumor that precipitates an adverse price move relative to the trader's current position may cause the trader to exit her existing position. This is simply good money management and risk control. These actions are based on the behavior of market prices and are independent of whether the news report that precipitates the price change turns out to be correct. Put differently, traders need to be able to adjust their positions to reflect the current realities of the market independent of whether the factors driving price changes are correct. In this case, the news report precipitated a significant change in exchange rates even though the report later turned out to be false.[13] These changes may have been significant enough to cause some traders to exit their positions.

Dollars or Shares?

At approximately 10:35 A.M. on Monday, November 15, 1999, the market for Nasdaq 100 stock index shares traded on the American

Stock Exchange (AMEX) was $139 7/8 bid and $140 1/8 offered for 25,000 shares.[14] The market for the S&P 500 stock index shares traded nearby stood at $137 5/8 bid and $137 13/16 offered.[15] According to market participants, a broker representing Bear Stearns entered the market with an order to sell 2.5 million shares of the Nasdaq 100 stock index and 2 million shares of the S&P 500 stock index shares. The broker requested a single price to sell all 2.5 million Nasdaq 100 stock index shares and a trade was soon executed at $138 3/4. The broker was able to sell two million S&P 500 stock index shares at an average price of $137 1/2 at about the same time.

The fact that Bear Stearns was able to quickly sell several hundred million dollars worth of index shares at one time is a testament to the depth of the exchange traded fund (ETF) market. It is also an illustration of the impact that large trades can have on market prices. Notice that the Bear Stearns order was 100 times what the Nasdaq 100 market makers were willing to buy (sell) at the existing bid (offer). The price impact of the large ETF trades was $1.125 for the Nasdaq 100 stock index shares ($139 7/8 – $138 3/4) and only $.125 for the more liquid S&P 500 stock index shares. The order also caused the effective bid/ask spread to widen.

A common trading thesis is that large sell orders should depress market prices, whereas large buy orders should boost market prices. This reflects the belief that the demand curve for securities is downward sloping and the supply curve for securities is upward sloping. It also reflects the suspicion that the party placing a large trade may have information that other market participants do not have. The impact of the Bear Stearns order was not limited to the AMEX ETF market. The AMEX traders who had bought Nasdaq 100 and S&P 500 stock index shares immediately attempted to protect themselves by selling stock index futures to hedge any unwanted portion of their newly acquired long position. Information about the large sell order in the ETF market put additional downward pressure on stock index futures prices even before the order was filled.

However, the original order was a mistake. According to an AMEX trader on the floor that day, a customer order to sell 2.5 million shares of the Nasdaq 100 stock index and 2 million shares of the S&P 500 stock index was misinterpreted. It was supposed to be an order to sell $2.5 million of the Nasdaq 100 stock index and $2 million of the S&P 500 stock index. This interpretation was validated by the subsequent behavior of the Bear Stearns broker. About 14 minutes after selling 2.5 million Nasdaq 100 index shares and 2 million S&P 500 index shares, the Bear Stearns broker returned trying to buy 2 million index shares of the Nasdaq 100 stock index and 2 million shares of the S&P 500 stock index.

The Nasdaq 100 index shares market stood at $139 1/2 bid and $139 7/8 offered for 25,000 shares immediately before Bear Stearns came in to reverse most of its earlier trade at 10:49. Bear Stearns was able to buy 2 million Nasdaq 100 stock index shares at $140 1/2. Bear Stearns was able to buy two million shares of the S&P 500 stock index in two transactions at an average price of $137.84. Bear Stearns absorbed the multi-million dollar loss that resulted from executing the erroneous initial customer order and subsequently reversing it.[16]

As noted earlier, many Nasdaq 100 and S&P 500 index AMEX traders hedge their risk exposure to large positions by taking an off-setting position in the corresponding futures market. Many of the AMEX traders who took the other side to the initial erroneous Bear Stearns order and shorted the related futures contracts lost money on their hedged positions because the futures market had already adjusted downward to reflect the size of the erroneous Bear Stearns order. In retrospect, the $138 3/4 bid price that AMEX traders quoted to buy the entire 2.5 million share lot was too high. This illustrates how information about order size (and the potential information it may contain) can quickly travel across related markets.

This raises another issue: The attempt by many ETF market makers to keep both their bid/ask spread and the quantity that they are willing to buy or sell constant regardless of the volatility or lack of liquidity of the underlying security (or hedging vehicle) is an example of *mental anchoring*, a cognitive error. The pursuit of such a strategy may have an adverse effect on market maker profitability in an environment where the price volatility of the underlying security increases and liquidity decreases. It may also exacerbate volatility in financial markets as market makers attempt to cut their losses short.

Finally, the preceding example illustrates how a trading catalyst may exert a powerful, yet short-lived, effect on market prices. Trading days are often comprised of many relatively small trading catalysts that buffet the market. Market participants with longer time horizons may choose to ignore the intraday fluctuation in prices these trading catalysts induce. However, a short-term trader cannot ignore such price swings.

Trading Lessons and Summary

Trading catalysts routinely impact financial market prices and volatility. The preceding examples demonstrate how even errors can act as trading catalysts. These accidental trading catalysts can have widespread—albeit transitory—effects on financial markets.

This book begins with an example of how a surprise cut in the targeted Fed funds rate on January 3, 2001 sparked a massive 20% plus intraday move in Nasdaq stock index futures prices and ends with an example of how an erroneous customer order on November 15, 1999 pushed the price of the Nasdaq 100 index shares down and then up when the order was later reversed. The numerous examples in between demonstrate that trading catalysts can come from many different sources. These examples range from natural disasters to elections to market interventions to company-specific announcements to factors internal to the markets, among many others.

The market impact and duration of trading catalysts varies across catalysts and over time. Some trading catalysts affect only a single security or commodity. Other trading catalysts precipitate price changes in many markets. Some trading catalysts influence market prices and volatility for a considerable period of time, whereas the influence of most trading catalysts on prices and volatility is short-lived.[17] The market reaction to similar trading catalysts may vary over time. For instance, weekly announcements of changes in the money supply used to exert a big impact on Treasury bond prices. They no longer do. The forecast errors from other key economic reports still impact the market most, but not all of the time and not always in the same way. Finally, the market reaction to a trading catalyst may not always increase with the absolute size of the forecast error.

Trading catalysts are seen through the twin prisms of news reports and price changes. There is a natural tendency for reporters to use action words like "plunge" or "soar" that accentuate the reported reaction of a market to a given catalyst. There is also a tendency among reporters to frequently simplify matters by ascribing all, or most, of the price change during a trading period to a single factor when it is possible that multiple factors played a role. In addition, reporters may inadvertently report stories that contain the spin of the individuals that they interview. And, it is always possible that the reported "catalyst" for a price move is simply a convenient rationalization by market participants for what they were intending to do already. Despite the potential for getting it wrong, contemporary news media accounts of what prompted many price moves provide a reasonably accurate view of the market's movements as seen by traders. This interpretation of why the market reacted to a given trading catalyst may not be shared by academics and policymakers or accord with financial economic theory.

The reaction of market prices to perceived trading catalysts is often puzzling. Sometimes, the market's reaction seems disproportionate to the news that the trading catalyst brings—either too large or too small. Often, the market seemingly overreacts. This seemingly anomalous behavior might be explained, in many cases, by *market dynamics*. That is, by the presence of internal trading catalysts as market participants put on or unwind positions and positive feedback trading accentuates the price move. However, internal trading catalysts do not explain all of the anomalous behavior associated with the market reactions to trading catalysts.

Although this book has largely focused on trading catalysts that precipitated large changes in financial market prices, it should be emphasized that many trading catalysts exert only a modest impact on prices. Indeed, the trading day is often comprised of the reactions to a number of trading catalysts whose impact is far smaller and shorter-lived than many of the examples of trading catalysts discussed in this book.

Market Conditions, Sentiment, and Trading Theses

The speed, magnitude, and duration of the market's reaction to a trading catalyst also depend upon *market conditions and sentiment*. An apparently bullish trading catalyst may be discounted or ignored in a bearish market environment, and vice versa. Similarly, the price move that a trading catalyst precipitates may be exacerbated if positive feedback trading is triggered. The presence of positive feedback trading may cause the market's response to similar trading catalysts to differ over time.

Which markets are expected to be most affected by a trading catalyst depend on the relationships that traders and other market participants perceive. (For example, a widely held belief is that higher crude oil prices cause lower stock prices overall.) These perceptions are encapsulated in the form of *trading theses*. At any point in time, there is usually a dominant trading thesis that prevails in the market. However, sometimes, there may be multiple trading theses operating simultaneously in the market. These theses often have a different time dimension and apply to a subsector of the market.

For instance, the market reaction to a terrorist action might trigger a flight to safety (one trading thesis) that bids up bond and gold prices and at the same time sparks a selloff in travel industry stocks and triggers a rally in defense and security stocks (another trading thesis). The flight to safety effect (i.e., higher bond and gold prices), for example, may not last as long as the adverse impact on travel industry stocks.

One lesson, from an examination of past market reactions to the forecast errors of economic reports, is that traders often have misconceived ideas of how economists think the economy works. Simply put, many trading theses are often what economists call partial equilibrium analyses. Some trading theses are combinations of conflicting economic theories. For example, a casual survey of traders would likely reveal a variety of responses to the question of how an unexpected increase in the rate of growth of the money supply would affect interest rates and would likely include some combination of competing monetary theories.

In a similar vein, many traders believe that economic theory has something to say about the relationship between certain economic releases (e.g., durable goods) and interest rates when it does not. In addition, many widely held beliefs among traders, other market participants, and policymakers—such as the notion that budget deficits affect interest rates—lack empirical support.

The fact that traders confuse the concept of stocks with *flows* (e.g., the price level versus the rate of inflation), use partial equilibrium analysis, or don't understand the nuances of macroeconomic or monetary theories is largely irrelevant to other traders. The principal objective of trading is to make money. Traders must react to how other market participants and prices behave and not to how economic theory suggests the market should behave. For this reason, economic theory is often a poor indicator of how markets will react to a given trading catalyst. This has been shown repeatedly in the foreign exchange market.

Sometimes, the focus of market participants is not on the economic implications of the report directly but rather the potential policy implications of the report. For example, will the Federal Reserve tighten or loosen monetary policy in response to the latest economic data? That is, what do policymakers watch? The potential reaction of economic policymakers to economic reports justifies, to some extent, the focus on the forecast errors of economic reports by traders.

Trading Is a Game

One recurrent theme of this book is that trading is a game. Although the objective of the game remains constant—to make money—the rules of the game seemingly change over time. As a game, it is imperative to know how other participants in the game are likely to behave under various conditions or react to various catalysts. Even more valuable is knowledge of the positions that key traders have on. For instance, if most macro hedge funds are in the yen-carry trade, a sudden increase in the value of the yen against the dollar (when yen interest rates are below dollar interest rates) may precipitate a more dramatic rise in the yen as hedge funds seek to cut their losses short by buying yen and selling dollars. Simply put, the risk characteristics of a trade changes over time and increases with its popularity among large players.

News: Information versus Noise

Financial markets react to news. And, news may consist of *information* (i.e., economic fundamentals) or *noise* (nonfundamental information that affects prices). Markets react to both.[18] As noted earlier, there is often a seeming disconnect between the apparent news content of a trading catalyst and the market's reaction to it. Past relationships between or among economic variables may not hold. Transitory periods of correlation may be followed by a seeming lack of relationship.

Some news releases, and hence potential trading catalysts, are scheduled in advance, whereas others are not. Periodic macroeconomic reports are examples of scheduled news events. The scheduled nature of economic reports means that there are often well-formed expectations about the probable information content of key economic reports. The information content of economic reports lies in the forecast error. Other things being equal, the surprise potential of scheduled economic reports is probably lower than the surprise potential of unscheduled news. Put differently, the power of trading catalysts from scheduled economic reports is lower than unscheduled news, everything else staying the same.

As explained in Chapter 6, "Market Interventions," what is "in the market" (i.e., the implicit consensus forecast of traders) may differ from the consensus forecast of economists usually reported in economic surveys. Moreover, the consensus forecast of economists may be dated and not reflect the latest developments in the market. Of course, traders care about more than the consensus forecast. Traders are also interested in the dispersion of individual forecasts. However, as noted earlier, the size of the market response does not always increase with the absolute size of the forecast error even when it is adjusted for the dispersion of forecasts. In any case, an ability to forecast the information content of economic reports accurately is no guarantee of profitable trading off of the catalyst. It is also important to be able to assess the likely response of the market to the presumptive trading catalyst. Simply put, the market does not always respond as expected to trading catalysts.

Unscheduled news may be more difficult to trade off of than scheduled news events because both the news and the timing of its release are uncertain. Moreover, it is often difficult to assess what the consensus forecast (and hence forecast error) is for such events. Even when one is not able to obtain a consensus forecast of the unscheduled news event, there may be opportunities to trade on the event (if the full reaction is delayed) or on an overreaction after the news comes out.[19]

The Origin of Trading Catalysts

Some trading catalysts, like earthquakes and natural disasters, may be impossible to predict. Other trading catalysts may be difficult to predict. However, opportunities to trade may still exist. Even in cases where the trading catalyst is difficult to predict, the market reaction to the trading catalyst may be relatively easy to predict. Certain trading theses like the flight to safety thesis are common for some kinds of trading catalysts, and other trading theses are common for other types of trading catalysts. Moreover, as the delayed response to the Kobe earthquake of January 1995 or the Indian parliamentary elections of May 2005 indicate, there may be plenty of time to put on trading positions after a catalyst has occurred. Recall that in both instances, the largest reaction occurred days after the trading catalyst occurred. Other trading catalysts, like the weather, may be easier to predict. Not surprisingly, some agricultural traders subscribe to private meteorological services to get a trading edge.

The origin of a price change may influence how traders interpret its potential impact on other markets and on how a trader trades off of it. For instance, a shock originating in Asia or Europe may well have a less dramatic effect by the time it reaches the U.S. This means that a U.S.-based trader could play the likely overreaction of market prices to the trading catalyst. Conversely, a shock originating in the U.S. may have a more dramatic impact on foreign markets, and foreign traders would take that into account. Similarly, the source of a change in commodity prices may influence the validity of a trading thesis and explain apparently inconsistent reactions to it. For instance, a price increase in a commodity could result from an increase in demand—a demand shock—or a decrease in supply—a supply shock. There is no reason to expect that the implications for other markets, like equities or fixed income, are the same for both kinds of shocks.

Although external trading catalysts often receive substantial press attention, internal market catalysts may be far more important in determining the extent and magnitude of the market's reaction to an external trading catalyst. Internal trading catalysts are especially important in bubbles, crashes, corners, and market crises. Although an external trading catalyst may precipitate a market move, internal trading catalysts may exacerbate the price move. This means knowledge of market conditions that might exacerbate a price move (via positive feedback trading) is very valuable to traders. Positive feedback trading may arise from technical analysis, stop-loss orders, margin calls, portfolio insurance, momentum investing, and dynamic hedging.

Extreme Events

Extreme events occur more frequently than what would be expected if changes in prices were normally distributed. This book has shown that the trading catalysts that precipitate those extreme market events are many and varied.

Because the market reacts to a host of different factors, it is important to know if a trader has an edge in certain trades. For instance, some individuals may have a comparative advantage in forecasting the outcome of certain potential trading catalysts such as geopolitical events and government interventions in the marketplace. Such traders have an edge. The only caveat is that it is not enough to be able to forecast outcomes better than the market consensus; the trader also needs to know how the relevant markets are likely to react to the trading catalyst. Similarly, the probability distribution from which changes in financial market prices are drawn need not be constant over time. This means that traders who can recognize situations where the distribution is skewed while others do not have an advantage because their trading positions are less risky than it otherwise would appear. In extreme cases, such as when central banks defend an indefensible exchange rate, one-sided bets may result. This situation arose in September 1992 when legendary trader George Soros "broke" the Bank of England.

Independent of their origin, trading catalysts create both risk and opportunity for traders and other market participants. The large price moves that trading catalysts induce create the opportunity for substantial gains in a short period of time. The large price moves that trading catalysts induce also create the risk for substantial losses in a short period of time.

Many traders contend that only a handful of trades during the year account for the vast bulk of their trading profits. In theory, the large changes in market prices that many trading catalysts induce make possible substantial gains or losses from a handful of trades. In practice, traders are unlikely to limit their trades to trading off of trading catalysts because both the occurrence of the trading catalyst and the market response to the trading catalyst may be difficult to assess in advance.

Whether traders elect to bet directly on a trading catalyst, on the presumed market reaction (or overreaction) to it, or not at all, the potential impact on market prices and volatility means that all traders must pay attention to trading catalysts and the market reactions that they precipitate. A trader who eschews trading on the release of economic reports, for instance, should nevertheless, be cognizant of the scheduled release times of periodic economic reports because the volatility that often follows the release of economic reports may affect the timing of the trader's entry or exit of positions. Similarly, uncertainty generated by geopolitical events, for example, may cause a trader to reduce his position size even though the trader is not placing a direct bet on the geopolitical event or the market reaction that follows its occurrence.

References

Associated Press. "World Currencies Roiled by China Currency Talk, People's Daily Newspaper Feeds Speculation of a Yuan Revaluation." May 11, 2005, 12:22 p.m. ET, as reported on the MSNBC Web site (http://www.msnbc.msn.com/id/7815053/).

Bloomberg News. November 15, 1999.

Browne, Andrew. "How a News Story, Translated Badly, Caused Trading Panic." *The Wall Street Journal*, May 12, 2005, p. A1.

Hyuga, Takahiko. "UBS to Return Money from Tokyo Trading Error." Bloomberg News, *International Herald Tribune*, Thursday, December 15, 2005.

MoneyWeek. "What Was Your Worst Day at Work? Not as Bad as This..." December 9, 2005 (http://www.moneyweek.com/file/5335/mm-0912.html).

Samuelson, Paul. "Is Real-World Price a Tale Told by the Idiot of Chance?" *Review of Economics and Statistics*, 58(1), 1976, pp. 120-123.

Samuelson, Paul. "Proof That Properly Anticipated Prices Fluctuate Randomly." *Industrial Management Review*, 6, 1965, pp.41-50.

Moffett, Sebastian. "Japanese Economic Growth May Not Translate to Stocks." *The Wall Street Journal*, January 6, 2006, p. C14.

The Tokyo Stock Exchange. "Recent IPOs on Mothers 2005." March 7, 2006 (http://www.tse.or.jp/english/listing/companies/data/statistics_m-y.pdf).

The Tokyo Stock Exchange. "Summary of Report on Service Improvements and Report on the Overall System Inspection." January 31, 2006 (http://www.tse.or.jp/english/news/2006/200602/060210_a.html).

The Tokyo Stock Exchange, Japan Securities Clearing Corporation. "Settlement of Shares of J-Com Co., Ltd." December 12, 2005 (http://www.tse.or.jp/english/news/2005/200512/051212_c.pdf).

The Tokyo Stock Exchange. "To All Investors and Concerned Parties: Concerning the Stock/Convertible Bond Trading System Irregularity Relating to Processing of Cancel Order for Shares of J-Com Co., Ltd. on December 8." December 12, 2005 (http://www.tse.or.jp/english0/news/2005/200512/051212_a.html).

Wee, Larry. "Yuan Revaluation Report Sparks Asian Currency Surge." *Business Times Singapore*, May 12, 2005.

Endnotes

[1] The Tokyo Stock Exchange. "To All Investors and Concerned Parties: Concerning the Stock/Convertible Bond Trading System Irregularity Relating to Processing of Cancel Order for Shares of J-Com Co., Ltd., on December 8." December 12, 2005. Basically, the TSE system assumed that the J-Com order had started to be processed and would not allow the Mizuho trader to cancel the order in the midst of processing.

[2] Traders had good reason to believe that the order was an error. First, the size of the order dwarfed the available stock outstanding. Second, a similar incident had occurred in 2001 during the IPO of Dentsu, a large Japanese advertising company, when a trader at the Japanese branch of UBS inadvertently sold 610,000 shares of the newly listed firm for ¥16 per share resulting in a loss of ¥16.2 billion for UBS. Incredibly, the Tokyo Stock Exchange did not adjust its trading system after the UBS trading error. Takahiko Hyuga. "UBS to Return Money from Tokyo Trading Error." Bloomberg News, *International Herald Tribune*, Thursday, December 15, 2005.

[3] The Tokyo Stock Exchange. "Recent IPOs on Mothers 2005." March 7, 2006 (http://www.tse.or.jp/english/listing/companies/data/statistics_m-y.pdf).

[4] The Tokyo Stock Exchange, Japan Securities Clearing Corporation. "Settlement of Shares of J-Com Co., Ltd." December 12, 2005 (http://www.tse.or.jp/english/news/2005/200512/051212_c.pdf).

[5] The Tokyo Stock Exchange, Japan Securities Clearing Corporation. "Settlement of Shares of J-Com Co., Ltd." December 12, 2005 (http://www.tse.or.jp/english/news/2005/200512/051212_c.pdf).

[6] J-Com shares were split 3:1 during early 2006.

[7] Sebastian Moffett. "Japanese Economic Growth May Not Translate to Stocks." *The Wall Street Journal*, January 6, 2006, p. C14.

[8] *MoneyWeek*. "What Was Your Worst Day at Work? Not as Bad as This..." December 9, 2005 (http://www.moneyweek.com/file/5335/mm-0912.html).

[9] The Tokyo Stock Exchange. "Summary of Report on Service Improvements and Report on the Overall System Inspection." January 31, 2006.

[10] As the name suggests, a non-deliverable forward contract is simply a forward contract on a currency that is settled in cash at maturity. The party that is long receives (pays) money from (to) the party that is short if the RMB rises (falls) against the dollar by more than the forward rate before the contract matures. The difference between today's spot exchange rate and the NDF rate is a measure of the market's expectations of whether the future spot foreign exchange rate will be higher or lower than today's spot exchange rate. Offshore NDF markets exist for a number of foreign currencies.

[11] Larry Wee. "Yuan Revaluation Report Sparks Asian Currency Surge." *Business Times Singapore*, May 12, 2005.

[12] Ibid.

[13] *The Wall Street Journal* reported on May 12, 2005 that the "news": "... roiled the world's trillion-dollar-a-day foreign exchange market and sparked panicky emails and phone calls among currency traders and fund managers from Singapore to Stockholm as the U.S. dollar tumbled. The dollar later recovered against major currencies." Andrew Browne. "How a News Story, Translated Badly, Caused Trading Panic." *The Wall Street Journal*, May 12, 2005, p. A1.

[14] The Nasdaq 100 stock index shares are commonly called *QQQs* or *cubes* or the *Nasdaq 100 ETFs*.

[15] The S&P 500 stock index shares are commonly called *Spiders* or *SPDRs*, Standard & Poor's Depositary Receipts or S&P 500 ETFs.

[16] Bloomberg News, November 15, 1999.

[17] Academic research suggests that volatility in some financial futures markets is clustered around days that economic reports are released and within those days, around the time that the reports are released.

[18] In contrast, financial economic theory suggests that, in an efficient capital market, prices react only to the arrival of new information and prices bouncing between bid and ask. Volatility mirrors the arrival of new information in an efficient capital market.

[19] In some cases, online trading services offer market participants an opportunity to wager on the occurrence of these unscheduled news events (e.g., the revaluation of the Chinese yuan or the outcome of a referendum), which, in turn, create market measures of the probability of the occurrence of the trading catalyst. The advent of various online trading services like Tradesports.com has sharply increased the array of events that one can wager directly on.

INDEX